SOUT
ENGLAND
BY
TRAIN

by PAUL ATTERBURY

Published by The Automobile Association,
Fanum House, Basingstoke, Hampshire RG21 2EA

The Automobile Association acknowledges the
invaluable assistance given in the preparation
of this book by Network SouthEast

Whatever the chosen destination for a day out, travelling by train makes a leisurely way to appreciate the urban and rural landscape of south east England
Below: An autumnal day in rural Surrey
Title page: Rhododendrons flank the line in north Hampshire
Cover: The River Thames at Windsor, with the castle behind and (inset) trains crossing the Thames in London on Blackfriars Bridge, with fine views across to St Paul's Cathedral

Researched and written by Paul Atterbury

All cartography based on the AA's Automaps database

Typeset by
Avonset, Midsomer Norton, Bath, Avon

Colour reproduction by
LC Repro and Sons Ltd, Aldermaston

Printed and bound in Great Britain by
William Clowes Ltd, Beccles and London

A catalogue record for this book is available from the British Library.

ISBN 0 7495 0168 5 (Softback)
ISBN 0 7495 0242 8 (Hardback)
ISBN 1 55650 200 1 (US edition)

Contents

ROUTES FROM

USING THE NETWORK

Network SouthEast covers a vast area of southern England, bounded by Exeter and Weymouth in the west, Bedford and Northampton in the north and King's Lynn and Harwich to the east. It also includes England's southern shore, from Essex and east Kent to Dorset and east Devon. Within the area are hundreds of interesting, exciting and unusual places to visit, served by over 930 stations, not forgetting the miles of attractive landscape to be enjoyed on the journey.

The train is the best way to combine a great day out with relaxing and quick travel, and the Network SouthEast area offers a wide choice of destinations, for visits to castles, country houses and museums, to seaside resorts, ports and harbours, to picturesque villages, to cathedrals and churches, and to large towns and cities for shopping and tourism. Network SouthEast offers a wide range of outings for individuals, families and groups, whatever their interests or tastes, and the routes can be valuable starting points for walks and cycle tours.

London is at the heart of the Network SouthEast area, but many journeys need not start from or end in the capital. There is a wide choice of cross-country routes, and listed on pages 5 and 6 are many of the major provincial towns and cities within the area, with the rail journeys that are directly accessible from them.

This is a book about travelling by train for pleasure within the Network SouthEast area, with routes selected both for the quality of the journey and for the appeal of the destination and the places *en route*. By making the most of the various types of tickets described on page 7, this book can be the inspiration for many great days out.

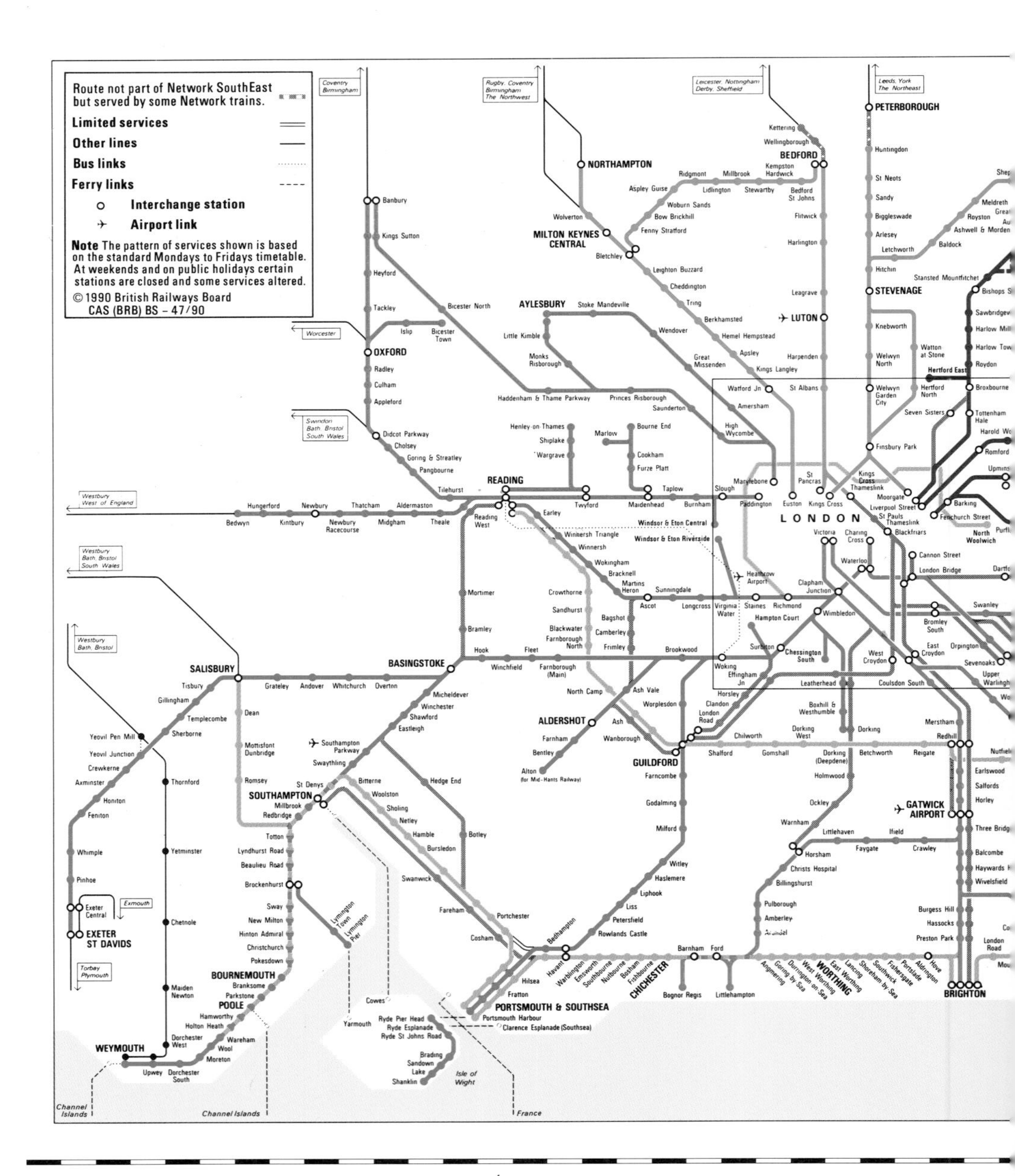

KEY TO ROUTES

The Network SouthEast routes included in this book are highlighted in colour on the map. Other routes in Network SouthEast are shown in grey.

Routes from	Pages
Paddington and Marylebone	14–25
Euston, St Pancras and Kings Cross	30–37
Liverpool Street and Fenchurch Street	42–51
Charing Cross and Victoria	56–71
Waterloo	76–93
Cross-Country Routes (including the North London line)	94–111

Not all stations are shown within the boxed area.

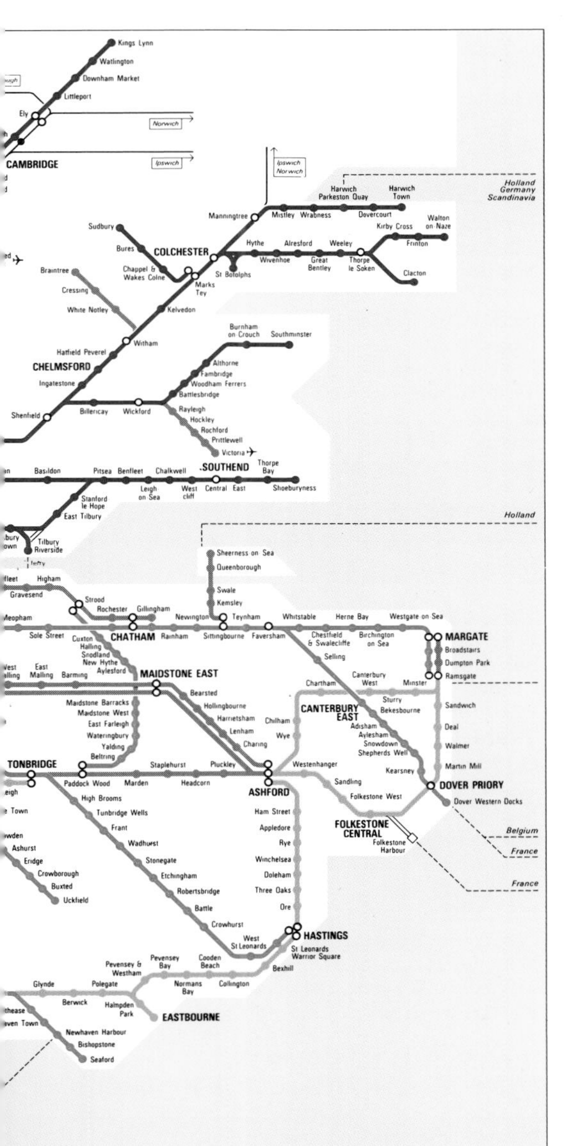

MAKING THE CONNECTION

Listed below are main out-of-London stations, and the direct Network SouthEast routes available from them. Journeys from these stations which are a route or part of a route described in the book are highlighted in bold. This list can be used to plan journeys that do not necessarily start or finish in London.

ASHFORD

Direct services to London Charing Cross via Tonbridge or Maidstone and London Victoria via Maidstone. Through services to **Hastings** via Rye, **Dover**, Folkestone and via Canterbury to **Ramsgate** and Margate.

BANBURY

Direct services to **London Paddington** via Oxford and Reading, and **London Marylebone** via High Wycombe. Also through services to Brighton via London Kensington, Olympia and to Poole via Reading, Basingstoke, Winchester, Southampton and Bournemouth.

BASINGSTOKE

Direct service to **London Waterloo**. Through services from **Waterloo to Weymouth** via Winchester, Southampton, Bournemouth, Poole and Dorchester, and from **Waterloo to Exeter** via Salisbury. Also services from Waterloo to Portsmouth via Fareham, and Poole to Oxford via Bournemouth, Southampton, Winchester and Reading.

BEDFORD

Direct services to **London St Pancras, Kings Cross Thameslink** and **St Pauls Thameslink** via Luton and St Albans. Through Thameslink services to Croydon, Gatwick Airport, Brighton, Guildford, Bromley and Sevenoaks. **Local service to Bletchley.**

BOURNEMOUTH

Direct service to **London Waterloo** via Southampton, Winchester and Basingstoke. Through services to **Weymouth** via Poole and Wareham, to **Portsmouth** via Southampton and to Reading and Oxford via Basingstoke.

BRIGHTON

Direct service to **London Victoria**, St Pauls Thameslink and Kings Cross Thameslink. Through Thameslink services to Luton and Bedford. Direct services to Bognor Regis, Chichester, Gatwick Airport, Littlehampton and Worthing. Also services to **Bournemouth** via Portsmouth and Southampton, to **Eastbourne and Hastings via Lewes**, and to Exeter via Salisbury.

CAMBRIDGE

Direct services to **London Kings Cross** via Stevenage, and **London Liverpool Street** via Harlow. Also services to **Ely and King's Lynn.**

CANTERBURY EAST AND WEST
Direct services to **London Victoria** via Faversham and Chatham and London Charing Cross, Ashford and Tonbridge. Through services from **Ashford to Ramsgate** and Margate.

CHATHAM AND GILLINGHAM
Direct services to **London Victoria**, and to London Charing Cross via Strood and Gravesend. Through services to **Dover via Canterbury East**, and to **Margate and Ramsgate.**

CHICHESTER
Direct service to **London Victoria.** Through services to **Worthing, Brighton**, Gatwick Airport and **Littlehampton** and to **Southampton** via Portsmouth.

COLCHESTER
Direct service to **London Liverpool Street** via Chelmsford. Through services to **Clacton and Walton, Harwich and Ely**. Local service to **Sudbury**.

DOVER PRIORY
Direct services to **London Victoria** via Canterbury and Faversham and London Charing Cross via Ashford and Tonbridge or Maidstone.

ELY
Direct service to **London Liverpool Street via Cambridge**. Through services to **King's Lynn**, Colchester and Harwich.

EXETER
Direct service from **London Waterloo**, via Basingstoke and Salisbury. Through services to Southampton, Portsmouth and Brighton via Salisbury.

GATWICK AIRPORT
Direct service to **London Victoria** and London Kings Cross and St Pauls Thameslink. Thameslink services to Luton and Bedford. Direct services to **Brighton**, Chichester, Guildford, Portsmouth, Southampton and Worthing. Also services to Newhaven and Seaford, to **Eastbourne** and Hastings via Lewes.

GUILDFORD
Direct services to **London Waterloo** and London Kings Cross and St Pauls Thameslink. Also through services to **Reading**, Gatwick Airport, **Tonbridge, Portsmouth** and Croydon.

HARWICH
Direct service from **London Liverpool Street**. Through services from **Colchester** and Ely.

MAIDSTONE EAST AND WEST
Maidstone East: Direct services to London Victoria and to London Charing Cross. Through services to Ashford and to Dover. Maidstone West: Through service to Paddock Wood from Strood.

OXFORD
Direct service from **London Paddington** via Reading. Through services to **Banbury**, and to Poole via Reading, Basingstoke, Winchester, Southampton and Bournemouth. Local service to **Bicester**.

PORTSMOUTH
Direct services to **London Waterloo**, via Guildford and via Eastleigh. Through services to **Brighton** via Chichester and Worthing, to Gatwick Airport, to **Salisbury and Southampton**, to **Bournemouth and Wareham**, to Bognor Regis and Littlehampton, to Exeter via Salisbury and ferry service to **Ryde, Isle of Wight**.

READING
Direct services to **London Paddington** and London Waterloo. Through services to **Banbury via Oxford, to Newbury and Bedwyn, to Tonbridge via Guildford**, to Poole via Basingstoke, Winchester, Southampton and Bournemouth and to Bicester.

ST ALBANS
Direct service to **London St Pancras** and London Kings Cross and St Pauls Thameslink. Through service to Bedford. Through Thameslink services to Guildford, Sevenoaks, Brighton and Gatwick. Local service to Watford Junction (from St Albans Abbey).

SALISBURY
Direct service to **London Waterloo**. Through services to Exeter, Westbury and to **Southampton and Portsmouth**.

SEVENOAKS
Direct services to **London Charing Cross** and London Kings Cross Thameslink and St Pauls Thameslink. Through Thameslink service to St Albans, Luton and Bedford. Through services to **Hastings**, Ashford, Canterbury, Ramsgate, Margate, Folkestone, Dover.

SOUTHAMPTON
Direct service to **London Waterloo** via Basingstoke and Winchester, and to London Victoria via Chichester and Worthing. Through services to Gatwick Airport, **Weymouth** via Bournemouth and Poole, to **Salisbury** and to **Portsmouth** and to Reading and Oxford via Basingstoke.

TONBRIDGE
Direct services to **London Charing Cross**. Through services to **Hastings**, Canterbury, Ramsgate, Margate, Folkestone and Dover, and to **Reading** via Guildford.

WAREHAM
Direct service to **London Waterloo** via Poole, Bournemouth, Southampton, Winchester and Basingstoke. Through services to **Weymouth** via Dorchester and to **Portsmouth** via Southampton.

WATFORD JUNCTION
Direct service to **London Euston**. Through services to **Milton Keynes and Northampton**. Local services to St Albans and Croxley Green.

USING THE TRAINS

RAIL INFORMATION

British Rail operates Britain's national rail network covering England, Scotland and Wales. Almost all train services in South East England are provided by Network SouthEast, the largest urban rail operator in the world. InterCity operates the Gatwick Express trains non-stop between Gatwick Airport and London Victoria, and a few longer distance services in East Anglia and across country in South East England. Network SouthEast is rapidly introducing new train carriages, and will speed you in comfort on your selected journeys.

TICKETS

Tickets can be purchased in advance or at the time of travel. Full details of prices of rail tickets including any special offers, together with information about train services, can be obtained from British Rail stations and Travel Centres and BR Appointed Travel Agents.

There is a range of rail tickets available to suit different travel requirements. Cheap Day Return tickets are available for most journeys between any two stations in Network South-East. They can be used any time on Saturdays, Sundays and Bank Holidays. For use on Mondays to Fridays, local stations will advise on the first available train after the morning peak period. Network AwayBreak tickets are available if you are staying away for up to five days and are widely available between stations more than about 30 miles apart (40 around London). Both these tickets are attractively priced for off-peak travel. The Network Card is a rail card which gives discounts on leisure fares in the Network SouthEast area for the individual, their family or friends. Considerable savings can be made, with one third off most Standard Class rail fares for up to three adults and four children travelling with the card holder. Discounts are also available to holders of Senior, Family, Young Persons and Disabled Persons Railcards.

Within the London area, One Day Travelcards give freedom of train, bus and tube. Rover tickets, where available, offer substantial savings and are an ideal way to tour South East England by rail. Overseas visitors should enquire about the 'London Extra' Pass which must be bought before leaving home.

In general, there are some time restrictions on off-peak, leisure tickets, and customers should enquire about these before travelling.

Children under five travel free provided that not more than four accompany each fare-paying passenger. Children aged between five and 15 travel at half fare.

At many stations Barclaycard/Visa, Access and American Express credit cards can be used.

PETS

Dogs and most other domestic pets can usually accompany passengers, but a fare is charged if larger animals travel in passenger carriages.

DISABLED FACILITIES

Principal stations are fully accessible to wheelchairs. On older trains there is limited access for wheelchairs, with entry via the guard's compartment, but most modern carriages have wide or sliding doors for direct wheelchair access. Some trains have a removable seat space for a wheelchair.

SMOKING

On most longer distance trains there are smoking and non-smoking sections, or carriages, but not on surburban trains or some local services.

LUGGAGE

Most carriages are equipped with adequate storage space for luggage and other personal possessions, but bulky items can travel in the guard's compartment, sometimes upon payment of a fee.

BICYCLES

On many trains a bicycle can be taken free of charge. On certain routes there are restrictions and charges because of limited space. Reservations are required on some services. Restrictions vary from route to route and details should be obtained from stations before travelling.

REFRESHMENTS

Most longer distance trains have either a buffet on board where you can get meals, hot and cold snacks and drinks 'on the move'; or a trolley service where light refreshments and drinks are provided. Refreshment facilities are found at stations in most large towns and cities. See the Station Index.

PARKING

Parking facilities are available at most stations. Stations with no car park are marked accordingly in the Station Index.

CAR HIRE

In association with British Rail, Hertz offer immediate and comprehensive car rental facilities at 71 principal Network SouthEast stations during normal office hours. Cars can also be arranged to be available at virtually any BR station, provided they are booked at least 24 hours in advance. Further details are available from Hertz or main British Rail stations.

TAXIS

Stations with a taxi rank are marked accordingly in the Station Index.

PRIVATE STEAM RAILWAYS

British Rail tickets are not valid on preserved railways and separate ones need to be purchased, although special tickets are sometimes available covering the BR journey and the preserved railway. Brief operating details are given with the preserved railways featured in this book, but many preserved railways run some services out of season which may vary from year to year and cannot be detailed in this guide.

USING THE BOOK

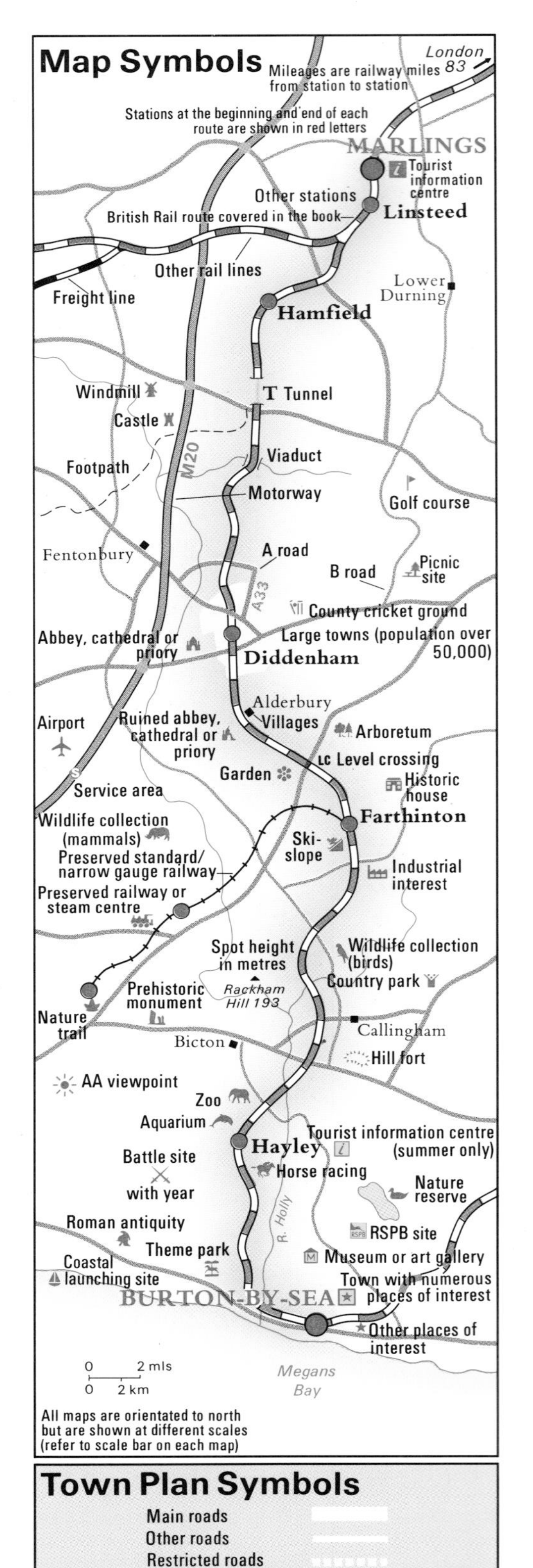

Town Plan Symbols

Main roads
Other roads
Restricted roads
Building of interest
Church
Tourist information centre
Public convenience

THE ROUTES

South East England By Train is presented as a series of journeys within the area covered by Network SouthEast. Most of the routes start from a main line London station, and are grouped in the book accordingly. A selection of routes between stations elsewhere in the area is given in the cross-country routes section. The Network SouthEast map on page 4 highlights the routes described in the book.

Any route can, of course, be joined outside London, nor does it have to be travelled in the declared direction. See Making the Connection on pages 5 and 6 if you are starting a journey out of London.

THE MAPS

The maps show the railway line and its immediate surroundings, with railway features, roads, towns, villages and places of interest clearly marked. All maps are orientated to the north, but are shown at different scales (refer to the scale bars).

PLACES TO VISIT

Each route is accompanied by a selection of places to visit, also shown on the route map, that lie within 3 miles of a station on that route. They are open all year unless otherwise stated, but it is always advisable to check the current details before making a special trip. The relevant Tourist Information Centres are listed with each route. Both these and the stations near which there are places to visit are listed in the described route order.

PRIVATE STEAM RAILWAYS

Seven private railway companies (listed on the Contents page) are featured in the book, all of which use steam for haulage. These have direct, or bus, connections with Network SouthEast.

WALKING FROM STATIONS

South East England is criss-crossed with waymarked and long distance footpaths and those which can easily be reached from a station are listed on the relevant route. These paths are indicated on the route maps, but you will need to consult an Ordnance Survey map or contact a local Tourist Information Centre for more detailed information. The TICs may also have information on other walks in the area, on guided walks or, occasionally, on walks which may be available from railway stations.

There are many opportunities in the area for walking from one station to another, either on the same route or between different routes, making a round trip possible. As a taster, five such routes are given on pages 96–7 but, with a little ingenuity, and the use of an Ordnance Survey map, it is possible to devise many other similar excursions. Always check the times of the return trains and allow yourself a good safety margin for catching them.

WALKING AND CYCLING ON DISUSED RAILWAYS

Over 8,000 miles of railways have been closed in Britain since 1947. Of this total there are still thousands of miles untouched since the track was lifted, quietly left as linear nature reserves. Many have been re-opened as public footpaths, and some connect with other footpath networks.

By their nature, the routes are predominantly level and fairly easygoing and there is always plenty to see in terms of landscape, urban settings, railway history and natural history. Sustrans, the railway and cycle route company (address below), can supply detailed information on officially designated railway paths.

Right: The Mid Hants preserved railway shares the British Rail station at Alton. Below: The railway line runs beside the Grand Union Canal at Berkhamsted, where there is access to the towpath

INDEXES

There are two indexes in the book. The first is to all the stations on the routes in the book, and here you will find information about car parking, refreshments and disabled facilities at each station, and whether there is a London Underground connection.

The second index includes towns, villages and places of interest mentioned in the book.

ADDRESSES

The following organisations are concerned with various aspects of the countryside, places to visit, walking, cycling and tourism and are happy to supply detailed information on request.

The Countryside Commission
John Dower House
Crescent Place
Cheltenham
Gloucestershire
GL50 3RA

Cyclists' Touring Club
69 Meadrow
Godalming
Surrey GU7 3HS

English Heritage (EH)
PO Box 43
Ruislip
Middlesex HA4 0XW

Forestry Commission
231 Corstorphine Road
Edinburgh
EH12 7AT

The National Trust (NT)
36 Queen Anne's Gate
London SW1H 9AS

Nature Conservancy Council
Northminster House
Peterborough
PE1 1UA

Royal Society for the Protection of Birds (RSPB)
The Lodge
Sandy
Bedfordshire
SG19 2DL

Sustrans Ltd
35 King Street
Bristol BS1 4DZ

The Ramblers' Association
1/5 Wandsworth Road
London SW8 2XX

TOURIST BOARDS

London
26 Grosvenor Gardens
London SW1W 0DU

South East
Warwick Park
Tunbridge Wells
Kent TN2 5TA

South
The Old Town Hall
Leigh Road
Eastleigh
Hampshire
SO5 4DE

Thames & Chilterns
The Mount House
Church Green
Witney
Oxon OX8 6AZ

West Country
37 Southernhay East
Exeter
Devon EX1 1QS

1 The entrance to the Royalty and Empire Exhibition, Windsor & Eton Central station

2 A Reading line train passes a field of oilseed rape in full bloom near Twyford

3 The grand clock over the main entrance, Platform 1, to Brunel's Paddington station

4 A rowing eight on the River Cherwell, Oxford with Merton and Christ Church Colleges behind

5 Approaching Great Bedwyn, with the Kennet and Avon Canal running alongside the railway line

6 Morris dancing in the street, part of the May Day celebrations in Oxford

1

2

3

4

ROUTES FROM
PADDINGTON AND MARYLEBONE

The Great Western Railway's line between London and Bristol, completed in 1835, quickly became the backbone of a vast network that covered the west of Britain from Cornwall to the Black Country. Even today the old traditions of the GWR still survive, with Brunel's great Paddington station the starting point for journeys to the West Country, South Wales, the Thames valley, Oxford and the Cotswolds, the Welsh borders and the West Midlands. Included in this section are journeys selected to show the varied nature of Network SouthEast's routes west of London, from the fast main lines to Reading, Oxford, Banbury, Newbury and Hungerford to the quiet branch lines serving the Thames valley.

Marylebone, the London terminus of the Great Central Railway, the last main line to be built in Britain, originally competed with Paddington and the GWR for West Midlands traffic, and the legacy of those days are the two routes to Banbury. Today, such competition is a part of history and Marylebone offers a range of commuter services to the Chilterns and beyond.

5

6

LOOKING AT STATIONS

Below: Slough's central pavilion roof is an elaborate confection of scale-like metalwork, bull's eye windows and finely worked, French-style iron railings

Above: Fenny Stratford station is one of a series on the Bedford to Bletchley line built to match the Duke of Bedford's estate at Woburn

Right: LNER's 1920s station at Clacton. Its imposing, pseudo-Georgian façade, typical of many public buildings of the period, is unusual for a railway station

The frontage at Brighton, which supports the clock, right, was built in 1840–1. The glass and iron porte-cochère was added later

Left: Mortimer's 1848 brick station is typical of Brunel's Italianate style, with its broad-hipped roof extending on all four sides

Below: the corner clock tower is the prominent feature of Eastbourne's Italianate French Renaissance style station

Recent repainting at Great Missenden station highlights the decorative detailing of the ironwork

Contemporary styles of architecture are reflected in the stations being built anew or redeveloped by British Rail. Below: the recently rebuilt station at Littlehampton, West Sussex

ONE OF THE PLEASURES OF travel on Network SouthEast is the discovery of the extraordinary variety of stations that exists throughout the region. As the railways were built by many independent private companies, every imaginable architectural style has been used over the years, from medieval and classical to modern, and much else in between, with every company trying to make its mark and attract traffic by its own distinctive style. This tradition survived well up to the formation of British Rail in 1948, and now these idiosyncratic buildings are increasingly being preserved as part of Britain's railway heritage. At the same time, Network SouthEast is busy restoring and redeveloping existing stations and opening new ones to satisfy changing demands.

LESSER-KNOWN STATIONS

Marylebone, which serves the Chiltern Lines, is one of London's hidden treasures, an elegant structure full of discreet qualities. One of the last of London's many termini, Marylebone was completed in 1899 by the Great Central Railway, whose new rail route from the North East and the Midlands to London, an ambitious undertaking, used up most of its finance. Its London terminus was therefore rather modest, its style determined by an economical simplicity rather than the conventional Victorian exuberance. Recent restoration work has made the most of this particular quality, while leaving intact many original features, including the glazed *porte-cochère* and walkway that links it to the flamboyant Great Central Hotel, whose façade on the Marylebone Road completely conceals the station from view. The hotel, designed by Robert Edis and decorated with Art Nouveau terracotta panels by John Broad, is set to return to its former use after serving as offices over many years.

A very different structure is Fenchurch Street. When completed in 1854, it was the first station in the City of London. Designed by George Berkeley, and built as its terminus by the little-known London and Blackwall Railway, the station was shared from the outset by the much larger London, Tilbury and Southend company. To this day it remains the terminus for destinations along the Essex side of the Thames estuary. Extensively redeveloped inside, Fenchurch Street still has its distinctive classical façade, whose long curving pediment gives it the flavour of some European station. The formal severity of the design is softened by the zig-zag line of the wooden canopy.

GOTHIC AND MEDIEVAL

Victorian architects were particularly fond of gothic and medieval styles, and there are, as a result, many stations that reflect this enthusiasm. In some cases a medieval or Tudor style was thought appropriate for a historic setting, with notable examples including Battle, designed in 1852 by William Tress, and Hampton Court, Sir William Tite's 1849 response to the challenge posed by the palace. Other Tudor-style stations of a similar date include Wateringbury and Aylesford, the latter marked by a careful use of local materials, while the local golden Ham stone also adds character to the Tudor details of Crewkerne, also by Sir William Tite. The more decorative, or picturesque, aspects of the medieval style are echoed by the remarkable group of half-timbered, cottage-style stations on the Bedford to Bletchley line, including Fenny Stratford (see opposite).

RENAISSANCE AND CLASSICAL

From the 17th century onwards, Renaissance and classical styles of architecture were dominant in Britain, and these were also favoured by many Victorian railway architects. Italian and Dutch influences can be seen at Hertford East, 1888, and Wareham, 1886, particularly in the decorative gables, while the simpler Italian style favoured by Brunel in the late 1840s, with its broad-hipped roof, can be seen at Mortimer and Dorchester West. Different aspects of the Renaissance can also be seen in the two Windsor stations. The earlier, Windsor & Eton Riverside, was completed in 1849 in an ornate English Renaissance style, while Windsor & Eton Central was completely rebuilt in 1897 in a style that was more French than Italian. French influences can also be seen at Slough, in the chateau-like façade of Portsmouth & Southsea and, in a far more rural manner, at Boxhill & Westhumble, which dates from 1867.

Much more common among railway stations is the more formal classicism of the late 17th and 18th centuries. Early examples include the long, arcaded 1845 façade of Cambridge, the symmetry of Audley End, also of 1845. Other good examples of classical symmetry are Micheldever, 1840, Rye, 1851, and the 1866 stations on the St Denys to Fareham line. The survival of the classical style into this century is underlined by Hatch End of 1911, with its Lutyens-like details, and the imposing but rather stark version used in 1926 at Margate and at Ramsgate.

1930s AND MODERN

Art Deco is a rare style in British architecture, and good 1930s stations are even rarer. All the more remarkable, therefore, is Surbiton's 1937 station, a major building of its period in the modern Odeon cinema style. Other examples include Bishopstone and the set of stations on the Chessington branch, with their curved concrete canopies. Modern styles of architecture are also reflected in the stations that British Rail are building now, ranging from the post-modernism of Oxford's grand 1989 structure to the conscious use of vernacular details at Dorchester South.

IN LOCAL STYLE

Also worth noting are stations built for a particular purpose. Seaside and harbour stations are a group with their own particular qualities. They can be grand and ornate, as at Eastbourne with its Italianate tower and French details, classical and pompous as at Brighton or Clacton, or workmanlike, as at Dover Marine, Weymouth or Harwich. The best seaside atmosphere is inevitably achieved by those where the train enters the station over the sea, as at Portsmouth Harbour, Ryde Pier Head and Folkestone Harbour.

The Thames and the Cherwell

PADDINGTON – BANBURY *86¼ miles*
and The Bicester Branch

This is a journey of three parts, first westwards from London to Reading, second following the route of the Thames to Oxford via Didcot and third along the valley of the Cherwell to Banbury. The scenery and the surroundings are continuously varied and full of interest, reflecting the colourful history of a part of England where centuries of development can be seen, from prehistory to the present. Above all, it is a landscape forged by rivers and the line crosses the Thames no fewer than six times on its way to Oxford.

Upstream from Maidenhead's railway bridge: Boulter's Lock on the Thames

Paddington – Reading
Trains for Oxford and Banbury leave from beneath the vaulted and glazed roof of London's most elegant station. Paddington, completed in 1854, was designed by I K Brunel, the engineer of the Great Western Railway, and this cathedral of the railway age is a fitting starting point for a journey that still bears the clear stamp of Brunel's genius. The line to Reading is fast and straight, and marked by engineering on a generous scale. Notable features include major bridges and viaducts, high embankments and long cuttings, all reflecting Brunel's desire to give his railway the fastest possible route to the West.

Leaving Paddington, the train follows the elevated M40 motorway briefly before emerging into an area of high-rise development. Kensal Green cemetery and Old Oak Common depot are passed to the north, while to the south are the pinnacles of Wormwood Scrubs. London tube trains share the route for much of the way to Ealing Broadway and then the surroundings become more suburban as the line is carried high over the River Brent on the eight-arched Wharncliffe Viaduct of 1837.

The French-style, domed station at **Slough** dates partly from 1838.

Tourist Information Centres
MAIDENHEAD The Library, St Ives Rd (0628) 781110
READING Town Hall, Blagrave St (0734) 566266
ABINGDON (for Radley) The Old Gaol, Bridge St (0235) 22711
OXFORD St Aldates (0865) 726871
BANBURY Banbury Museum, 8 Horsefair (0295) 259855

Walks
Kennet and Avon Canal (see page 18). The towpath can be joined from stations between Reading and Bedwyn.
The London Countryway A 205-mile circular route around London, including the North Downs and the Chilterns. The route can be joined from Maidenhead.
The Ridge Way Path Runs 85 miles, from East Kennett near Marlborough (Wilts) to Ivinghoe Beacon (Herts). The path can be joined from Goring & Streatley.

Places to Visit
BURNHAM (stopping train only) **Burnham Abbey ruins.**
MAIDENHEAD **Courage Shire Horse Centre,** Maidenhead Thicket, 3m W. Working stable with up to 12 prize-winning Courage shire horses. Free tours (open Mar–Oct).
READING **Abbey ruins and Forbury Gardens,** The Market Place.

continued on page 15

One of the gentle giants of the Courage Shire Horse Centre, Maidenhead

This is the place to change for the branch to Windsor (page 20).

Before this was opened, in 1850, Queen Victoria used Slough when she travelled to Windsor Castle. A number of interesting factories line the route, notably the impressive brick home of Horlicks.

After Slough, the landscape becomes more rural, while to the south can be seen the continuous stream of planes on their final approach to Heathrow. To the north is Taplow's 1912 church with its distinctive green spire, and then the train makes its first crossing of the Thames. Maidenhead bridge, with its two graceful shallow brick arches spanning the river, is one of Brunel's masterpieces. Opened in 1837, it confounded its critics, who firmly believed that such flat arches were bound to collapse. The bridge also features in J M W Turner's painting, *Rain, Steam and Speed.* **Maidenhead** still retains echoes of its Edwardian charm by the river.

This is the place to change for the branch to Bourne End and Marlow (page 21).

To the west of **Twyford** station, where the Henley branch (see page 21) joins the main line, are the lakes and flooded gravel pits that surround the River Loddon, a Thames tributary. A deep cutting south of Sonning carries the train towards Reading, and it enters the town with the Thames right by the track. To the north is the white façade of Caversham Park, an 1850s mansion that now houses the BBC's foreign language section. Before it arrives at Reading's newly expanded station, the line crosses the River Kennet, the Thames's link with the Kennet and Avon Canal and the recently reopened waterway route to Bath and Bristol.

Reading

A thriving university town and shopping and business centre, Reading still has a good variety of 19th-century architecture, notably the Royal Berkshire Hospital of 1837 and the 1870s municipal buildings by Waterhouse. The ruins of the Cluniac abbey, founded by Henry I in the 12th century, underline the town's importance in the past.

Reading station is an important junction, with lines running to Oxford and the Midlands, the West Country and the South West via Basingstoke. Another line, running to Waterloo, (see pages 92–3) also connects with routes to Surrey and Kent.

Reading – Oxford

Leaving Reading, the line turns north-west to follow the Thames valley. Just west of **Tilehurst** station there is a glimpse of Mapledurham House, sited by the river, and there are fine views of the Thames at **Pangbourne**. West of Pangbourne, 18th-century Basildon Park can be seen to the south-west. The scenery is at its best as the line, and the river, pass through the Goring Gap, with rolling hills to the south and the wooded banks of the river to the north. The train crosses the river before reaching **Goring & Streatley**, and again shortly after, and then the landscape becomes more open as the Thames swings away northwards. After **Cholsey**, the former branch line to Wallingford can still be seen and to the south are the distant Downs that mark the route of the Ridge Way. As the line approaches Didcot, a distinctive feature to the north are the twin, rounded mounds of the Sinodun Hills with their Iron Age fort. At **Didcot Parkway**,

Blake's Lock Museum, Gasworks Rd. Illustrates the history of industrial and commercial life in Reading. **Museum of English Rural Life,** University of Reading,

Reading station's decorative clock tower

Whiteknights Park. Agricultural, domestic and crafts exhibits.
TILEHURST **Mapledurham House**. Elizabethan manor, watermill and country park (Etr Sun–1 Oct).
GORING & STREATLEY **Child Beale Wildlife Trust,** Church Farm, Lower Basildon, with exotic birds, Highland cattle and rare sheep. Playground, craft centre, river trips (open Etr–Sep). **Basildon House & Park** (NT), 3m S. 18th-century house overlooking Thames (open Apr–Oct).
DIDCOT **Gt Western Society Didcot Railway Centre.** Largest collection of ex-Great Western rolling stock (open Mar–Dec).
APPLEFORD **Pendon Museum of Miniature Landscape and Transport,** Long Wittenham. Model railway and village

continued on page 16

The Elizabethan mansion at Mapledurham

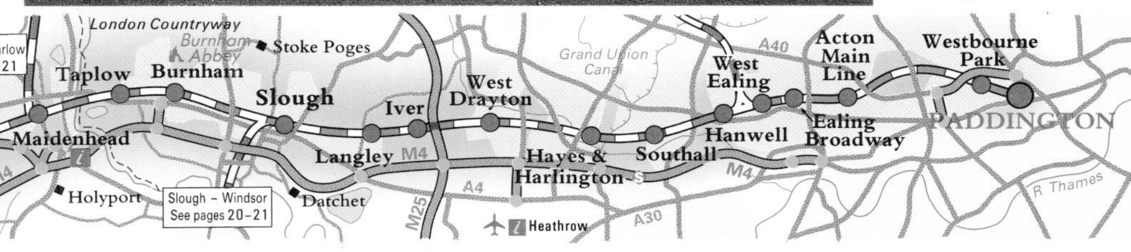

scenes depicting 1930s. RADLEY (for Abingdon) **Abingdon Museum,** County Hall, the Market Place. Built

Chinese porcelain boys in the Ashmolean, Oxford

1678, local history, archaeology. OXFORD **Ashmolean Museum of Art and Archaeology,** Beaumont St. Extensive display of archaeology. Art includes Old Master and modern drawings, European oil paintings, watercolours and prints. **Bate Collection of Historical Instruments,** Faculty of Music, St Aldates. **Carfax Tower.** Only remaining part of St Martin's church (open Mar–Nov). **Christ Church Cathedral**, St Aldates. Mainly Norman church, built on the site of Anglo-Saxon nunnery. **Christ Church Picture Gallery,** Canterbury Gate. Important Old Masters. **Museum of the History of Science,** old Ashmolean building. Finest collection of early astronomical, mathematical and optical instruments in the world. **Museum of Modern Art,** 30 Pembroke St. Changing exhibits of contemporary art. **Museum of Oxford,** St Aldates. Displays the archaeology and history of the city. **The Oxford Story,** Broad St. University's history in audio-visual displays. **Oxford University Museum,** Parks Rd. Natural history collection. **Pitt Rivers Museum,** South Parks Rd. Ethnology and prehistoric archaeology. **Sheldonian Theatre.** 16th-century assembly hall built by Wren. **University Colleges.** Many college buildings are open to the public,

continued on page 17

another major junction, the Oxford line turns north, while the main line continues westwards towards Bristol. Many Oxford trains bypass the timber station of 1885 but pass close to the preserved carriages, wagons, buildings and steam engines that are all part of the Great Western Society's Railway Centre. While the cooling towers of Didcot power station dominate the view to the west, there is a changing view of the Sinodun Hills to the east. At **Appleford** there is an original GWR corrugated-iron station building, known as a Pagoda shelter, while **Culham** still boasts a chalet-style station of 1845, designed by Brunel. The train makes two more crossings of the meandering Thames and then there is a good view of 18th-century Nuneham Courtenay, set in its park high above the curving river. From **Radley** station there was once a branch to Abingdon. Approaching Oxford, the line runs by the Thames again, and an iron bridge carries the Kennington branch that serves the Austin Rover car factory at Cowley. Oxford suburbs now dominate, and then from Hinksey there are the first views of the famous skyline of spires and towers. Oxford station, the third on the site, is a brand new post-Modernist style structure, opened in 1990.

Change at Oxford for the branch to Bicester Town (see page 17).

Oxford

One of the great centres of European learning and a university town since the 12th century, Oxford has a quality of timelessness that somehow survives the clamour of modern tourism, commerce and industry. Its gothic towers and cloisters, and its wealth of handsome stone buildings from the 17th to the 19th centuries make it an excellent city to explore on foot. There are over 650 buildings of interest in the city, including a major cathedral, Wren's Sheldonian Theatre, the 18th-century Radcliffe Camera, and the Victorian gothic University Museum. However, the city's most famous features are inevitably the colleges, with their chapels, cloisters and quadrangles, and exploring both the colleges and their gardens is one of Oxford's great pleasures. The city has plenty of other attractions, however, including the Thames, the Ashmolean Museum, the covered market and the great shopping streets – the High, Cornmarket and Broad Street. Famous also for books and bookselling, marmalade and motor cars (William Morris built his first car in Oxford in 1913), the city is an enjoyable blend of town and gown.

Oxford – Banbury

The train leaves Oxford with the broad expanse of Port Meadow and its wild ponies to the west and the Oxford Canal, whose terminus is just by the station, to the east. The canal is a constant presence by the line between Oxford and Banbury, with plenty of opportunities to enjoy its locks, its distinctive lifting bridges and its meandering course along the Cherwell valley. With Wytham Hill and Wood forming a distant view to the west, the line passes Wolvercote and Yarnton, with its church and manor. At Thrupp, to the west, lines of narrow boats flank the canal, and beyond is Shipton Church and Manor. Directly opposite, to the east, is the delightfully isolated 18th-century church of Hampton Gay, and beyond it the ruins of Hampton Manor, destroyed by a fire in 1887. The line follows the Cherwell and the canal to **Tackley**, where there is a fine partly 11th-century cruciform church. North of the station is a good view of

One of the world's greatest libraries, the Bodleian, Oxford, has some five million books

the old oxbow bends of the Cherwell, with the canal beyond, its route marked by distinctive arched bridges. As it approaches **Heyford**, the line runs close to Rousham Park, to the west, giving excellent views of the landscape garden and its buildings designed by William Kent from 1738. At Heyford, canal and railway run side by side, while to the west Steeple Aston church overlooks the valley. Frequently to be seen are planes from the USAF at Upper Heyford. Following the Cherwell valley, the line runs through landscape dotted with farms and houses in the soft Cotswold stone. To the east is Somerton church, with its fine 15th-century, battlemented parapet on the tower, and then two large handsome brick viaducts carry the line from Bicester to its junction with the Banbury line at Aynho. The new M40 crosses the line and then the tall spire of King's Sutton Church forms a prominent landmark to the east. Just south of **King's Sutton** station are the remains of the old line to Kingham via Chipping Norton. As the train approaches Banbury there are plenty of signs of its former importance as a major junction, with the remains of old lines westwards to Northampton and Bletchley and its link with the old Great Central route to London. Old semaphore signals are another link with Banbury's railway past.

Banbury
Well known for its cross, its nursery rhyme and its cakes, Banbury is a busy market town with a handsome main street lined with 18th- and 19th-century buildings in the distinctive, rich brown Northampton stone. The famous cross was actually erected in Victorian times.

The Bicester Branch

OXFORD – BICESTER TOWN *11¾ miles*

Reopened to passengers in 1989, this line was originally part of a route from Oxford to Cambridge via Bletchley and Bedford. Part of the old terminus, a striking cast-iron and timber building of 1852, still survives near Oxford's brand new station, in use as a tyre depot. Leaving Oxford, the train follows the main line north past Port Meadow and then branches east to **Islip**, a pretty, stone village set on a hill, before running to the north of Ot Moor, a natural wildness of wetlands. To the south is Merton's fine 14th-century church, while to the north is the site of the Roman town of Alchester. Approaching Bicester, with the mound of Graven Hill dominant to the south, the line is flanked by hedgerows and the water meadows of the River Ray. **Bicester Town** is the end of the line for passengers.

The Marylebone – Banbury route (pages 24–5) runs through Bicester North, a 20-minute walk from Bicester Town station.

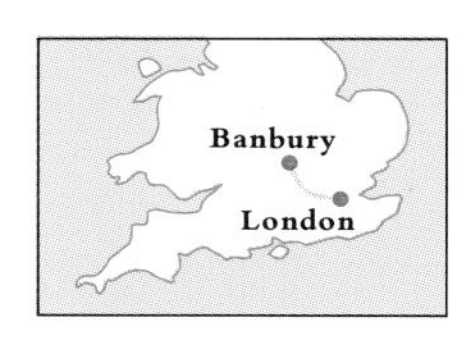

but access to some is restricted to certain times. Contact TIC for further details.
University Botanic Gardens, High St. Oldest botanical gardens in Great Britain.
HEYFORD **Rousham House and Gardens.** 17th- and 18th-century house near River Cherwell, with Civil War associations (open Apr–Sep; gardens all year; children under 15 not admitted).
BANBURY **Banbury Museum,** 8 Horsefair. Small museum, local history, etc.
Broughton Castle, 2m SW on B4035. Moated Tudor mansion (open May–Sep).

'Ride a cock-horse to Banbury Cross' – a rhyme that dates from medieval times, but the present cross was erected in 1859

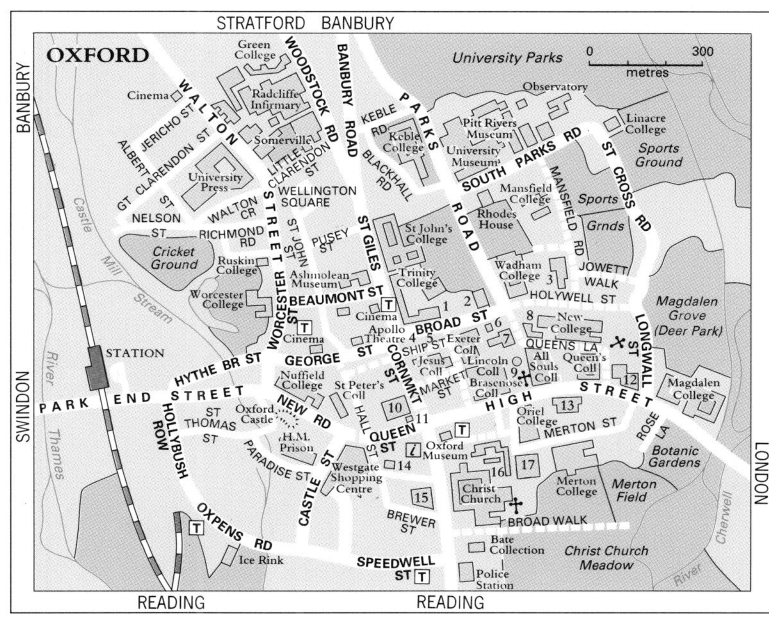

Main roads
Other roads
Restricted roads
Building of interest
Church
Tourist Information Centre
Public convenience

PLACES OF INTEREST

1 Balliol College
2 New Bodleian Library
3 Manchester College
4 Saxon Tower
5 The Oxford Story
6 Sheldonian Theatre
7 Bodleian Library
8 Hertford College
9 Radcliffe Camera
10 Clarendon Centre
11 Carfax Tower
12 St Edmund Hall
13 University College
14 Museum of Modern Art
15 Pembroke College
16 Picture Gallery
17 Corpus Christi College

The Kennet and the Avon

PADDINGTON – BEDWYN *via Reading* *66½ miles*

The leisurely journey from London to the heart of rural Wiltshire generally involves a simple change of trains at Reading. The route actually forms part of the main high-speed line to Devon and Cornwall, but the atmosphere of the stopping train to Bedwyn is far more relaxed as it follows the Kennet and Avon Canal westwards.

Tourist Information Centres
MAIDENHEAD The Library, St Ives Rd (0628) 781110
NEWBURY The Wharf (0635) 32196
READING Town Hall, Blagrave St (0734) 566226

Walks
The Kennet and Avon Canal connects the Avon at Bath to the Kennet at Reading. The towpath can be joined between Reading and Bedwyn. See Walk 1 on page 96.
The London Countryway (see page 14). The path can be joined from Maidenhead.

The imposing gatehouse of Donnington Castle, just north of Newbury

Paddington – Reading
For the journey from London Paddington to Reading, see pages 14–15. There is nothing to be gained by taking the slower, stopping trains for this part of the route.

Reading – Bedwyn
Reading station has a gracious Italianate façade of 1870, crowned with a decorative clock tower, but to the side lies a new station complete with shopping arcade. The town centre, enclosed by the Thames to the north and the Kennet to the south and east, is conveniently reached on foot from the station. Although the remains of the abbey founded by Henry I give a hint of the town's early history, Reading is predominantly Victorian, and its most striking buildings include the classical Royal Berkshire Hospital of 1837, Woodyer's Christ Church of 1861 and the wonderfully decorative municipal buildings designed by Waterhouse in 1872.

Trains for Bedwyn leave from the south-west part of the station, run past housing estates to **Reading West**, and then soon enter open country as they cross the Kennet. From this point the river and the Kennet and Avon Canal are never far from the line, and the canal with its newly restored locks, its handsome brick bridges and its brightly painted narrow boats is an enjoyable feature of the journey. With the gravel works and lakes of the Kennet valley to the south, the line passes under the M4 and then **Theale** comes into view, marked by its large early Victorian church. The next station is **Aldermaston**, but the village with its pretty brick cottages and its famous pottery is over a mile south of the station. Closer to hand is Midgham Church, Victorian and decorative, and attractively placed in a field just west of **Midgham** station. At **Thatcham**, another station some distance from its town, there is a canal lock just to the south. Approaching Newbury, the train passes the racecourse, whose old weather-boarded station, **Newbury Racecourse**, retains its GWR name boards. At **Newbury** station, little of the town can be seen, but the centre is

Paddington – Banbury
See pages 14–17
Didcot 17¼
Reading
Reading West
A340
Theale
A329
Waterloo 43
M4
Bucklebury
0 2 mls
0 2 km
Old Rectory Garden
Burghfield
Reading – Tonbr
See pages 108–
A33
Aldermaston
Midgham
Aldermaston
Mortimer
Thatcham
Kennet & Avon Canal
A339
Newbury Racecourse
Newbury
A4
A34
Donnington
R Lambourn
Hamstead Marshall
Kintbury
Hungerford
A338
Froxfield
Little Bedwyn
29 Westbury
BEDWYN
Great Bedwyn

Newbury Racecourse, right beside the railway, has its own station

Places to Visit

For information on Reading see pages 14–15

MAIDENHEAD **Courage Shire Horse Centre**, Maidenhead Thicket, 3m W. Working stable with up to 12 prize-winning Courage shire horses. Free tours (open Mar–Oct).
THEALE **The Old Rectory Garden, Burghfield,** 2½m SE. Old-fashioned cottage plants and many rare plants from China and Japan (open last Wed of month, Feb–Oct).

continued on page 19

The railway between Reading and Great Bedwyn is never far from the Kennet and Avon Canal

not far away, easily accessible on foot. Newbury has plenty to offer the visitor. The great 16th-century church and the 17th-century cloth hall, which now houses the museum, reveal the town's former wealth as a centre of the wool trade. In the 15th century over 1,000 wool weavers were employed here, in what was England's first true factory. Prosperity continued in later centuries, particularly after the opening of the Kennet and Avon Canal, which winds its way through the town centre, and the legacy is an interesting variety of buildings of all periods, including some groups of almshouses and a Victorian corn exchange.

Leaving Newbury, the train enters a wooded stretch, with glimpses of the pretty village of Hamstead Marshall to the south as it passes the close group of the mill, the pub and the canal lock. To the north is the classical façade of 18th-century Benham House, set in its Capability Brown park. **Kintbury** village is to the south of its station, clustered round its large church. After Kintbury the river valley becomes more defined and the line runs along the southern slopes with good views across to the northern side, beyond the river and the canal. **Hungerford** is a handsome town, with all its main buildings in one street which climbs southwards away from the river. From the railway bridge just west of the station, there is a clear view of the town centre, with its good range of 18th- and 19th-century buildings, but trains approaching from the west offer the best view of the church and its vicarage, pleasantly set beside the river and the canal. West of Hungerford the line overlooks the canal and the river valley, and then it crosses the canal again near Froxfield, where the decorative gothic façade of the almshouses founded by the Duchess of Somerset in 1694 can be clearly seen.

Railway and canal now run close together to Little Bedwyn, a delightful village with its 12th-century church, its row of 1860s estate cottages, all in coloured brick, and the 18th-century buildings by the canal and lock. Locks appear quite frequently now as the canal climbs towards its summit, a few miles to the south-west, and the train soon reaches **Bedwyn**, the end of the line for Network SouthEast travellers. Near the station is Great Bedwyn's large church with its grand central tower and pretty graveyard, and a short walk away is the attractive village whose delights include the eccentric Stone Museum, where examples of the stonemason's art show how the carvings have a language of their own. There is a fossilised footprint of a dinosaur. A pleasant walk westwards for two miles along the canal towpath leads to Crofton, where the oldest steam pumping engine in the world that is still in working order can occasionally be seen on duty, adding water to the canal to maintain its level. To the north-west is the dense woodland of Savernake Forest, formerly a Royal hunting park.

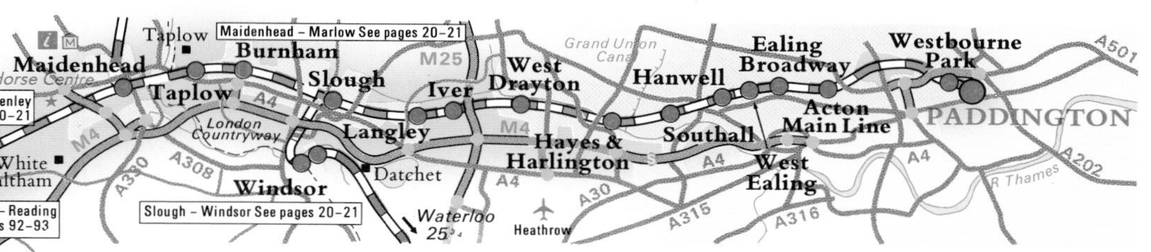

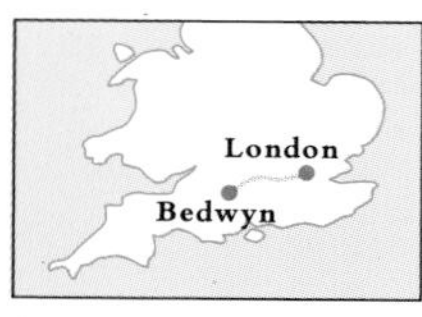

NEWBURY **Donnington Castle,** 2m N. 14th-century rectangular castle. **Newbury District Museum,** the Wharf. 17th- and 18th-century buildings housing displays of ballooning, the Kennet and Avon Canal, traditional crafts, costume and the Civil War battles of Newbury.
Newbury Racecourse (contact TIC for details of race meetings).
Civil War battle sites – one to the north (1644), centred on Donnington Castle, and the second to the south-west (1643).
BEDWYN **Bedwyn Stone Museum.** Open air museum, displays stonemason's art in monuments,

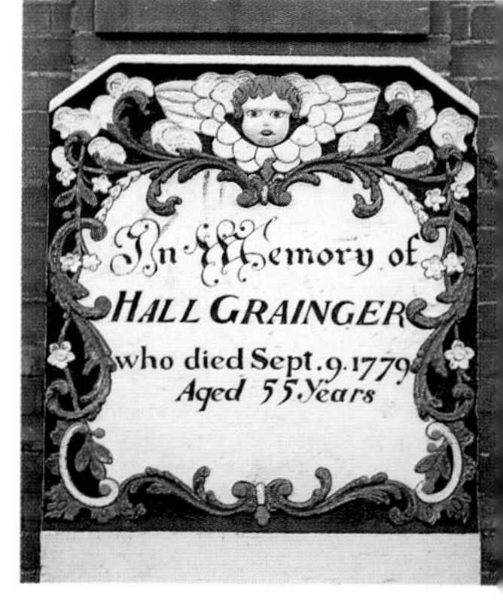

Exhibit at the Great Bedwyn Stone Museum

gravestones, busts and sculpture going back to the 18th century.
Crofton Beam Engines, 2m SW. Early 19th-century building containing two restored Beam Engines. Both are coal-fired and pump water into the canal with a lift of 40ft. Trips can be taken on the canal (open Apr–Oct).

Thames Valley Branches

PADDINGTON – WINDSOR *via Slough* *21 ¼ miles*
PADDINGTON – MARLOW *via Maidenhead* *31 ½ miles*
PADDINGTON – HENLEY *via Twyford* *35 ½ miles*

A day spent exploring the Thames by train is an enjoyable and unusual way to see Britain's most famous river. Thames-side castles and mansions, pretty villages and attractive landscapes are all features of these branch lines, along with ample opportunities to witness the delights, or otherwise, of messing about in boats.

The starting point in London for all these journeys is Paddington station and travellers can take any of the stopping services that run to Reading and change to connecting services at Slough for Windsor & Eton, Maidenhead for Marlow or Twyford for Henley. See pages 14–15 for a description of this part of the journey.

Tourist Information Centres (*summer only)

HENLEY* Town Hall, Market Place (0491) 578034
MAIDENHEAD The Library, St Ives Rd (0628) 781110
MARLOW* Court Garden, Leisure Complex, Pound Lane (06284) 3597
WINDSOR Central Station, Thames St (0753) 852010

Walks

The London Countryway (see page 14). The path can be joined from Maidenhead.
The Oxfordshire Way Runs 65 miles across Oxfordshire, from Henley-on-Thames to Bourton-on-the-Water (Glos), linking the Chilterns and the Cotswolds. The path can be joined from Henley.

SLOUGH – WINDSOR & ETON
2 ¾ miles

Windsor still has two stations and their palatial grandeur is a reflection of the desire by rival railway companies to attract royal travellers. The Great Western opened its short branch from Slough to Windsor & Eton Central in 1850 but what survives today dates largely from 1897, an ostentatious celebration of Queen Victoria's Diamond Jubilee. The train leaves **Slough**'s imposing French-style station and takes initially a rather domestic route among back gardens and allotments until it passes under the M4. There is then a dramatic change as it makes an elevated, curving approach to Windsor. Much of the route is on a brick viaduct, from which there are splendid views of the castle and the Thames, with Eton College chapel on the skyline to the east. The Thames is crossed on an 1849 wrought-iron bridge, Brunel's oldest surviving iron bridge, and the line then swings high above **Windsor** into the terminus. It is an excellent example of railway theatre, and it must have satisfied the royal family, whose huge private station stands alongside, a massive roofed structure complete with royal waiting rooms and big enough to accommodate a full military escort with their horses. Fully restored and complete with period details, this now houses the Royalty and Empire Exhibition. The station, a mass of red brick, buff stone and glass, richly detailed overall, opens directly into the heart of Windsor, facing the towering castle walls. Bus and walking tours start directly from the covered cab drive attached to the station.

The stations at Windsor have seen royalty come and go since opening in 1850

Places to Visit

For information on Maidenhead see pages 14–15

SLOUGH – WINDSOR & ETON
WINDSOR & ETON
Eton College. Largest English public school, founded in 1440 by Henry VI. Chapel, Lower School and Cloisters open Apr–Oct. **Household Cavalry Museum**, Combermere Barracks. Exhibits of Life Guards, Royal Horse Guards and 1st Royal Dragoons. **Royalty and Empire Exhibition,** Windsor & Eton Central Railway Station. Recreates the celebrations of Queen Victoria's Diamond Jubilee of 1897 using full-size wax figures. **Windsor Castle.** Restored Norman royal castle with additions by George IV (castle precinct open daily but subject to sudden closure). **St George's**

continued on page 21

MAIDENHEAD – MARLOW
7¼ miles

Maidenhead station, with its decorative cast iron and its pretty little glazed trainshed over the Marlow line platforms, is certainly to be enjoyed while changing trains. The older parts of Maidenhead are surrounded by new development, but by the river the town retains some echo of its Edwardian charm. There is a fine view of Boulter's Lock from the elegant 1772 stone bridge, and a short walk southwards along the Thames leads to Maidenhead's greatest feature, Brunel's magnificent 1838 bridge. With its two 128ft span arches, this is the longest, and the flattest, ever built in brick. Leaving the station, the Marlow train curves round Maidenhead, touring its suburbs and back gardens on its way to **Furze Platt** station. The town is then left behind as the train moves into a more open landscape, with good views to the east towards the Thames. The Astor family's great mansion at Cliveden can be seen above the trees

Cliveden: its grounds include woodland walks with magnificent views over the Thames

Chapel, Windsor Castle (open most of year). **State Apartments** (open most of year). **Queen Mary's Dolls House & Exhibition of Drawings**, Windsor Castle. **Queen's Presents & Royal Carriages Exhibition**, Windsor Castle. **Windsor Great Park**, 3m S. **Windsor Safari Park and Seaworld**, Winkfield Rd. Wild animal reserves, killer whale and dolphin shows, butterfly house, children's farmyard and boating lake.

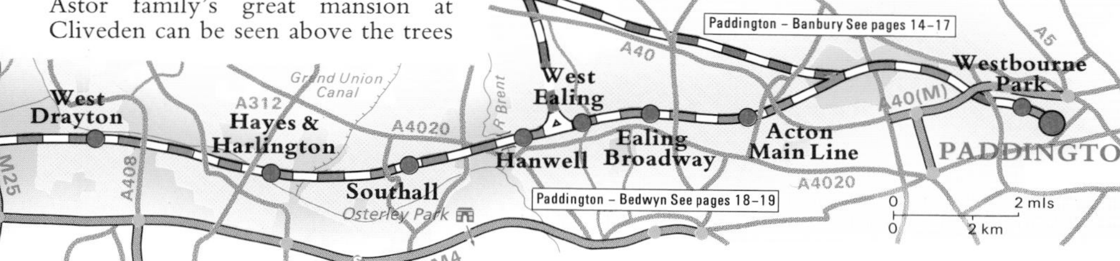

all the way to **Cookham**, set high above the river. Now a luxury hotel, the classical-style house was designed by Sir Charles Barry. Cookham village is well to the east of its station but is worth a visit for its 13th-century church, its decorative cast-iron bridge and riverside cottages and, above all, for the Stanley Spencer Gallery. Leaving Cookham, the line drops down towards the Thames and then crosses the river before coming to a dead end at **Bourne End**. Formerly, the line continued northwards towards High Wycombe, but the train now reverses and sets off along the pretty riverside journey to **Marlow**, with good views back towards Bourne End and over the river to Winter Hill. Marlow is the end of the line and the rather minimal station is well placed for the town. There is plenty to see, notably the riverside setting with the lock and the weir, best seen from Tierney Clark's splendid suspension bridge of 1831, and Marlow Place, dating from 1720.

The Thames is particularly attractive between Marlow and Henley and both towns are good bases for explorations of the river and its valley and for walks along the Thames towpath.

TWYFORD – HENLEY-ON-THAMES *4½ miles*

Twyford is a typical Thames valley station, with plenty of coloured brick and decorative cast iron. Leaving Twyford, the Henley train curves round the village with its Victorian church visible among the trees, and then runs straight to **Wargrave**, which is well to the east of the station, but worth a visit for its variety of 18th-century cottages, and its unexpected Arts and Crafts and Art Nouveau buildings, by the local architect Cole Adams. Wargrave Church has a distinctive 17th-century brick tower. Leaving the village, the train crosses the Thames rather slowly, allowing plenty of time to enjoy the view of the river. Rather grand is the heavy white-painted classical façade of Wargrave Manor, seen in the wooded hills to the east. The next station is **Shiplake**, approached across the Thames watermeadows, but the only parts of the village that can be seen from the train are the riverside mansions with their wealth of Edwardian and Art Nouveau details. North of Shiplake the Thames is seen at its best as it flows below steeply wooded banks, and then the train reaches its terminus. **Henley's** new station is convenient for visits to the town, one of the most attractive on the river and well known for its annual regatta. The best way to see Henley and its pleasant river-front is to cross the 18th-century stone bridge and look back to enjoy the variety of decorative 18th- and 19th-century buildings that surround the pretty gothic church. The 1805 theatre and the famous Henley brewery are among things not to be missed.

MAIDENHEAD – MARLOW
COOKHAM

Cliveden House and Gardens (NT), 2m E. Extensive and historic gardens, home of Astors (garden open Mar–Dec, house Apr–Oct). **Stanley Spencer Gallery**, High St. Devoted to local artist Stanley Spencer.

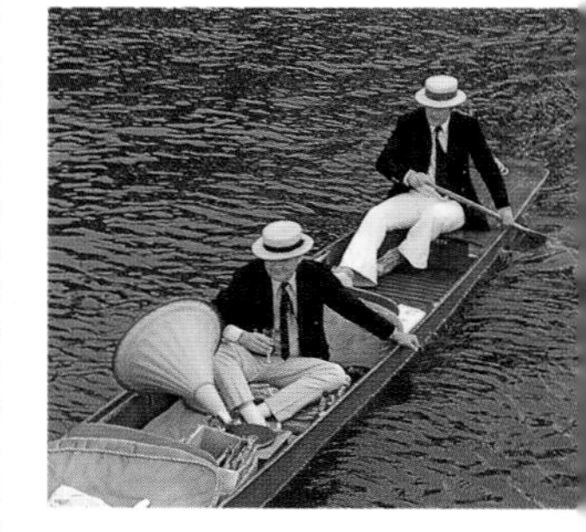

Boating in style at Henley Regatta

TWYFORD – HENLEY-ON-THAMES
HENLEY

Chantry House, nr bridge. Church Hall, formerly school, dating back to 1400 (open by appointment only). **Greys Court** (NT), 2½m W. 16th-century house with gardens, donkey wheel. (Open Apr–Sep).

Through the Chilterns

MARYLEBONE – AYLESBURY *via Amersham* *37¾ miles*

There are two routes from London to Aylesbury. Both leave from Marylebone, London's least known and most relaxed terminus, both cross the Chilterns on their way, and the journey time is much the same. Passengers can therefore choose either the High Wycombe or the Amersham route and a round trip can add interest to a day out.

For the High Wycombe route, see pages 24–5.

Roof-top view of Amersham, with St Mary's Church and the Town Hall clock tower in the centre

AYLESBURY
A41
A413
Stoke Mandeville
High Wycombe 15¼
Princes Risborough – Aylesbury See pages 24–25
Wendover
Ridgeway Path
Great Missenden
Holmer Green
0 2 mls
0 2 km
A404
Amersham
Chalfont & Latimer
M25
Grand Union Canal
Chorleywood
Chalfont St Giles
Rickmansw
A412

Marylebone – Amersham

The train leaves Marylebone's simple glazed canopy, with the minaret of the Regent's Park mosque standing high above the sidings, and at Neasden swings north-west, passing the huge London Regional Transport depot. British Rail trains share the route with London Regional Transport's Metropolitan line trains all the way to Amersham, and all the intermediate stations carry LRT rather than NSE-style name boards. This is a legacy of the old Metropolitan Railway's ambitious development of its routes into London's growing north-western suburbs during the early years of the 20th century – a period when communities such as Pinner, Northwood, Moor Park, Rickmansworth and Chorleywood were developed under the broad banner of Metroland. The route is still largely suburban as the train makes its way past villas and back gardens to **Moor Park**, where the Colne valley and the Grand Union Canal help to divide London from its surrounding countryside. The famous Moor Park golf course is by the track, and the grand, early 18th-century mansion that now serves as a club house is a short walk to the west. Woods flank the line to **Chorleywood**, allowing only glimpses of the salubrious suburban mansions whose decorative details carry the spirit of Metroland westwards. At Chorleywood there are two houses by C F A Voysey, the best-known being The Orchard, which the architect built for himself in 1901. After **Chalfont & Latimer**, the point to change for the Metropolitan line's branch to Chesham, the train reaches **Amersham**, a town with plenty of architectural interest, including a 17th-century Town Hall and almshouses, a variety of 18th-century and earlier houses, a church with a wealth of striking monuments, and some famous 1930s International Modern style houses, notably Connell's High and Over of 1931.

Tourist Information Centres
AYLESBURY County Hall, Walton St (0296) 382308
RICKMANSWORTH 46 High St (0923) 776611
WENDOVER The Clock Tower (0296) 623056

Walks
Grand Union Canal Connects the River Thames at Brentford to the Midlands. The towpath can be joined from Aylesbury.
The London Countryway (see page 14). The path can be joined from Great Missenden.
The North Buckinghamshire Way Runs 30 miles from Chequers Knapp on the Chiltern Ridge Way to Wolverton. The path can be joined from Aylesbury.
The Ridge Way Path (see page 14). The path can be joined from Wendover. See Walk 2 on page 96.

Places to Visit
RICKMANSWORTH **Moor Park Mansion**, 1m SE. Palladian house reconstructed in 1720, incorporating house built in 1678–9 for Duke of Monmouth.
CHORLEYWOOD **Chiltern Open Air Museum**, Newland Park, 1½m S. Historical buildings representing 500 years of Chiltern life, set in 44 acres of parkland. Toll-house, furniture factory, Iron Age house. (open Etr–Oct).
CHALFONT & LATIMER **Milton's Cottage** and **Shire Horse Centre**, Chalfont St Giles, 3m S – (see Seer Green and Jordans page 24).
AMERSHAM **Amersham Museum**. Local artefacts from Roman times to the present.
AYLESBURY **Buckinghamshire County Museum**, Church St. Local collections.

The canal basin in Aylesbury, barges making an attractive scene

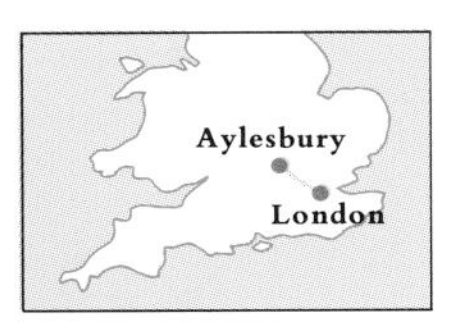

THE GREAT CENTRAL RAILWAY

The two routes to Aylesbury are a legacy of the competing companies who created the English railway network in the 19th century. The High Wycombe line was built by the Great Western Railway, while the Amersham route was constructed by the Metropolitan Railway as part of its expanding network into London's outer suburbs. In 1899 these two routes were given a new lease of life by the Great Central Railway, an ambitious undertaking built to link the network operated in the North East by the Manchester, Sheffield & Lincolnshire Railway with London, the South East and, ultimately, with the Continent via the Channel Tunnel. A completely new high-speed route, now called the Great Central, was constructed from Nottingham southwards. The cost of getting it into London, however, proved to be an enormous burden, and so the company's new London terminus at Marylebone had to be built cheaply and never fulfilled the hopes enshrined in it. Despite its reputation for good time-keeping, and its efficient and immaculate locomotives designed by John G Robinson, the Great Central was never really successful. In 1923 it became a part of the London, Midland and Scottish Railway, and in 1948 a part of British Railways, but it did not survive the route rationalisation of the Beeching era. Today, the only memorials in the South to the Great Central Railway's ambition and enterprise are Marylebone station and the two lines to Aylesbury with their well-engineered and handsomely built routes out of central London.

Amersham – Aylesbury
From Amersham the train climbs into the Chilterns along the valley of the River Misbourne, a delightful stretch of woodland and rolling hills seen at its best in spring or autumn. As the train approaches **Great Missenden**, the church can be seen in the valley to the east, and near by is the 18th-century gothic-style abbey, now a college. From Missenden onwards all the stations are similar in style, stock brick with grey banding and pretty canopies, a mark of the concern for quality that was a feature of the Great Central, whose main line to London this used to be. The attractive landscape continues to **Wendover** as the train begins its downward descent through Chiltern beechwoods. Wendover is a pretty town set in the valley to the east of the station and it marks the end of the Chilterns. With the wooded scarp of Bacombe Hill to the west and beyond it the obelisk of Coombe Hill, the hills are left behind as the train drops into the flatter landscape of the Vale of Aylesbury. For passengers travelling towards London, there is an excellent view of the approaching Chiltern woodlands. After **Stoke Mandeville**, another original Great Central station, the train passes the famous hospital and then makes its elevated way into **Aylesbury**.

Aylesbury
The county town of Buckinghamshire, Aylesbury has managed to preserve its market town atmosphere despite much modern development. A good shopping centre, the town has at its heart a fine market square, with its early 18th-century County Hall, 1876 clock tower and three statues – Disraeli, Lord Chesham flanked by French lions, and a dashing figure of the Parliamentarian John Hampden with sword in hand. The church, at heart 13th-century but mostly Victorian, is set away from the centre, but the streets and squares that link it to the market place are the prettiest part of the town, with a wealth of 17th- and 18th-century buildings, classical and timber-framed. The former grammar school now houses the Museum. Also attractive is the canal basin, the terminus of a branch of the Grand Union Canal, with its moored boats and the locks climbing away from the town.

Great Missenden station bears witness to the Great Central's attention to detail

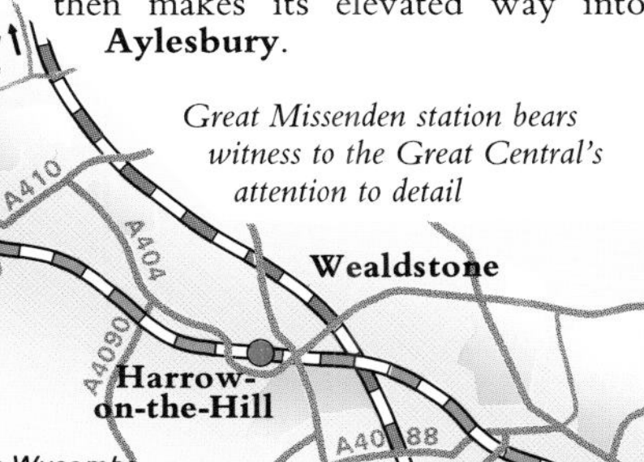

The Vale of Aylesbury

MARYLEBONE – BANBURY *and Princes Risborough – Aylesbury*

There are two routes from London to Banbury, one a high-speed run from Paddington via Oxford along the Thames and Cherwell valleys (see pages 14–17) and this, a more leisurely journey through the Chilterns and the Vale of Aylesbury. The Oxford–Bicester Town branch (see page 17) links the two routes (with a 20-minute walk between Bicester Town and Bicester North) and so there are plenty of opportunities for planning interesting round trips. Trains from Marylebone to Aylesbury via High Wycombe share this route as far as Princes Risborough, and then branch north-eastwards for the short run to Aylesbury via Little Kimble.

Tourist Information Centres
HIGH WYCOMBE 6 Cornmarket (0494) 421892
BANBURY Banbury Museum, 8 Horsefair (0295) 259855
OXFORD St Aldates (0865) 726871
AYLESBURY County Hall, Walton St (0296) 382308

Walks
The London Countryway (see page 14). The path can be joined at West Wycombe, 3m from High Wycombe station.
The Ridge Way Path (see page 14). The path can be joined from Princes Risborough.
Grand Union Canal (see page 22). The path can be joined from Aylesbury.

Places to Visit

For information on Banbury see page 17. For information on Aylesbury see pages 22–3.

SEER GREEN AND JORDANS **Spindrift Garden**, Jordans, 1m. 1½-acre, split-level garden. Fine trees, shrubs and hedges, sunken rock garden. (Open by appointment for parties only). **Shire Horse Centre**, Chalfont St Giles, 2m N. Home of the Chalfont shire horses. Demonstrations, café. **Milton's Cottage**, Chalfont St Giles, 2m N. 16th-century cottage in which John Milton completed *Paradise Lost* and began *Paradise Regained* (open Mar–Oct).
BEACONSFIELD **Bekonscot Model Village**, Warwick Road. Oldest model village in the world (open Mar–Oct).
HIGH WYCOMBE **Hughenden Manor**

continued on page 25

MARYLEBONE – BANBURY *68¼ miles*

The train leaves the peace and quiet of Marylebone and a long tunnel takes it under Lord's Cricket Ground, St John's Wood and Hampstead. At Neasden the High Wycombe trains branch westwards, passing Wembley Stadium, and then the route is predominantly suburban as it makes its elevated way out of London through Sudbury, Northolt and Ruislip, with part of the journey shared with London tube trains. After crossing the Grand Union Canal and the River Colne, whose valley is filled with reservoirs, London is left behind. **Denham**, a pretty village of mellow, red brick, lies to the south, with at its heart the 17th-century Denham Place, and then there is the first of the many golf courses near the track, this one with its own station, **Denham Golf Club**. **Gerrards Cross** is the next stop, an attractive brick and stone station in a cutting, with Bulstrode Park and its Iron Age hillfort to the south. The train now climbs through the beechwoods of the Chilterns, crossing a landscape of woodland and rolling fields in alternating cuttings and embankments. Attractive throughout the year, the route is at its best in spring and autumn. Passing the wooden station at **Seer Green and Jordans**, famous for its 1920s garden village and the 1688 Quaker Meeting House, the train reaches **Beaconsfield**, another station in a cutting with the town hidden from view.

After a short tunnel, the train emerges high on the side of the Wye valley which it follows to **High Wycombe**, with fine views across the valley to the distant M40. High Wycombe fills the valley, a town with plenty of good 18th- and 19th-century buildings, notably the 1757 Guildhall. The big 16th-century church, with its gothic revival tower of 1755, can best be seen from trains travelling towards London. Long a centre for furniture making, Wycombe still has many small craft factories, with G-Plan and Ercol beside the track. Leaving the town, there is a view of the hillfort, Desborough Castle, to the south, and then, as the train follows the valley, the 18th-century dilettante Sir Francis Dashwood's West Wycombe Park comes into view, the 1765 mansion set high on a hill, its tower crowned by a golden ball. Garden buildings, grounds landscaped by Repton, a pretty village, a medieval church, and the caves made famous as the setting for the extraordinary activities of Dashwood's Hell Fire Club, all add to West Wycombe's attractions. Across the valley to the east is Benjamin Disraeli's house, Hughenden Manor. The train now climbs through woods and rolling fields, passing **Saunderton**, with Bledlow Ridge to the west.

The next station is **Princes Risborough**, whose size reveals that it was once a busy junction, with lines serving Oxford, Rugby and Watlington, as well as Aylesbury and Banbury. Soon after leaving the station, Banbury trains swing north-west, towards the Vale of Aylesbury. With good views of the Chilterns to the south, and to the north the distant line of hills framing the Cherwell valley, the train makes its elevated way across the flat landscape. To the west is the

The cottage at Chalfont St Giles, where John Milton came to escape the plague in 1605

spire of Ilmer Church with its pretty, isolated village, then Kingsey's big church, set in woods, and to the east tiny Aston Sandford. **Haddenham & Thame Parkway** is a new station, opened recently to serve the growing commuter traffic from the area. The train then crosses the River Thame, with the remains of Notley Abbey to the west, and enters a more varied landscape, and a little-known part of England that has a wealth of attractive villages and handsome 18th-century houses. Among the best are Chilton, Dorton and Brill, high on its hill to the west, and to the east Wotton Underwood. Soon after passing the enormous ordnance depots at Arncott and Graven Hill, the train reaches **Bicester North**. Bicester is a small market town notable for its grand parish church of 13th- to 15th-century date. Rarely for a town of its size, Bicester now boasts two stations, since the recent reopening of Bicester Town.

The recently restored Banbury line station, Bicester North, is well away from the town centre, and travellers changing stations should allow at least 20 minutes for the walk through the heart of Bicester.

Leaving Bicester, views are limited by a long cutting followed by a tunnel, but as it leaves the tunnel the train is met by a panoramic view of the Cherwell valley, with the villages of Souldern and Aynho cresting the hills to the east, and Deddington to the west. The line then makes its elevated way to join the main Oxford–Banbury line at Aynho Junction, with high viaducts offering even better views over the Cherwell and the Oxford Canal. For the route from Aynho Junction to Banbury, see page 17.

PRINCES RISBOROUGH – AYLESBURY *43¼ miles*

From Marylebone to Princes Risborough trains for Aylesbury share the Banbury route (see page 24). At Princes Risborough they branch north-east, leaving the Chilterns on the southern horizon as they enter the rich agricultural plain of the Vale of Aylesbury. Passing the small stations at **Monks Risborough** and **Little Kimble**, with the mound of Cymbeline's castle to the east, the train crosses the flat landscape towards **Aylesbury**, to join the Amersham line just south of the town. Now the end of the line for passenger trains, Aylesbury was formerly served both by Great Central expresses on their way to London from the north and the Midlands and by the Metropolitan Railway's outer suburban network. For Aylesbury, see pages 22–3.

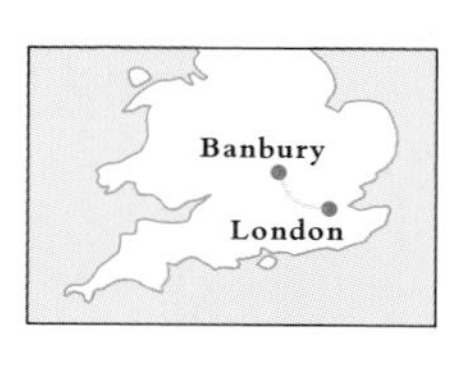

(NT), 2m N. Home of Benjamin Disraeli, Earl of Beaconsfield. Houses the Disraeli Museum which displays Disraeli relics, furniture, pictures and books (house and gardens open Mar–Oct). **Wycombe Chair Museum**, Castle Hill. Fine house set in gardens, with museum of Windsor chair making. Exhibitions of chair caning, rushing and lace-making. SAUNDERTON **West Wycombe Park** (NT), 2½m S. Rebuilt for Sir Francis Dashwood in 1765 and situated in a fine park containing garden temples (house and grounds open Jun–Aug). **West Wycombe Caves**, West Wycombe Hill.

Banbury's character lies in its ancient streets, old houses and inns

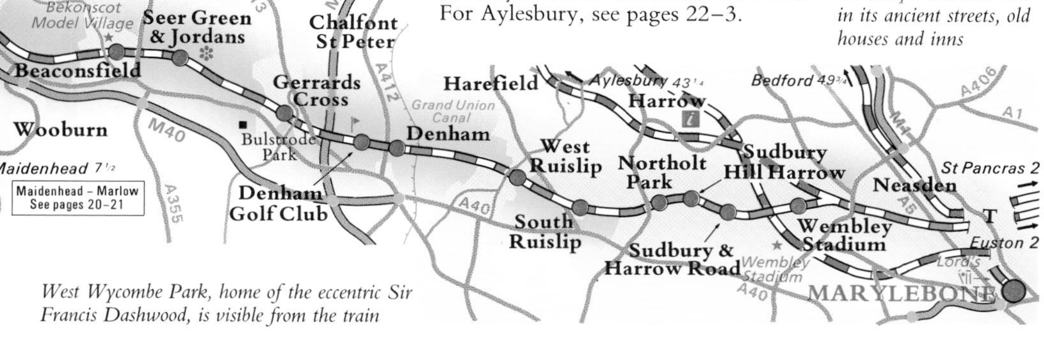

West Wycombe Park, home of the eccentric Sir Francis Dashwood, is visible from the train

Built between 1748 and 1752, and reputedly used by the black magic Hell Fire Club. From a large forecourt a brick tunnel leads back into caves. PRINCES RISBOROUGH **Princes Risborough Manor House** (NT), 1m. 17th-century brick house, containing Jacobean oak staircase (open by appointment only). **Pulpit Hillfort**, 1m E on Pulpit Hill.

1 The unmistakable skyline of Gilbert Scott's hotel block at St Pancras – opened in 1868

2 Oilseed rape in full flower brightens the Northamptonshire landscape near Linslade

3 A signal box and semaphore signals between Bedford and Bletchley recall the past

4 King's College Chapel and the Backs – quintessential Cambridge

5 Speeding alongside the Grand Union Canal just outside Berkhamsted

6 The ruins of Berkhamsted Castle – a former haunt of royalty – lie near the station

1

2

3

4

5

ROUTES FROM

EUSTON, ST PANCRAS AND KINGS CROSS

6

In the first half of the 19th century the industries of the Midlands and the North were the driving force behind Britain's main line railway network. The first route to reach the capital was George Stephenson's London & Birmingham line to Euston, and this was soon followed by the Great Northern who built their London terminus at Kings Cross. The Midland Railway came later, but it made up for its lateness with its huge station at St Pancras, whose extravagant gothic hotel façade is still one of London's greatest railway landmarks. Later these stations became part of the LMS and LNER empires and have continued to the present to be famous starting points for journeys to the Midlands, the North, Scotland and Ireland.

Network SouthEast journeys to Northampton, Bedford and Huntingdon enable travellers from London to sample the flavour of these termini and their historic routes northwards. By contrast is the new Thameslink network linking Bedford and north of London destinations directly with others south of the capital. New routes through Kings Cross and other London Thameslink stations establish patterns of travel based on convenience rather than old regional boundaries.

WATER AND RAIL

A Solent Link train crosses the River Hamble at Bursledon

BRITAIN'S WATERWAYS ARE ONE of the country's best kept secrets, a 2,000-mile network of canals and river navigations that link major cities and towns, and hundreds of villages. There are canals in Scotland, north Wales, the West Country and East Anglia, but the heart of the network is in central and southern England and a surprising amount is accessible by train.

Since prehistory, rivers have been used for travel and transport, and the first artificial waterways, or canals, in Britain were dug by the Romans. However, the development of water transport was always hindered by tides, currents, gradients and seasonal variations, so no real progress was made until the lock came into general use. It was first developed in Italy and then spread westwards to France and England during the 16th and 17th centuries.

The canal age in Britain really started in the middle of the 18th century with the building of the main cross-country routes linking the Trent and the Mersey, the Thames and the Severn, and the industrial cities of the Midlands and the North with London. Existing river navigations, such as the Thames, the Medway, the Nene and the Great Ouse, were improved and upgraded but the major investment went into the miles of artificial canals built to link together rivers, cities and ports.

FORGING A WAY

Routes followed rivers and river valleys wherever possible, to avoid expensive changes in level, but the early canal engineers were quick to respond to the challenge posed by the physical changes in the landscape they were crossing by digging great tunnels, erecting huge embankments and aqueducts and by constructing flights of locks. Indeed, the early canal engineers with their horses and primitive instruments produced such efficient routes that the later railway builders often followed closely in their footsteps. Even today, motorways and trunk roads are often built along the routes selected by the canal builders in the 18th century.

THE END OF AN ERA

With the opening of Britain's first long distance railway routes in the 1830s, the canal age was effectively at an end. Small canal companies merged to form bigger groups, some routes were abandoned, and others were taken over by railway companies. For example, the Thames and Medway Canal was filled in to form a railway and trains on the Gravesend to Strood line still pass through a great tunnel built originally for boats. By the end of the 19th century most canals were in railway ownership and the network continued to decline and diminish through the first half of this century. In the 1960s the emphasis finally switched from commercial trading to leisure, and a canal revival got under way, with a number of routes that had formerly been closed being restored. The best example is the Kennet and Avon, a major link in the waterway route from London to Bristol, abandoned in the 1950s and reopened throughout its length in 1990.

WATERS OF THE THAMES

Because they often share the same route, trains are a good way to see canals and river navigations, and there are plenty to visit in the Network SouthEast region. At the heart of the region is the Thames, and the classic Thames journey is the London to Oxford route, with the train crossing the river no less than six times. The best stretches are between Maidenhead and Goring where the river is never far from the track, and traditional Thames views are a feature of the Henley, Marlow and Windsor branches. Another face of the Thames is London itself, and the river is

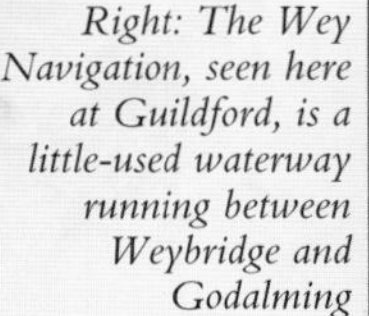

Right: The Wey Navigation, seen here at Guildford, is a little-used waterway running between Weybridge and Godalming

Above: Castles and roses are traditional decorations for bargeware

Below: Hamstead, near Kintbury, where the Kennet & Avon Canal and the railway run through an attractive wooded stretch

Left: The lock at Little Bedwyn. The railway from Reading to Bedwyn follows the same course as the Kennet & Avon Navigation

The line between Oxford and Paddington makes several crossings of the River Thames. Below: near Cholsey, Oxfordshire

well seen from the bridges that serve Victoria, Charing Cross and Cannon Street stations. However, best of all is the view of St Paul's and the City enjoyed by Thameslink passengers travelling from Blackfriars. East of London the Thames becomes a mighty tideway and it is a powerful presence on the journey along the Essex shore from Fenchurch Street to Shoeburyness.

The Thames's network of connecting waterways can also be seen by train. From Oxford to Banbury the line closely follows the Oxford Canal through the delightful Cherwell valley.

AWAY FROM LONDON

At its eastern end the Thames is joined by the Medway, a confluence of mighty waterways by the Isle of Sheppey. Inland the Medway is a quieter river, and its attractive course southwards through Kent to Tonbridge can be explored all the way by train. Equally accessible by train is the Lea navigation and its branch the Stort, linking the Thames with Hertford and Bishop's Stortford. Another, rather more secret, navigable tributary is the Wey, seen briefly at Weybridge, Guildford and Godalming – all good starting points for visits on foot to this little-known river. Near Weybridge the newly restored Basingstoke Canal branches westwards, and the line from Weybridge towards Basingstoke offers plenty of views of pretty locks set in woodland.

The backbone of the English canal system is the Grand Union, linking London and the Thames with Birmingham. Its route was so well engineered that the railway builders had little choice but to follow it and so trains from Euston to Northampton are never far from the canal, its locks and its colourful narrow boats.

Less familiar are the river navigations of central and eastern England. The Cam, navigable between Cambridge and Ely, is best known for its scenic route through the Cambridge Backs, but this is actually one of the few rivers in the Network SouthEast area whose entire course can be followed by train, from its source near Elsenham in Essex to its confluence with the Great Ouse south of Ely in Cambridgeshire.

Finally there is the Great Ouse itself, perhaps the least known of all Britain's great river navigations. It can be explored from Bedford, the upper limit for boating, and the line between Sandy and Huntingdon follows its course closely. However, this river is seen at its best in the flat Fenland landscape between Ely and its estuary into the Wash by King's Lynn, and the train is never far from the high dykes that contain its waters.

Stephenson's Line

EUSTON – NORTHAMPTON *65¾ miles*

The route to Northampton forms part of Robert Stephenson's pioneering London to Birmingham railway, which in turn became a part of the West Coast main line to Scotland. Euston is the starting point for a scenic journey full of interest, much of which is often missed by travellers on high-speed Intercity trains.

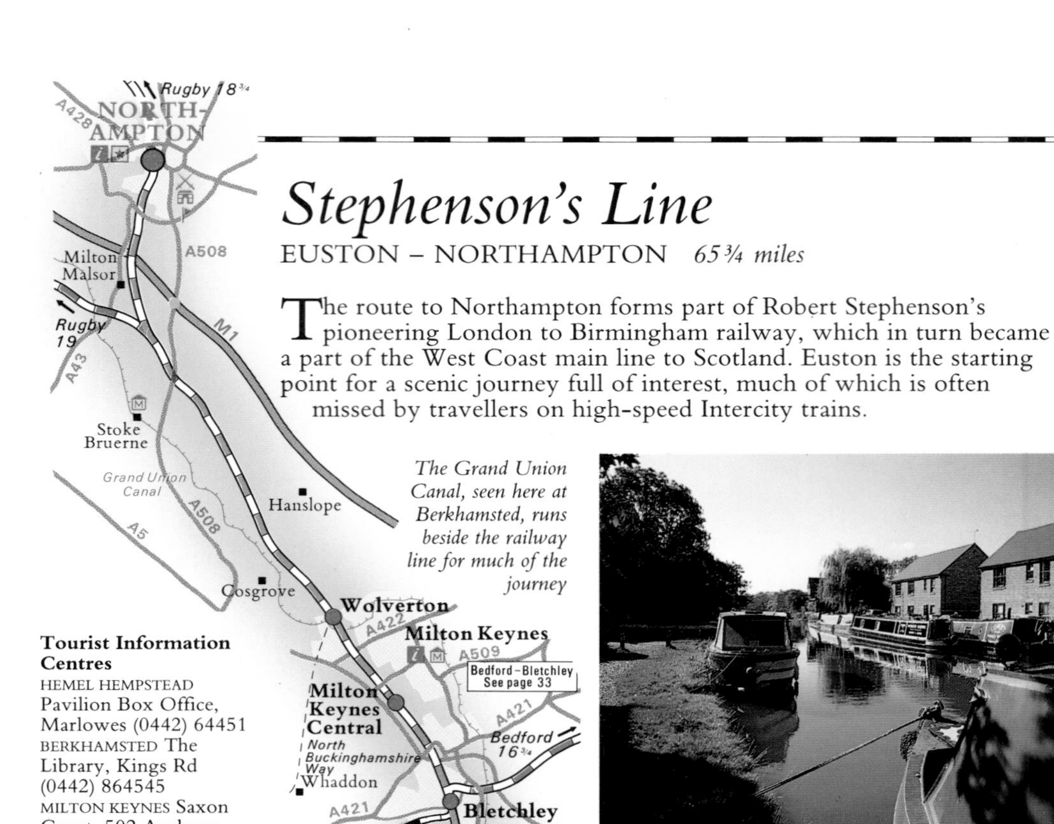

The Grand Union Canal, seen here at Berkhamsted, runs beside the railway line for much of the journey

Tourist Information Centres
HEMEL HEMPSTEAD Pavilion Box Office, Marlowes (0442) 64451
BERKHAMSTED The Library, Kings Rd (0442) 864545
MILTON KEYNES Saxon Court, 502 Avebury Boulevard (0908) 691995
NORTHAMPTON 21 St Giles St (0604) 22677.

Shoe heels in the Central Museum, Northampton

Walks
The Grand Union Canal (see page 22). The towpath can be joined from all stations along the line except Northampton.
The London Countryway (see page 14). The path can be joined from Kings Langley.
The North Buckinghamshire Way (see page 22). The path can be joined from Wolverton.
The Ridge Way Path (see page 14). The path can be joined from Tring. See Walk 2, page 96.

Places to Visit
WATFORD **Watford Museum**, 194 High St. Local history, printing, brewing and wartime Watford.

continued on page 31

Euston – Berkhamsted
As is usual with London stations serving the north, trains leaving Euston pass through northern London in a series of cuttings and tunnels, and the most striking features of this part of the journey are the famous Round House at Camden Town, a former engine shed built in 1847, and the great classical portal of Primrose Hill tunnel, dating from 1837. The train makes its way out to the suburbs, passing Willesden, Wembley, Harrow and Bushey on its way to Watford. Worth a look are the stations at Harrow & Wealdstone and Hatch End, built in a distinctive Arts and Crafts style by the architect Gerald Horsley in 1910. Another feature of this route are the food factories, with great names such as Heinz, McVitie's and Ovaltine, to be seen beside the line not far from London. From **Watford Junction** there is a branch to St Albans and a Railair link to Heathrow. North of Watford the suburbs are left behind as the train enters a pleasantly rolling landscape, following the Gade valley and the Grand Union Canal through **Kings Langley**, a former royal town with the remains of a Dominican Friary founded in 1312, a 15th-century church and an attractive main street. The Grand Union Canal is a major feature of the journey and its winding route northwards is never far from the line, with plenty of views of narrow boats, locks and the distinctive brick arched bridges. **Apsley**, famous for paper-making, is followed by **Hemel Hempstead**, whose pleasant High Street and fine Norman church are in marked contrast to the expanding acres of post-war new-town housing. Leaving Hemel, there is a good view westwards across the canal and its locks towards a typically English landscape of rolling fields framed by hedges and copses.

Berkhamsted – Northampton
At **Berkhamsted** the remains of the castle can be seen just to the south-east of the station. The original castle was built soon after William the Conqueror accepted the English throne in 1066. Destroyed in a rebellion, it was rebuilt, and many

subsequent royal figures stayed here, including the Black Prince. With its Tudor school, large church and 18th-century buildings, Berkhamsted still has the atmosphere of the busy market town it once was.

The next station is **Tring**, over a mile from its town, and to the east are the wooded hills behind Aldbury. Leaving Tring, the train enters a long cutting, one of the major engineering works of Stephenson's line, 2½ miles long and up to 60 feet deep, which is followed by a long elevated section through **Cheddington** to **Leighton Buzzard**, with enjoyable views to east and west. This attractive area was popular with grand families in the 19th century, several of whom, notably the Roseberys and the Rothschilds, built their country houses here. Mentmore can briefly be seen from the train to the west, while Ascott, Tring and Waddesden are not far away. Ascott, now owned by the National Trust, is two miles south-west of Leighton Buzzard station, near the village of Wing, which boasts one of the best Anglo-Saxon churches in Britain. After Linslade tunnel, with its gothic portico, there is a fine view to the east of Linslade Old Church, set on a mound with a manor near by. It was near Linslade that, in 1963, the Great Train Robbery took place. An armed gang held up an overnight Royal Mail train running from Glasgow to London and stole mail-bags worth over £2½ million.

The train now follows the canal and the River Ouzel through an attractive landscape to **Bletchley**, where the line to Bedford branches eastwards (see page 33). Bletchley now spreads in-determinately into the modern town of **Milton Keynes**, whose new station is well placed for the shopping centre. Apart from the great variety of modern architecture visible from the train, Milton Keynes also has some more eccentric features, notably the herd of concrete cows to be seen in a field just to the east of the track, with the 13th-century tower of Bradwell Church beyond. At **Wolverton** there is a new town of an earlier age, built from 1838 to serve the railway-carriage work, whose history is painted as a long mural beside the canal. North of Wolverton the countryside returns, with good views westwards towards Cosgrove, thanks to a long embankment and the high six-arched brick viaduct of 1838. Cuttings now limit the views, but the fine spire of Hanslope Church, nearly 200 feet high, is hard to miss to the east. At Hanslope junction the West Coast main line swings away to the north, and the train then drops down towards the Nene valley, passing Milton Malsor Church, with its unusual tower, to the west and running over the M1. Crossing both canal and river, the train enters **Northampton**.

Northampton

A major medieval town, Northampton was destroyed by a fire in 1675. The new Northampton was described by Defoe as 'the handsomest and best built town in all this part of England' and this description is still remarkably apposite. Virtually nothing remains of the castle now, but it was once one of the most famous Norman castles in Britain and was the setting for the trial of Thomas à Becket.

At its heart is a massive market square and near by a wealth of exciting buildings, including the 17th-century All Saints' Church with its delicate baroque interior, the classical Sessions House of the same date, a striking Guildhall by the eccentric Victorian architect E W Godwin, richly decorated with sculpture, stained glass and paintings, and plenty of interesting 18th- and 19th-century façades. Elsewhere in the town are other fine churches, including two of Norman date, St Peter's in Marefair and the round Holy Sepulchre, one of only four such churches in England. An easy town to explore on foot, Northampton is full of interest, with plenty of echoes of its importance in the shoe industry, not least in the unusual examples on show in the Central Museum. Other buildings worth seeing include 16th- to 17th-century Delapre Abbey and Abington Abbey, the latter also a museum. With its lively market, excellent shops and great variety of architecture, Northampton is one of Britain's better kept secrets, and it makes a good day out.

BERKHAMSTED
Berkhamsted Castle Begun soon after 1066. Ruins only.

TRING **The Zoological Museum** (1892), Akeman St. Branch of the British Museum. Mounted specimens of worldwide mammals, birds, insects and shells. **Pitstone Windmill** (NT), 2¾m N. Restored 17th-century postmill in full working order (May–Sep). **Bird Sanctuary and Nature Reserve**, 1½m N of Tring.

LEIGHTON BUZZARD
Ascott House (NT), Wing, 2m SW. Rothschild collection of pictures, furniture and porcelain. Fine gardens (gardens open Apr–Sep, house Jul–Sep). **Leighton Buzzard Narrow Gauge Railway**, Page Park Station, 3m E. Built 1919 to carry sand.

NORTHAMPTON
Delapre Abbey. Built on site of Cluniac nunnery. **Site of Battle of Northampton** (1460), S of city, near Delapre Abbey. **Central Museum and Art Gallery**, Guildhall Rd. Collections of footwear, paintings. **Museum of Leathercraft**, The Old Blue Coat School, Bridge St. Tells the story of leather.

Leighton Buzzard Narrow Gauge Railway, built to carry sand from nearby quarries, now takes visitors out into the open countryside

Bedfordshire's Lowlands

KINGS CROSS – BEDFORD *and Bedford – Bletchley*

The highlights of this journey across the distinctive low-lying landscape of Hertfordshire and Bedfordshire are St Albans and Bedford, one a great cathedral city with some of the best Roman remains in Britain, and the other a riverside town of great character. An added bonus is the rural railway from Bedford to Bletchley with its timber-framed stations, old fashioned atmosphere and interesting landscape.

The fastest trains to Bedford leave from St Pancras, but many of these stop only at Luton. For St Albans and other intermediate stations it is best to take a Thameslink train from Kings Cross Thameslink, Farringdon, St Paul's Thameslink or Blackfriars (see pages 110–11).

KINGS CROSS – BEDFORD
49¾ miles
Trains leaving St Pancras and Kings Cross Thameslink pass through the network of cuttings and tunnels typical of lines heading north from London before finally surfacing at **West Hampstead Thameslink**, where connections can be made with London Regional Transport's tube trains. At **Cricklewood** there is a large Express Dairy depot and then the line runs into the suburbs alongside the M1, passing the RAF museum between Hendon and Mill Hill Broadway, which is not easily accessible by train. **Elstree**, famous for its film studios, is followed by **Radlett**, where the line runs briefly beside Watling Street before crossing the River Colne and then entering the outskirts of St Albans. One of two stations serving the town, **St Albans** station is to the east of the city centre. St Albans is a remarkable blend of the Roman and the medieval, and as such probably without equal in England. Roman Verulamium was one of the largest towns in Britain and the few buildings that survive, notably the theatre, indicate its importance. The Verulamium Museum is an excellent record of Roman life in Britain. Near by is the cathedral, a gaunt, Norman brick structure greatly expanded in the 13th and 14th centuries, and impressive mainly because of its great size. Around the cathedral is the city's medieval heart, its narrow streets, with erratic overhangs, leading from the old abbey gatehouse to the 15th-century clock-tower.

After leaving St Albans the train passes **Harpenden** and enters Bedfordshire, following the valley of the Lea, with attractive views to the west towards Sir Julius Wernher's great mansion at Luton Hoo. The house is hidden by trees, but Capability Brown's park runs down to the river. With the airport to the east, the train enters **Luton**, a vast sprawling town whose wealth was based initially on straw-plaiting and hat-making, and since 1905 on Vauxhall cars. The attractive church, with its fine collection of monuments, and the local museum retain links with the town's past. Luton and the M1 are left behind as the line turns north to cross a more varied landscape. At **Harlington**, the church can be seen on a hill to the east and then the train passes **Flitwick** before curving round the pleasant village of Ampthill. After a tunnel there is a fine view of the 18th-century façade of Ampthill Park House to the east.

The early 15th-century Clock Tower in St Albans. The nearby streets still have a medieval atmosphere

Bedford
The line now crosses a flat landscape to **Bedford** with plenty of reminders of the brick industry. As the train enters the town, the remains of Elstow nunnery can be seen to the east, shortly before the bridge over the Great Ouse. John Bunyan was born in Elstow in 1628, and he wrote *The Pilgrim's Progress* in Bedford gaol, imprisoned for his nonconformist beliefs. His statue stands on St Peter's Green, but far better are the rather Art Nouveau statue of John Howard, by Alfred Gilbert, the sculptor of Piccadilly Circus' Eros, and Jagger's powerful war memorial sculpture of St George, both by the river. Bedford is seen at its best from the river, with parks and trees lining both banks and handsome buildings set back. Boats can be hired. There are four medieval churches, a fine ornamental Shire Hall of 1881 by Waterhouse, the architect

Tourist Information Centres
BOREHAMWOOD Civic Offices, Elstree Way (081) 207 2277
MILTON KEYNES Saxon Court, 502 Avebury Boulevard (0908) 691995
ST ALBANS Town Hall, Market Place (0727) 864511
LUTON Grosvenor House, 45–47A Alma St (0582) 401579
BEDFORD 10 St Paul's Square (0234) 215226

Walks
Grand Union Canal (see page 22). The towpath can be joined from Bletchley.
The Icknield Way The eastern continuation of The Great Ridge Way which runs from Wessex, north-east, into East Anglia. The path can be joined from Luton.
The London Countryway (see page 14). The path can be joined from St Albans.

Places to Visit
ELSTREE
Borehamwood Country Park.
ST ALBANS **Clock Tower**, Market Place. Fine views of the city (open Etr–mid-Sep). **Kingsbury Watermill Museum**, St Michael's St. 16th-century cornmill with working waterwheel. **Margaret Harvey Gallery**, Hertfordshire College of Art and Design. Changing exhibitions (contact TIC for open hours). **Royal National Rose Society Gardens**, Chiswell Green, 2m S. Over 30,000 rose plants (open mid-Jun–Oct). **Gorhambury House**, 3m W. Late Georgian mansion (1777–84) by Sir Robert Taylor. 16th-century enamelled glass, Chippendale furniture (open May–Sep). **St Albans Cathedral**. Norman abbey church (*c*1077). **St Albans City Museum**, Hatfield Rd. Natural history and geology craft workshops. **St Albans Organ Museum**, 320 Camp Rd. Automatically operated organs and other instruments (recitals Suns all year). **Site of the Battle of St Albans** (1455) during the War of the Roses. West of the city.

continued on page 33

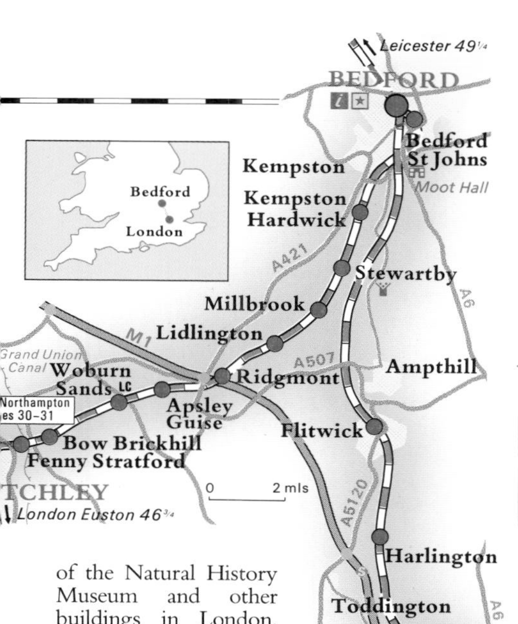

of the Natural History Museum and other buildings in London, and a picturesque Town Hall, while the High Street has a number of interesting 18th- and 19th-century buildings. The Cecil Higgins Art Gallery and Museum in Castle Close contains one of the best collections of 19th-century decorative arts to be found anywhere in Britain, much of it being displayed in Victorian room settings.

Luton Hoo houses one of the finest private collections of works of art in the country, including pieces by the Russian court jeweller, Carl Fabergé

Bedford: the statue of John Bunyan

Moot Hall, a medieval market hall, stands in a field at Elstow

BEDFORD – BLETCHLEY
16¾ miles

In its day Bedford was an important railway junction, but all that survives today, apart from the main Midland line, is the branch to Bletchley, itself part of a line that originally linked Oxford to Cambridge. This rather unexpected survival is an interesting journey and a useful way of combining visits to St Albans, Bedford and Northampton into one round trip.

Leaving Bedford, the train enters a landscape dominated by the brick industry. Clay pits, active and flooded, surround the line at **Kempston Hardwick**. At **Stewartby** the train goes through the heart of one of the largest brickworks in the world, with the giant kilns and their tall chimneys all around, an awe-inspiring sight that gives the journey a particular quality. **Millbrook** is the first of a series of cottage-style, timber-framed stations. From here to **Lidlington** the line runs beside a motor industry proving ground, and then at **Ridgmont** the train passes under the M1 and to the south-east is Ridgmont's Victorian church and the woods that surround Woburn Park. **Aspley Guise**, with its pretty village spread over the hillside to the south, is next and then the train comes to **Woburn Sands**, where a signal box and old semaphore signals add to the traditional atmosphere of a country railway. (Woburn Abbey is four miles away to the south-east.) After **Bow Brickhill**, an isolated station, the line crosses the River Ouzel and the Grand Union Canal before reaching **Fenny Stratford**. From here the train makes its slow way into **Bletchley**, to join the main London–Northampton line (pages 30–1).

Verulamium Museum and Hypocaust, St Michaels. Roman finds, including tessellated pavements.
Verulamium Theatre, St Michaels. Roman theatre, still in use.
LUTON **Luton Hoo**, 2¾m S. Mansion with Wernher collection of treasures (open Apr–Oct). **Luton Museum and Art Gallery**, Wardown Park. Natural history, culture and industries of Bedfordshire.
Stockwood Craft Museum and Gardens, Farley Hill. Rural crafts and trades, with period gardens (open Mar–Oct).
BEDFORD **Bedford Museum**, Castle Lane. Local and natural history.
Bromham Mill, Bromham, 3m W. Restored water mill and machinery with natural history room (open Apr–Oct).
Bunyan Meeting House and Museum, Mill St. Associated relics and collection of Bunyan's works (open Apr–Oct).
Cecil Higgins Art Gallery and Museum, Castle Close. English watercolours and drawings, foreign prints, ceramics, glass. Victorian and Edwardian room settings.
Moot Hall, Elstow, 1½m S. Medieval market hall with collection portraying life and times of John Bunyan (open Apr–Oct).
STEWARTBY **Stewartby Country Park.**

The Great Northern

KINGS CROSS – HUNTINGDON and CAMBRIDGE

There are two routes from London to Cambridge, one from Kings Cross via Stevenage, and the other from Liverpool Street via Harlow. The Liverpool Street route is the more direct, but the other is more varied in scenic terms. The fastest trains stop only at Stevenage, so for intermediate stations take a stopping service. Some of these terminate at Royston, with an onward connection to Cambridge. Trains for Huntingdon take a more easterly route from Kings Cross, via Hertford North. For intermediate stations on the Hertford North route it is necessary to take a stopping train from Kings Cross to Stevenage, and then take an onward connection to Huntingdon or Royston and Cambridge.

The Chinese-style bridge in Godmanchester, originally built in 1827

KINGS CROSS – HUNTINGDON *58¾ miles*

Leaving Kings Cross, the train is carried under Camden and Islington in tunnels before a long elevated section takes it to **Finsbury Park**, with views over terraced houses and busy shopping streets. Look out for an old Pullman carriage named Doris, encased on a siding at Finsbury Park, while to the north of the station is the depot that houses modern InterCity trains and other special carriage sets. The pinnacles of the recently restored Alexandra Palace, once served by its own branch line, crown the hill to the west and then Hertford line trains cross the main line to swing away to the east. The surroundings are now suburban, with plenty of trees, and after Enfield London is left behind. The train makes its elevated way towards Hertford through fields and woodland, crossing first the Lea and then the Mimram on high viaducts. The town is well to the east of **Hertford North**, a well-restored brick and stone station with big glazed canopies, and the view approaching the station is dominated by the Victorian spire of St Andrew's Church. Hertford is still a pleasantly traditional county town, with an open space at its centre, a good 18th-century Shire Hall by Robert Adam's brother James, a good range of timber-framed, 18th- and 19th-century buildings and the remains of a 12th-century castle, surrounded by parks that run attractively down to the Lea. North of the town a short tunnel leads the train into the valley of the Beane, a pretty landscape of woods, rolling fields and old farms. The train swings westward onto a long elevated stretch and then it rejoins the Great Northern main line just south of **Stevenage**.

The next station is **Hitchin** and here Cambridge trains branch to the east (see page 36). The station is well placed for visiting this attractive market town. Its large church reflects the town's importance as a centre of the wool trade in the Middle Ages, and it has a variety of timber-framed and 18th-century buildings. Leaving Hitchin, the train follows the course of the Rivers Hiz and then Ivel across a flatter landscape. **Arlesey** has a newly rebuilt station and to the north-west is Henlow, famous for its early 18th-century Grange and the RAF camp. The next station is **Biggleswade**, in the centre of the town, which is at its most attractive on the west side by the Ivel. Three miles to the west is Old Warden airfield, the home of the Shuttleworth Collection of historic aircraft. Approaching **Sandy**, the line runs beside the water-meadows of the Ivel, buttercup-filled

Tourist Information Centres
HERTFORD The Castle (0992) 584322
STEVENAGE Central Library, Southgate (0438) 369441
HITCHIN The Library, Paynes Park (0462) 434738
HUNTINGDON The Library, Princes St (0480) 425831
WELWYN & HATFIELD Campus West, The Campus (0707) 332880
CAMBRIDGE Wheeler St (0223) 322640

Walks
The Cole Green Way A 4-mile walk along a disused railway line from Hertford to Cole Green.
The Ely Nature Trail A 3-mile circular walk through the Isle of Ely.
Harcamlow Way Runs 140 miles, in a figure-of-eight, from Harlow to Cambridge and back. The path can be joined at Cambridge.
Icknield Way (see page 32). The path can be joined from Hitchin.
Wimpole Way Runs 11½ miles from Burrell's Walk in Cambridge to Wimpole Park.

Places to Visit
KINGS CROSS – HUNTINGDON
CUFFLEY (stopping train only) **Northaw Great Wood**, Cuffley, 1½m NW. Country Park with marked trails and picnic sites.
HERTFORD **Hertford Castle and Gardens.** Gatehouse and ruin of Norman castle (gardens open all year, castle 1st Sun each month, May–Sep).
Hertford Museum, 18 Bull Plain. Geology, archaeology, natural and social history of town and county.
WATTON-AT-STONE **Benington Lordship Gardens**. Edwardian terraced gardens overlooking lakes and parkland, on site of Norman castle (open Feb–late summer).
STEVENAGE **Stevenage Museum**, St George's Way. Tells story of town from present back to early days.
HITCHIN **Hitchin Museum and Art Gallery**. Local and natural history collections, costumes and Victoriana, Regimental Museum of Hertfordshire

continued on page 35

in early summer, with, to the east, the wooded slopes of Sandy Warren, now an RSPB nature reserve. After Sandy the train follows the Ivel valley to its confluence with the Great Ouse near Tempsford, to the west of the line. During the Second World War Tempsford was the main base of the Special Operations Executive and from here agents were flown to secret destinations in occupied Europe. **St Neots** station is set well to the east of its town, but it is worth the walk in for the grand 15th-century church, the market place with its central column and the river frontage. The river marks the boundary between Bedfordshire and the former county of Huntingdon. The line now runs close beside the Great Ouse, a river navigable to Bedford and much used by pleasure craft. Three churches stand close by the line to the east, Great Paxton, Offord D'Arcy and Offord Cluny, and of these Great Paxton is the most remarkable, a complete Anglo-Saxon building on a grand scale. The train then crosses the Ouse, with a fine view of Hinchingbrooke House to the west, a splendidly decorative building constructed by the Cromwell family between 1544 and 1627.

Huntingdon

Huntingdon station, in part an original Great Northern Railway structure of 1850, gives easy access to the town. Huntingdon is small and compact, a traditional market town whose qualities have not been affected by modern development. A traffic-free High Street makes it easy to enjoy its pleasant 18th-century buildings. The two late medieval churches are at its heart, and near the market place, with its pensive soldier war memorial by Lady Kennet, the widow of Scott of the Antarctic, are the 1745 Town Hall and the former Grammar School, attended by Cromwell and now housing the Cromwell Museum. Another famous Huntingdon citizen was the poet Cowper, whose early 18th-century house stands near the river. A short walk across the Ouse is Godmanchester, a town with a number of interesting buildings, including a Chinese-style bridge. Together the two towns and their surroundings offer plenty to fill a leisurely day out.

One of the historic aircraft in the Shuttleworth Collection at Old Warden Aerodrome, near Biggleswade

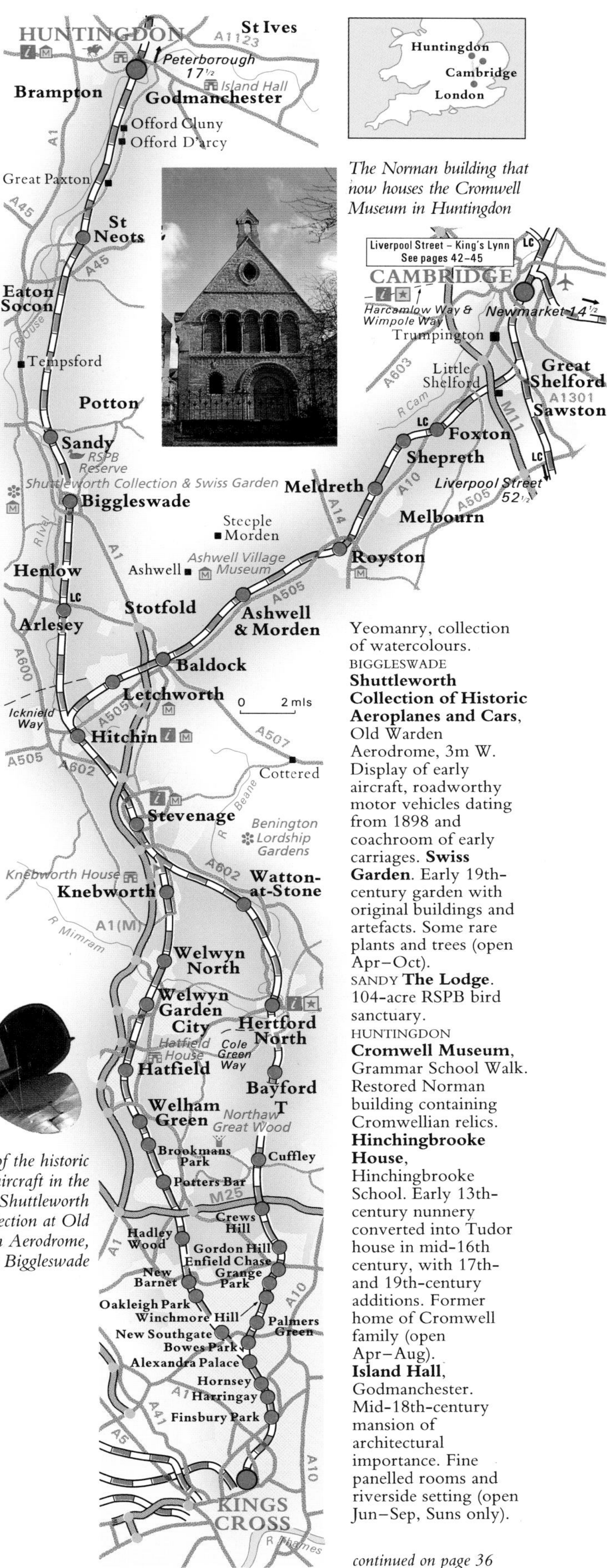

The Norman building that now houses the Cromwell Museum in Huntingdon

Yeomanry, collection of watercolours.

BIGGLESWADE **Shuttleworth Collection of Historic Aeroplanes and Cars**, Old Warden Aerodrome, 3m W. Display of early aircraft, roadworthy motor vehicles dating from 1898 and coachroom of early carriages. **Swiss Garden**. Early 19th-century garden with original buildings and artefacts. Some rare plants and trees (open Apr–Oct).

SANDY **The Lodge**. 104-acre RSPB bird sanctuary.

HUNTINGDON **Cromwell Museum**, Grammar School Walk. Restored Norman building containing Cromwellian relics.

Hinchingbrooke House, Hinchingbrooke School. Early 13th-century nunnery converted into Tudor house in mid-16th century, with 17th- and 19th-century additions. Former home of Cromwell family (open Apr–Aug).

Island Hall, Godmanchester. Mid-18th-century mansion of architectural importance. Fine panelled rooms and riverside setting (open Jun–Sep, Suns only).

continued on page 36

KINGS CROSS – CAMBRIDGE
For Stevenage and Hitchin, see page 34.
HATFIELD **Hatfield House** Jacobean mansion where Elizabeth I spent much of her childhood. Park, scented and knot garden (open Mar–Oct).
KNEBWORTH **Knebworth House and Country Park** Gothic mansion, home of Lytton family for 500 years. Park includes many attractions (open Apr–Sep).
LETCHWORTH **First Garden City Heritage Museum**, 296 Norton Way South. Exhibition of the Garden City Movement and social history of Letchworth. **Museum and Art Gallery**, Broadway. Displays north Hertfordshire archaeological material, natural history and art exhibitions.
ASHWELL & MORDEN **Ashwell Village Museum**, Swan St. Early Tudor timber-framed house. Illustrates village life from Stone Age to present day.
ROYSTON **Royston Museum**, Lower King St. Local history housed in former chapel schoolroom.

Welwyn Viaduct: its vast size makes a powerful impact on the landscape

CAMBRIDGE **Cambridge and County Folk Museum**, 2–3 Castle St. Houses large collection of domestic, agricultural and trade exhibits. **Cambridge Art and Holographic Centre**, Magdalene St. Collection of holograms. **Fitzwilliam Museum**, Trumpington St. Extensive art and archaeology collection. European paintings and manuscripts. **Great St Mary's Church**,

continued on page 37

Knebworth House, home of the Lytton family for 500 years

KINGS CROSS – CAMBRIDGE
58 miles

From Kings Cross the train follows the same route out of London to Alexandra Palace, and then takes the fast Great Northern main line through Barnet and Hadley Wood. Long cuttings restrict the view as the train speeds through the suburbs to Potters Bar, Brookmans Park and Welham Green. To the west is the picturesque, late Elizabethan grandeur of North Mymms House but this is nothing compared to Hatfield House, one of Britain's greatest Elizabethan mansions, built by Robert Cecil from 1608. The gates and the park can be seen to the east from **Hatfield** station but the house is out of sight beyond the church, a grand structure set on a hill in the old town. Near Hatfield House are the remains of the 15th-century Bishop's Palace, a major example of medieval domestic architecture and a reminder that Hatfield became a bishopric in 1109. Leaving Hatfield the line passes through the new town, one of a number of such developments that are a feature of this area, and then, having crossed the Lea, it enters another, **Welwyn Garden City**. Largely designed by Louis de Soissons and built from the 1920s, Welwyn became the model for many later new towns with its emphasis on curving streets, trees and green spaces, and well-planned shopping, residential and industrial areas. The little town that gave it its name is well away to the north-west. Between Welwyn Garden City and **Welwyn North**, the line crosses the Mimram valley on a massive, 40-arch, brick viaduct that carries the train 100 feet above the ground. Completed in 1850, this has to be seen from below for its scale to be fully appreciated. The next station is **Knebworth**, a town with a church, a mansion and a golf club-house by Lutyens, but the early 19th-century house and its park are over a mile to the west, beyond the A1(M).

Stevenage and **Hitchin** come next (see page 34) and then trains for Cambridge swing north-east away from the main line. The first stop is **Letchworth**, the first garden city to be built in Britain. Started in 1903 and laid out by Parker and Unwin, the new town was an attempt at translating Ebenezer Howard's late 19th-century ideals into a practical reality. The 1913 station has suitable Arts and Crafts detailing. This was built at the centre of the town to replace the rather simple timber structure that can be seen in S F Gore's famous painting. As the train approaches **Baldock** there is a good view of the town's 18th-century buildings spread round its handsome church, which has a small spire set on the big tower.

Ashwell & Morden station is unfortunately a long way from the two villages, and then the train runs through a varied landscape, with the wooded Pen Hills to the south. The downland of Therfield Heath, with its Bronze Age barrows, precedes **Royston**, a handsome town that grew up around the crossing of Ermine Street and the Icknield Way, and then the train crosses an open landscape with good views to the west to reach **Meldreth**. Approaching **Shepreth** there is a fine view of the church, and then the line swings east to follow the Cam through a low-lying landscape of water meadows. Another village station is **Foxton**, with its barge-boarded signal box and another good church view. The village itself lies half a mile to the east and is well worth a visit for its main street of timber-framed and thatched cottages. After Foxton, rounded Rowley's Hill dominates the landscape to the south and then Little Shelford Church stands in woodland to the south as the train crosses the Cam, shortly before the junction with the former Great Eastern main line from Liverpool Street. The approach to Cambridge is rather low key, with Trumpington to the west and the huge hospital complex to the east. There is no view of the city, and no equivalent of Oxford's enticing skyline of towers and spires.

Cambridge station is a distinctive 1845 building, with a façade of 15 arches with the arms of the colleges in the spandrels. Equally distinctive is the long main platform, served by trains in both directions. A frequent mini-bus service runs into the centre from the station, which because of the city fathers' resistance to the arrival of the railway, was built at some distance from the city centre.

Cambridge

A city with Roman, Saxon and Norman origins, Cambridge has been a centre of learning since the 13th century, when students from Oxford fled here to escape rioting. Of the 31 colleges, 12 were founded before the 16th century, and it is these that form Cambridge's ancient heart. With their quadrangles, chapels and gardens, or Backs, many of which run down to the river, these give the city a quality that puts it apart from other university cities. Seeing Cambridge from the river is an essential pleasure, a visual treat without equal in Britain. Another good way to see Cambridge is from the top of the 17th-century tower of Great St Mary's, the official church of the university. One of the most visited college chapels is King's, with its magnificent fan vaulting. The city's centre is small, compact and relatively traffic free, with the bicycle being the preferred means of transport, and so walking about is the best way to see its many treasures, which include the round church of 1130, one of only four in England, the open-air market, the Fitzwilliam Museum, one of the oldest in Britain, the mathematical bridge and Kettle's Yard, a shrine to British 20th-century art.

King's Parade. The University church with 17th-century tower providing sweeping views. **Kettle's Yard Art Gallery**, Castle St. Permanent collection of 20th-century art. Also temporary exhibitions. **Museum of Zoology**, Downing St. **Scott Polar Research Institute**, Lensfield Rd. Relics and equipment from polar expeditions, emphasis on Scott. **Sedgwick Museum of Geology**, Downing St. **University Botanic Garden**, Cory Lodge, Bateman St. 40 acres with fine botanical collection. **University Colleges** (to visit, contact TIC for details). **University Museum of Archaeology and Anthropology**, Downing St. Man's development since prehistory. **University Museum of Classical Archaeology**, Sidgwick Avenue site. Collections of casts of Greek and Roman sculpture. **Whipple Museum of the History of Science**, Free School Lane. Scientific instruments (may close vacations).

A leisurely punt along the Backs provides some of the best views of Cambridge Colleges and their grounds

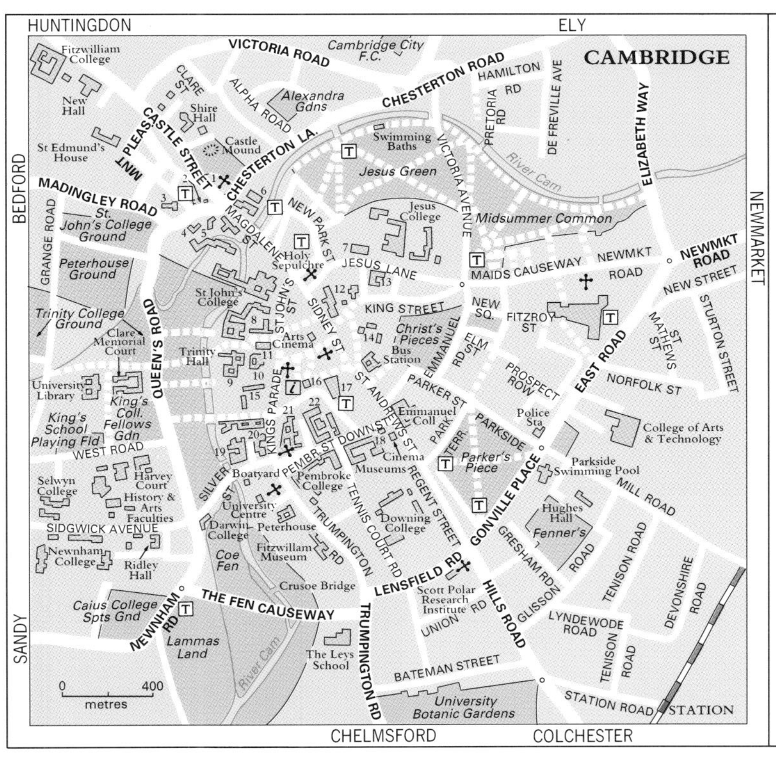

Main roads
Other roads
Restricted roads
Building of interest
Church
Tourist Information Centre
Public Convenience

PLACES OF INTEREST

1 County Folk Museum
2 Kettle's Yard Art Gallery
3 Westminster College
4 School of Pythagoras
5 Art & Holographic Centre
6 Magdalene College
7 Wesley House
8 Trinity College
9 Clare College
10 Old Schools
11 Gonville and Caius College
12 Sidney Sussex College
13 Westcott House
14 Christ's College
15 King's College and Chapel
16 Guildhall
17 Lion Yard Shopping Centre
18 Sedgwick Mus. of Geology
19 Queen's College
20 St Catharine's College
21 Corpus Christi College
22 Whipple Museum & Museum of Zoology

__1__ Clacton's development as a seaside resort, complete with pier, began when the railway first brought visitors in the 1870s

__2__ The sandy beach at Walton on the Naze

__3__ The forty arches of Welwyn Viaduct carry the track high over the Mimram valley

__4__ Concorde at the Imperial War Museum's Duxford collection of civic and military aircraft

__5__ The Gatehouse of King's College, Cambridge. The university fills most of the city centre

__6__ The soaring towers of Ely Cathedral dominate the town in its fenland setting

__7__ Liverpool Street's high glass roof. Beneath it, the station has been totally renovated

1

2

3

4

5

6

ROUTES FROM

LIVERPOOL STREET AND FENCHURCH STREET

7

Unlike its famous counterpart to the west of London, the Great Eastern Railway grew in a rather piecemeal fashion from a number of smaller companies, and it did not complete its London terminus at Liverpool Street until the 1870s. Historically, its routes served East Anglia, the East Coast and London's north-eastern suburbs, and this pattern is maintained today by the dramatically re-built station at Liverpool Street. The journeys included in this section have been chosen to show the contrasting routes operated by Network SouthEast in eastern England and the varied landscape of a region in which the coastline has always been important. There are main lines serving Cambridge, Ely and King's Lynn, Colchester and the international ferry port at Harwich, routes to the seaside and holiday resorts, rural branch lines and busy commuter lines to London's countryside.

The City of London's other main terminus is Fenchurch Street, a station built in the 1850s. Associated with routes along the Essex shore of the Thames, it was always primarily a commuter station, a reputation unchanged from the days of the London, Tilbury & Southend Railway to the present. At the same time, the development of Thames-side resorts such as Southend was largely due to the railway.

THE STORY OF THE RAILWAY

NETWORK SOUTHEAST IS A slightly misleading name, for its services operate not only all over south-eastern England, but also as far west as Weymouth and Exeter, to Banbury, Northampton and Huntingdon in the Midlands, to Cambridge and King's Lynn in the north-east of the region, and eastwards to Harwich. The network crosses, therefore, many of the traditional regional barriers of British Rail, the legacy of the 19th-century piecemeal development of the railway system by independent and often competing companies. Network SouthEast today incorporates routes built by the great names of the railway age, the Great Western, the Midland, the Great Northern and the Great Eastern, as well as many created by small local companies whose names are now buried in the byways of history. However, with the bulk of its routes south of the Thames, Network SouthEast has inherited, above all, the complex system formed by the London & South Western, South Eastern, London, Chatham & Dover, and London, Brighton & South Coast companies, all of which were subsumed in 1923 into the Southern Railway.

CREATING THE NETWORK

The first steam railway in the south, linking Canterbury to the port of Whitstable, opened in 1830 but London quickly became the hub of the network, with the first main lines, to Southampton and Brighton, in use in the early 1840s. Over the next two decades rival companies created a complex network of lines, each major company building its London terminus, and most places in Kent, Surrey and Sussex had some form of railway service before the end of the century. The inspiration for this was the commuter, for travelling to work by train became an accepted way of life during the Victorian period.

The lines themselves were often splendid feats of engineering. The North and South Downs were formidable barriers that required deep cuttings and long tunnels, laboriously carved by hand out of the white chalk by armies of navvies. Great engineering feats in the south, such as Rastrick's magnificent 1840 Ouse viaduct on the Brighton line, and the tunnel carved through the Shakespeare Cliff near Dover under the direction of William Cubitt in 1844, are among the finest achievements of the railway age. Just as significant in engineering terms are the miles of brick viaducts built to carry the lines out of London, and the series of cast-iron bridges crossing the Thames.

VITAL LINKS

Although the bulk of traffic in the South East was aimed at the commuter, there were

plenty of long-distance services, often operated by high-speed and de luxe trains. The *Atlantic Coast Express* and, later, the *Devon Belle*, served Exeter and the West Country, while other Pullman Belles ran to Brighton and Bournemouth. Some of the most famous expresses were the boat trains to the Channel ports, an area of intense rivalry between the various railway companies, and equally legendary were the boat trains connecting with the Atlantic liners at Southampton. At the same time, the routes were so numerous and the network so extensive that there were many quiet corners with lazy branch lines serving little villages in the depth of the country. In the days before the car and the lorry, everything went by train, milk and livestock, supplies to the local shops, parcels, flowers, and much else besides. Things ordered by post, from boots to bicycles, always included in the price delivery to the nearest station. And wherever you lived in the south of England, there always was a station near by. Today, the emphasis has changed completely, and railway freight is the carriage of bulk products over long distances in containers and specially designed wagons.

LEGACIES OF THE PAST

Rationalisation has resulted in the closure of many lines and stations, but there are plenty of reminders still to be seen and enjoyed of railway's colourful past. Closed lines can be traced on the map, and some are now official footpaths or bridleways, while others have been reopened by private steam railways. Many stations still have their old goods sheds, often attractive buildings in country areas, carefully built from local materials. Also to be seen from time to time are relics of the steam age such as engine sheds, water towers and, more rarely, turntables. Still common, but in some ways an endangered species, are signal boxes, decorative structures in brick or timber. At one time every level crossing had its keeper's box or cottage, but these are now a part of history. Equally redundant are the trackside huts where the linesmen kept their tools, and occasionally stayed.

THE FACE OF THE FUTURE

All these past echoes underline the changing face of Britain's railways, and the biggest change has been in levels of manning. Gone are the generations of porters and signalmen, shunters and platelayers, linesmen and ticket collectors who ran the railways 50 years ago, and in their place is a leaner, more efficient and highly automated business in which the human element is no longer the dominant feature. New trains, new stations and new routes are now a part of the future, and the Channel Tunnel beckons, to link Britain's railways firmly to Europe and to the 21st century. Ironically, a tunnel under the Channel offering direct services from Britain to the capitals of Europe was something ambitious Victorian railway companies dreamed about, and even tried to build. It was the enterprise of that century that built a railway network whose qualities we can still enjoy and appreciate from a modern high-speed train.

Charing Cross in 1864. The style of modern life makes a rather different scene for today's railway traveller

Tourist Information Centres
BISHOP'S STORTFORD Council Offices, 2 The Causeway (0279) 655261
CAMBRIDGE Wheeler St (0223) 322640
ELY Oliver Cromwell's House, 29 St Mary's St (0353) 662062
KING'S LYNN The Old Gaol House, Saturday Market Place (0553) 763044
HERTFORD The Castle (0992) 584322

Walks
Harcamlow Way (see page 34). The path can be joined from Harlow, Audley End (2m from station at Saffron Walden) or Cambridge stations.
The London Countryway (see page 14). The path can be joined from Broxbourne or Waltham Cross (at Waltham Abbey) stations.
The Cole Green Way (see page 34). May be joined at Hertford.

Places to Visit

For information on Cambridge and Hertford see pages 34–7

WALTHAM CROSS **Epping Forest District Museum,** 39-41 Sun St. Displays illustrate life in Epping Forest district from Stone Age to 20th century. **Waltham Abbey,** 1m E. 14th-century gatehouse and bridge, and cloister entrance dating from 12th century. The nearby Norman and later abbey church houses undercroft museum.
CHESHUNT **Hayes Hill Farm,** Stubbins Hill Ln. Traditional-style farmyard centred on a restored 16th-century barn. Farm animals in their natural surroundings.
BROXBOURNE **Hertford Heath Nature Reserve.** Paradise Park Woodland Zoo.
HARLOW **Harlow Museum,** Passmores House, Third Ave. Tudor and Georgian farmhouse set in landscaped grounds. Displays local archaeology and history, folk life and farming, geology and natural history. **Mark Hall Cycle Museum and Gardens,** Muskham Rd.

continued on page 43

Rivers and Fens

LIVERPOOL STREET – KING'S LYNN *via Cambridge and Broxbourne – Hertford East*

With no through trains to King's Lynn until the current electrification of the line is completed in May 1992, this is a journey of two parts. The route from London to Cambridge follows three rivers, the Lea, the Stort and the Cam, through varied scenery. From Cambridge to Ely and King's Lynn, the train crosses the distinctive landscape of the Fens in a journey that links together centres of architectural excellence.

Audley End House, a grand mansion near Audley End station. The Great Hall (above) and the moulded ceilings are particularly fine. The park was landscaped by Capability Brown

LIVERPOOL STREET – KING'S LYNN *97 miles*
London – Cambridge
Leaving the decorative splendour of newly rebuilt Liverpool Street, the train makes its way towards **Bethnal Green** through tunnels and cuttings. Here, it swings north away from the former Great Eastern main line, to make its elevated way through Hackney. Passing **Clapton**, it descends into the Lea valley, with the river largely surrounded by factories and reservoirs. At **Tottenham Hale** there is an interchange with London Regional Transport's Victoria Line and the line then follows the course of the Lea through undistinguished scenery. **Waltham Cross** marks the beginning of the end of London's sprawl and from here onwards there are pleasant views across the Lea valley lakes. From the station it is about a mile to the remains of the great Norman abbey, whose nave, still huge, was originally 400 feet long. Colourful additions by the Victorian architect William Burges increase the excitement. Waltham Cross takes its name from one of the four remaining Eleanor crosses. There were originally 12, erected by Edward I to mark the places where the body of his dead queen rested on the way from Leicestershire to Westminster Abbey. The next station is **Cheshunt**, and then at **Broxbourne** the Hertford East branch swings away to the north-west following the River Lea (see page 43). Broxbourne's large 15th- and 16th-century church is set in woods, just west of the station. After the junction, the train crosses the Lea and turns eastwards along the Stort valley. Like the Lea, the Stort is a river navigation and so there are frequent sights of pleasure craft. With the river never far away, the train makes its way to **Roydon**, a little village set in watermeadows whose simple church has some decorative woodwork and an entertaining font, and thence to **Harlow Town**, where the railway line forms the northern boundary of the New Town. Old Harlow, a former medieval market town, is well to the east, best approached from **Harlow Mill** station. Leaving Harlow Mill, there is a good view to the north of Pishiobury Park, a Tudor mansion rebuilt in the late 18th century and set in landscaped grounds.

Features of the Stort are the big old mills and maltings built originally to benefit from the opening of the river as a navigation, and good examples can be seen at **Sawbridgeworth**,

Pargeting on the old Sun Inn, part of Saffron Walden's decorative charm

adding extra interest to an attractive stretch of river. The next station is **Bishop's Stortford**, with the large battlemented church and the scant castle remains just to the north. The town is the head of the Stort navigation, but the line stays by the river to **Stansted**. The town, **Mountfitchet**, boasts a fine windmill and a medieval church with some splendid monuments, notably a recumbent 1614 effigy of Hester Salusbury complete with best dress and smart hat. North of the station the new high speed rail link to Stansted airport branches away to the east, with the M11 near by. **Elsenham**, an attractive, original timber station, is well away from its village and church, which has an unusual Norman doorway. Just beyond the station are the remains of the former branch line to Thaxted. With good views to the east, the line picks up the headwaters of the Cam, a little stream that grows steadily on its way north to Cambridge. **Newport** has a pleasant church and some good 15th-century cottages, just by the line. The next station is **Audley End**, a fine 1845 building with a handsome *porte-cochère*. This serves the delightful, unspoilt village of Wendens Ambo, the historic and decorative

Hertford Castle Gardens: band concerts are held here in the summer

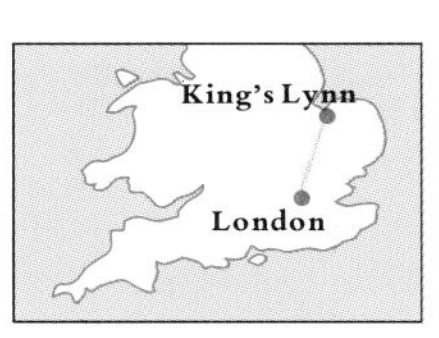

Converted 19th-century stable block containing a fine collection of historic bicycles (1818–present day).

BISHOP'S STORTFORD

Hatfield Forest Country Park, 3m E of Bishop's Stortford.

Rhodes Memorial Museum and Commonwealth Centre, South Rd. Early 19th-century house with exhibits illustrating life of Cecil Rhodes (open by appointment only).

continued on page 44

BROXBOURNE – HERTFORD EAST *7 miles*

You can reach Hertford East either by taking a Harlow and Bishop's Stortford train and changing at Cheshunt or Broxbourne, or by catching the direct service from Liverpool Street, which is a slow meander through north-east London via Bethnal Green, Hackney Downs, Stoke Newington, Seven Sisters, White Hart Lane, Edmonton, down into the Lea valley to join the main line at Cheshunt and then stopping only at Broxbourne and Hertford East.

After crossing a landscape dominated by the lakes and gravel pits of the Lea valley, the trains for Hertford East branch north-west, by the powerful brickwork of Gilbert Scott's power station, now disused. For trains from Cheshunt or Broxbourne, the first station is **Rye House**, and then the line follows the Lea to **St Margaret's** where the train leaves suburbia behind to enter an attractive landscape of farmland. Close by to the east is the Lea, with locks clearly visible against a background of hills, and to the west is another waterway, the New River, built in the 18th century to supply London with fresh water. Both waterways pass through the heart of **Ware**, an attractive old market town whose main street still retains an 18th-century atmosphere. A fine range of maltings stands by the station, while across the New River are the gardens created by John Scott, the Quaker poet, with a delightful 1770s grotto. Leaving Ware, the train crosses watermeadows to its terminus at **Hertford East**. The station is excellent, and well placed for the town centre. Built in 1888, it has a barrel-vaulted ticket hall, decorative ironwork, and a handsome exterior with delicate Dutch gables which are rather dwarfed by the grand *porte-cochère*. For Hertford, see also page 34.

STANSTED **Stansted Mountfitchet Windmill.** Restored red-brick tower mill of 1787, with machinery and furnishings still intact (open Apr–Oct).
NEWPORT **Mole Hall Wildlife Park,** Widdington, 2½m SE. Large collection of animals and birds, with a new butterfly and insect pavilion. Set in grounds of part-Elizabethan hall (house not open, park open daily). **Prior's Hall Barn,** Widdington, 2m SE. Fine medieval aisled barn (open Mar–Oct, weekends only).
AUDLEY END **Audley End House and Park.** 17th-century house built by Thomas Howard, Earl of Suffolk. Miniature railway in grounds (open Etr–Oct). **Saffron Walden Museum,** Museum St, Saffron Walden, 2m NE. Built in 1834. Housing local archaeology, natural history, costume and furniture. Castle ruins in grounds.

Wicken Fen: the windpump is the sole survivor of the Fens' drainage mills

WHITTLESFORD **Duxford Airfield,** Former Battle of Britain fighter station, with hangars dating from World War I. Housing Imperial War Museum's collections of military aircraft, fighting vehicles etc.
SHELFORD **Wandlebury Ring and Country Park,** 2m NE.
WATERBEACH **Anglesey Abbey,** Lode, 3m SE. 12th-century abbey converted to Elizabethan manor. Contains Fairhaven

continued on page 45

Restoration work on the Imperial War Museum's historic aircraft collection at Duxford Airfield

town of Saffron Walden, two miles to the east, and the splendid 17th- and 18th-century mansion of Audley End. The house cannot be seen from the train as it winds its way through the rolling landscape, but there is a glimpse of the 1774 obelisk above the trees. The pretty landscape continues as the train follows the Cam valley past Littlebury, the Roman town of **Great Chesterford** and Ickleton, whose church, with its dominant spire, contains a remarkable series of 12th-century wall paintings, unique in England. At **Whittlesford**, the hills are left behind, giving way to a flatter landscape. This is the station for Duxford, and the Imperial War Museum's collection of historic aircraft. A raised stretch takes the line past Sawston, known for its paper, parchment and leather industries, and Stapleford, with the Gog Magog hills and Wandlebury hillfort to the east. **Shelford** station serves the twin villages of Great and Little Shelford, full of delightful houses and colour-washed cottages, and then there is the junction with the Kings Cross to Cambridge line, which Liverpool Street trains share into Cambridge (see pages 36–7).

Cambridge – Ely and King's Lynn
Leaving Cambridge station, the train makes its way out of the city, passing the junctions with the line to Norwich and the goods line to St Ives. With the Cam and its guillotine locks to the east, it enters the strange landscape of the Fens, with the line running dead straight for miles to the distant horizon. The tower of Waterbeach Church can soon be seen and near **Waterbeach** station are Car Dyke, a Roman canal, and the remains of 12th-century Denny Abbey. The landscape is the characteristic blend of rich, brown earth, huge fields of vegetables, isolated farms and smallholdings and everywhere the dykes that control the water levels surround the line beneath huge skies. Sheep, cows and horses wander over the dykes, often standing higher than the roof of the train. To the east is Wicken Fen, 730 acres of original fenland carefully preserved as a nature reserve, and to the west is the tall chimney of the old steam pump at Stretham. The train crosses the Ouse, by its junction with the Cam, with the towers of Ely Cathedral gradually filling the horizon, like a great ship at anchor. **Ely** is the landmark of the journey, to be seen for miles in all directions, and its details will already be familiar by the time the train reaches the station.

Leaving the station, the train crosses the Ouse, with a fine view of the old quays and wharves against the background of the city huddled on the slopes of the cathedral mound. The lines to Norwich and Peterborough branch away to the east and west, and then the train continues north besides the Ouse to **Littleport**, a pleasantly old-fashioned timber station. The fine 15th-century church is best seen from the north. As the train approaches **Downham Market**, the windmill at Sluice Common can be seen to the east, while to the west is Denver Sluice, marking the tidal limit of the Great Ouse. Downham Market is a pleasant town of soft-coloured brick and stone, with gabled buildings showing Dutch influence. To the north, the great raised banks of the waterways dominate the landscape and limit the views, their height marked by chimneys and roofs peeping over the top. The next station is **Watlington**, and this is the stop for visits to the Wiggenhalls, including Wiggenhall St Mary the Virgin, whose church has some of the best carved benches in Britain. The romantic ruins of Wiggenhall St Peter are clearly visible across the dykes to the west. To the east is West Winch's windmill and then the train makes its rather private entry into **King's Lynn**, creeping round the back of the town to the station that once served much of north Norfolk, including the royal estate at Sandringham. It is a pretty building, well cared for and with plenty of decorative woodwork, and it makes a good gateway into King's Lynn itself.

King's Lynn

King's Lynn is one of England's treasures, a small town that has somehow survived the worst ravages of modern redevelopment. In the 14th century the town was one of England's busiest ports, and much of Lynn's wealth and style can be traced to that period. The 18th century was also important, and so what remains is a predominantly Georgian port town of great character, with a strong medieval heart. There are two medieval churches, one in each of the town's two great market squares, and a 15th-century guildhall. Decorative flintwork is the characteristic style, and the late Victorian Town Hall has matched it perfectly. The Georgian parts are all in brick, and the best streets lead down to the old quays and to the fine 1683 Customs House. Ships still use the harbour, and so Lynn has the lively atmosphere that is often lacking in better known, but more self-consciously preserved maritime towns. Famous also for its glass, King's Lynn is a delightful town to explore, and well worth the somewhat tortuous journey to the outer limits of Network SouthEast. Electrification, at present under way and with work visible from the train, will once again bring King's Lynn into Network SouthEast, with regular fast, through trains to London.

Ely Cathedral has been a landmark for miles around since the days of the Normans

King's Lynn has retained the lively atmosphere of a busy port from medieval and Georgian times to the present. Left, the seventeenth-century Customs House, and, below, the Tuesday market

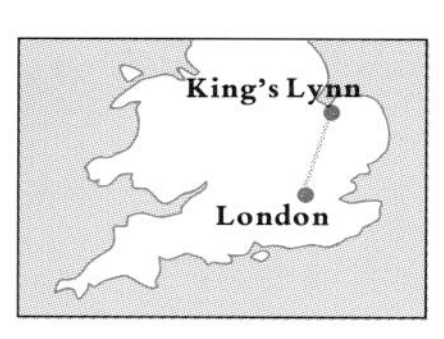

Collection of art treasures. Set in 100 acres of gardens with sculptures and Lode Watermill (open Apr–Oct). **Denny Abbey.** Originally a Benedictine Priory which passed on to the Knights Templar as a hospital. A 12th-century church with 14th-century additions still remains (open Mar–Oct).

ELY **Ely Cathedral.** Norman cathedral, mostly completed by 1189. Unique octagonal tower (1322). **Ely Museum,** High St. Illustrates social and natural history of Isle of Ely. Collection of Fenland farm and craft instruments. **The Stained Glass Museum,** North Triforium of Ely Cathedral. Founded to rescue and preserve fine stained glass (open Mar–Oct).

DOWNHAM MARKET **Denver Windmill.** Tower mill (open by appointment only).

KING'S LYNN **The Lynn Museum,** Old Market St. Natural, local and folk history and archaeology. **Museum of Social History,** 27 King St. Domestic life and dress, toys, dolls and glass. **St George's Guildhall**, King St. Largest surviving medieval guildhall in England. Now a theatre.

Tourist Information Centres
CHELMSFORD County Hall, Market Rd (0245) 283400 or 283339 (accommodation)
COLCHESTER 1 Queen St (0206) 46379
HARWICH Parkeston Quay (0255) 506139

Walks
The Essex Way. Runs 50 miles across Essex from Epping to Harwich. The path can be joined from Colchester, Manningtree, Mistley or Harwich stations.
The London Countryway (see page 14). The path can be joined from Shenfield.
Painter's Way. Runs along the River Stour, through landscape typical of Constable's paintings, from Manningtree to Sudbury, Gainsborough's birthplace.

Places to Visit
BRENTWOOD **Weald Country Park.**
CHELMSFORD **Chelmsford Cathedral. Chelmsford and Essex Museum** and **Essex Regiment Museum**, Moulsham St. Displays of prehistoric and Roman Essex, coins, costumes, paintings, industries.
KELVEDON **Paycocke's, Coggeshall**, 2m N. Early 16th-century merchant's house, with notable panelling, lace display, riverside garden (Apr–Oct).
MARKS TEY **Colchester Zoo, Stanway Hall**, 3m SE. 40-acre park. Zoo includes large mammal collection, reptile house, aquarium, and Birdland.
COLCHESTER **Bourne Mill.** Dutch gabled fishing lodge, dating from 1591 (open Apr–Oct, Suns only). **Colchester Castle**, N of High St, 11th-century. Housing collection of Roman and other antiquities. **Hollytrees Museum**, High St. Collection of costume and toys. **Minories Art Gallery**, 74 High St. Exhibitions of arts and crafts.

continued on page 47

Essex Landscapes

LIVERPOOL STREET – HARWICH *70¾ miles*

This journey links London with the Roman town of Colchester and the traditional port of Harwich, famous for many years as the starting point for ferry routes across the North Sea to Belgium and Holland. It explores the quiet landscape of Essex, the great river estuaries and the inland ports that have given the region its distinctive flavour. There is no need to take stopping trains, for the best part of the journey is beyond Colchester.

Colchester's Norman Castle: all that remains is the keep, which now houses a museum

Liverpool Street – Colchester
Trains for East Anglia leave from Liverpool Street. The recent total restoration of the station has meant the loss of some delightful bits of architectural eccentricity but the impact of the great forest of gothic cast-iron pillars and the huge space contained beneath the high roof is certainly exciting, and it shows that Victorian splendour can be combined with the functional demands of modern railway travel.

Trains take the old Great Eastern main line through Bethnal Green, Bow and Stratford, an elevated route past old terraces, back gardens and factories. West of Stratford the driverless trains of the Docklands Light Railway can be seen running alongside. Suburban London spreads eastwards through Ilford and Romford, and then ends suddenly as the fields take over just west of Brentwood. After **Shenfield** the line to Southend Victoria branches away to the east, and an open landscape of fields and woods flanks the line on its way towards Chelmsford. Ingatestone Hall, a grand 16th-century mansion, can be seen in woods to the south. **Ingatestone** station was built in a matching style in 1846. Soon after, the line passes close to Margaretting Church with its remarkable timber tower.

Chelmsford is a busy industrial town whose growth was encouraged first by the opening of the Chelmer & Blackwater Navigation in 1797, which linked it to the sea, and then by the arrival of the railway in 1843. The 15th-century parish church was given cathedral status in 1914. The world's first radio factory was set up by Marconi in Chelmsford's High Street in 1899. Leaving Chelmsford, the line runs close beside the A12 to **Hatfield Peverel**, where there is a big depot for London's milk supplies. At **Witham** the Braintree branch swings away to the north-west and then the line runs along the valley of the Blackwater to **Kelvedon**, which boasts a new station, built in a pleasant traditional style. As the train crosses the River Blackwater, there is a good view north along the valley towards Coggeshall. Marks Tey's pretty church stands in fields to the north of the line and just beyond is **Marks Tey** station, where the Sudbury branch (see pages 48–9) meets the main line.

Colchester
Soon Colchester's distinctive skyline of towers, spires and a giant water-tower comes into view, but **Colchester** station is a long way from the town centre. More convenient is St Botolphs, on the Walton and Clacton line. Colchester is England's oldest recorded town, and it was a regional capital before the Roman invasion. The Romans developed it further, and the street pattern today still follows the pattern laid down in the 2nd century AD. The town's continuing importance is reflected by the Norman castle, whose massive keep houses the museum. In the Middle Ages it was a wealthy cloth town and the ruined abbey and priory date from this period. There are plenty of medieval, 15th- and 18th-century buildings still to be seen, as well as a splendid late Victorian Town Hall by Sir John Belcher, whose extravagant 162ft tower can be seen for miles. Colchester is also known for its parks, its oysters and its harbour, still busy despite being tidal and a long way inland from the Colne's estuary.

Flatford Mill, near Manningtree, where Constable's cornmerchant father worked. The countryside is still clearly recognisable from Constable's paintings

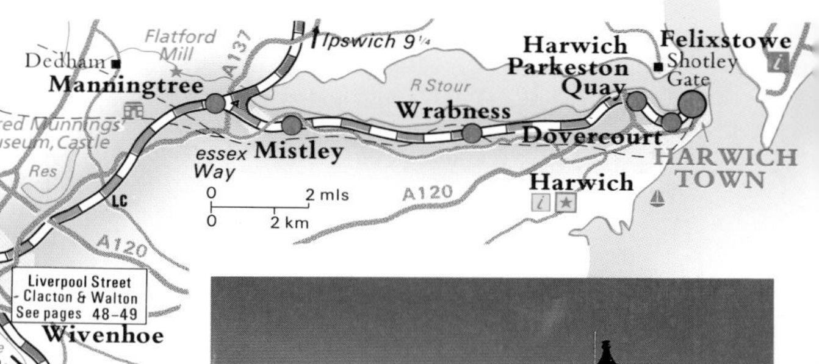

Colchester–Harwich
After Colchester, views are limited by cuttings and woods, but the train comes into a more open landscape as it approaches **Manningtree**. Passing Lawford Hall to the south, whose 18th-century façade conceals a Tudor mansion, and the church with its fine 14th-century chancel, the line reaches the wide expanse of the Stour estuary. Swinging south, away from the main line, the train passes through Manningtree village, and joins the Stour at **Mistley**, an attractive station set high above the old warehouses and granaries on the quays, still visited by coasters and red-sailed barges. Robert Adam's church and his lodge gates to the former Hall are visible from the station. The line runs along beside the Stour, but views across to the northern shore are limited by groves of chestnut. However, the tall tower of the Royal Hospital School can clearly be seen across the water. The next station is **Wrabness**, serving a little village whose church has a curious detached weather-boarded bell tower, and then the train drops down to the wilderness of the mudflats, a haven for seabirds. Harwich's international port is at **Parkeston Quay**. It is a busy sight, but it is quickly left behind as the line curves round a bay to **Dovercourt**, with fine views across the Stour estuary to Shotley and the mouth of the Orwell. Dovercourt is a curious little resort, with echoes of late Victorian ambition, but **Harwich Town** is a fine old seaside town. Georgian houses, some grand but faded hotels, and magnificent views out to sea and across the harbour make it a memorable place with a particularly English character.

Harwich has a strong seaside flavour: High Lighthouse (left) and (above) beach huts by the Maritime Museum

Museum of Social History, Holy Trinity Church, Trinity Sq. Displays of old country life and crafts.
Natural History Museum, High St. Local natural history.
Roman Walls. St John's Abbey Gate and Gardens. Ruins of Benedictine abbey.
Siege House, East St. A 15th-century house whose timbers are riddled with bullet holes from the 1648 Civil War siege.
Tymperley's Clock Museum, Trinity St. Colchester-made clocks (open Apr–Oct).

MANNINGTREE **The Sir Alfred Munnings' Art Museum**, Castle House, Dedham, 3½m W. The artist's former home and studio (open Apr–Oct). **Flatford Mill**, 1m N. Large mill complex. Subject of some of Constable's most famous paintings. **National Trust Field Centre** at nearby Bridge Cottage (open Etr–Oct).

HARWICH **Port of Harwich Maritime Museum**, Harwich Green. Disused lighthouse housing displays of RNLI, RN and commercial shipping (open Etr–Oct, Suns only).
The Redoubt, Main Rd. 80ft diameter circular fort, built 1808, housing three small museums (open Suns only).

Artists' Essex

LIVERPOOL STREET – SOUTHMINSTER *45½ miles*
LIVERPOOL STREET – SUDBURY *58½ miles*
LIVERPOOL STREET – CLACTON-ON-SEA *71¼ miles*
and WALTON ON THE NAZE *71¾ miles*

The main line from Liverpool Street to Colchester, a journey described on pages 46–7, is the starting point for a varied series of branch line excursions. The popular pleasures of sailing dominate the branch to Burnham and Southminster, and the rural line to Sudbury shows the face of Essex that has appealed to generations of painters. The traditional English seaside is the end of the line at Walton, while nearby Clacton is a more rumbustious resort.

Tourist Information Centres
(*summer only)
CHELMSFORD County Hall, Market Rd (0245) 283400 or 283339 (accommodation)
SUDBURY* Station Road (0787) 881320; in winter, Babergh District Council (0473) 825846
COLCHESTER 1 Queen St (0206) 712233
CLACTON-ON-SEA 23 Pier Avenue (0255) 423400
WALTON ON THE NAZE* Princes Esplanade (0255) 675542

Walks
The Essex Way (see page 46). The path can be joined from Colchester.
Painter's Way (see page 46). The path can be joined at Sudbury.
The Valley Walk. 3 miles along old railway line from Sudbury to Rodbridge.
St Peter's Way. Runs 45 miles from Chipping Ongar to Bradwell-on-Sea. The path can be joined from Ingatestone.
The London Countryway (see page 14). The path can be joined at Shenfield.

Places to Visit

For information on Brentwood, Chelmsford, Kelvedon, Marks Tey, and Colchester see pages 46–7.

WICKFORD – SOUTHMINSTER
BURNHAM-ON-CROUCH
The Burnham Museum. Collection of agricultural machinery and tools, maritime and prehistoric pieces from the Dengie Hundred region (open Mar–Dec).

MARKS TEY – SUDBURY
CHAPPEL & WAKES COLNE
East Anglian Railway Museum. 4-acre site with locomotives and large collection of signalling equipment.

continued on page 49

WICKFORD – SOUTHMINSTER
16½ miles

Trains for Southminster leave from Wickford. Passengers leaving from Liverpool Street should take a Southend Victoria train direct to Wickford (this follows the Colchester line as far as Shenfield) and then change.

Leaving Wickford, the branch crosses the little Crouch, and then turns east to follow the river valley. **Battlesbridge** station is little more than a hut, but much more substantial is **Woodham Ferrers**. The train then runs straight along the Crouch valley with, to the south, the dykes, ditches and mudflats that surround the tidal river. As the line passes **Fambridge** and **Althorne**, the horizon to the south is dominated by the massive tower of Canewdon Church. Approaching Burnham, the line drops closer to the river, now a wide tideway full of moored boats. The cottage-like station of **Burnham-on-Crouch** is set to the north of the town, and so there are no views of the quays and boatyards, its best features. Burnham's most exciting building is the Art Deco 1931 Royal Corinthian Yacht Club. After Burnham, the train runs inland through flat farmland to **Southminster**, with its typically Essex weather-boarded cottages. A quiet and rather forgotten place, with the Dengie Marshes stretching to the east, it is an unlikely terminus for a branch line whose creation must have seemed hard to justify.

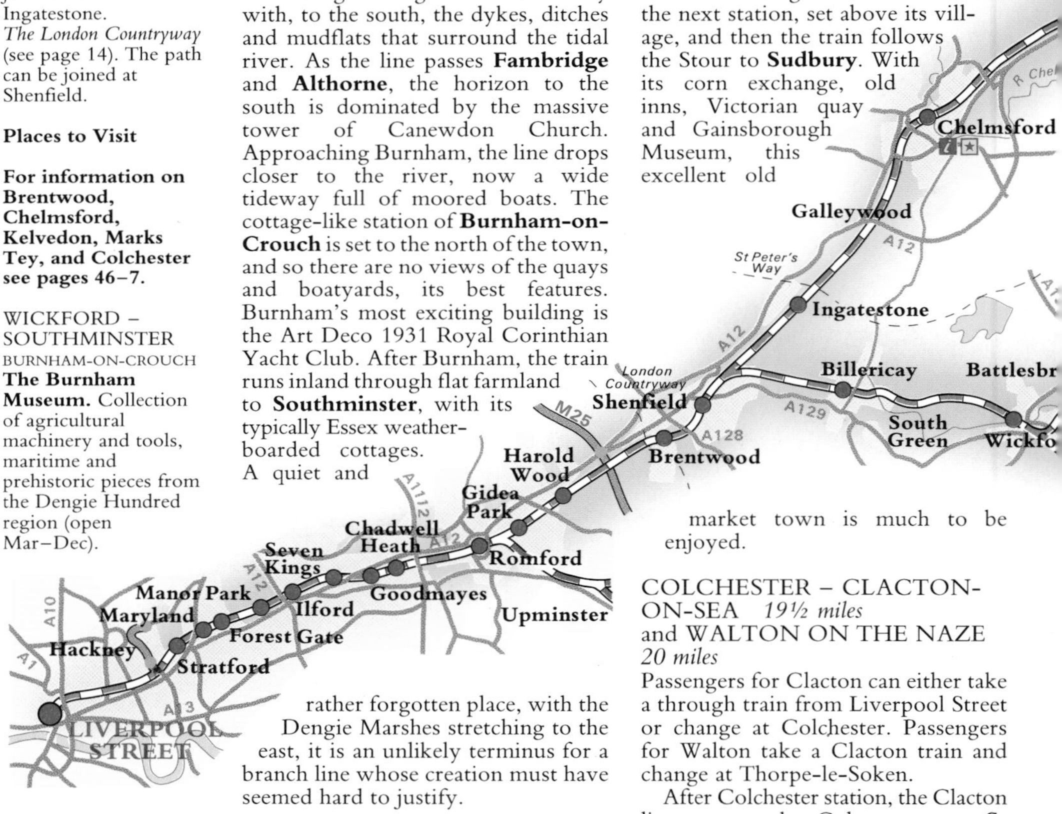

MARKS TEY – SUDBURY
11¾ miles

Trains for Sudbury leave from Marks Tey. Not all trains from Liverpool Street stop here, so passengers should either take the slower, stopping service, or go direct to Colchester and change to a local service for the five miles back to Marks Tey.

The Sudbury branch is a delightful rural journey through landscape straight out of Constable's paintings. Leaving Marks Tey, the train runs through leafy cuttings and then emerges to cross the great 1849 Chappel viaduct, whose 32 brick arches stride high above the River Colne and Chappel village. North of the viaduct is **Chappel & Wakes Colne** station, decorated in old LNER style and the home of the East Anglian Railway Museum. The train enters Suffolk with typical Constable views eastwards along the Stour. **Bures** is the next station, set above its village, and then the train follows the Stour to **Sudbury**. With its corn exchange, old inns, Victorian quay and Gainsborough Museum, this excellent old market town is much to be enjoyed.

COLCHESTER – CLACTON-ON-SEA *19½ miles*
and WALTON ON THE NAZE
20 miles

Passengers for Clacton can either take a through train from Liverpool Street or change at Colchester. Passengers for Walton take a Clacton train and change at Thorpe-le-Soken.

After Colchester station, the Clacton line crosses the Colne to enter **St Botolphs**, well placed for the town centre. The train now reverses out of the station and swings south, passing **Hythe** with its attractive old houses around the church and on the quay to the west. To the east is the University of Essex and the line now follows the widening estuary of the Colne. The next station is **Wivenhoe**, with its

Gainsborough's House Museum, Sudbury

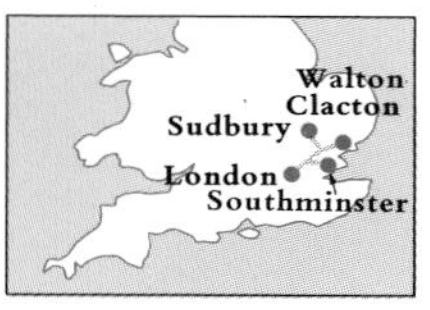

SUDBURY
Gainsborough's House, Gainsborough St. Birthplace of Thomas Gainsborough (1727–88), portrait and landscape painter. Contains 18th-century furniture and china and a loan collection of paintings by Gainsborough and his contemporaries.

pretty quay. From here there used to be a branch line south to Brightlingsea, and the elevated trackbed, clearly visible, makes a delightful estuary walk.

Leaving Wivenhoe, there is a fine view down the estuary and then the line turns inland to the flowery station at **Alresford**, whose simple and rather domestic classicism is typical of station buildings on this route. The train now runs through a landscape of fruit fields to **Great Bentley**, a station notable for its collection of gnomes, and then on to **Weeley** and **Thorpe-le-Soken** station, with a fine range of maltings. Handsome cast-iron brackets feature the GER monogram.

Change here for the Walton branch.

From Thorpe, Clacton trains soon enter the straggling outskirts of this famous seaside resort, with its piers and pavilions. The station, grand 1929 Georgian revival, is one of the town's best buildings.

For trains on the Walton branch from Thorpe, the first stop is **Kirby Cross** and then bungalows flank the line to **Frinton**, the station being well away from the heart of this rather exclusive resort with a distinctly old-fashioned atmosphere. Much more down to earth is **Walton on the Naze**. A homely resort with beach huts, seafood stalls and a pier striding out over the sandy beach, Walton is an unspoilt pleasure and it looks good from the rebuilt station with, to the north, its backdrop of estuaries, islands and mudflats painted so well by Ford Maddox Brown.

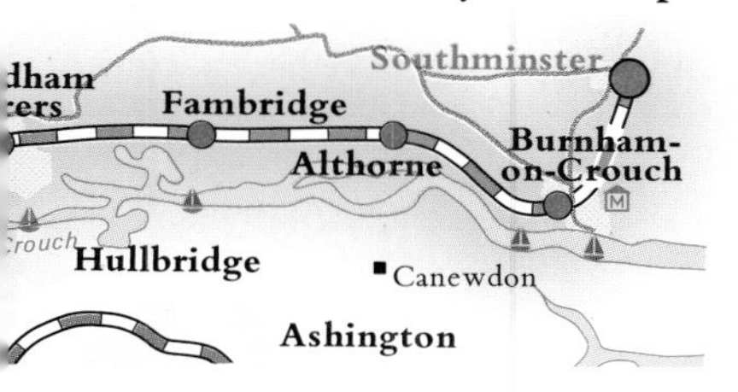

A preserved signal box at the Chappel & Wakes Colne Railway Museum

Melford Hall, Long Melford, 3m N. Turreted brick Tudor mansion (1578), with original panelled banquet hall, 18th-century drawing room, Regency library and Victorian bedroom. Special Beatrix Potter display (open May–Oct).

COLCHESTER – CLACTON-ON-SEA and WALTON ON THE NAZE
ALRESFORD **Beth Chatto Gardens,** nr Elmstead Market, ½m N. Contains variety of contrasting plantings, including dry garden, shade garden, five large pools surrounded by exotic bog plants and an adjoining nursery.

Walton on the Naze has all the ingredients of an unspoilt resort, including colourful beach huts

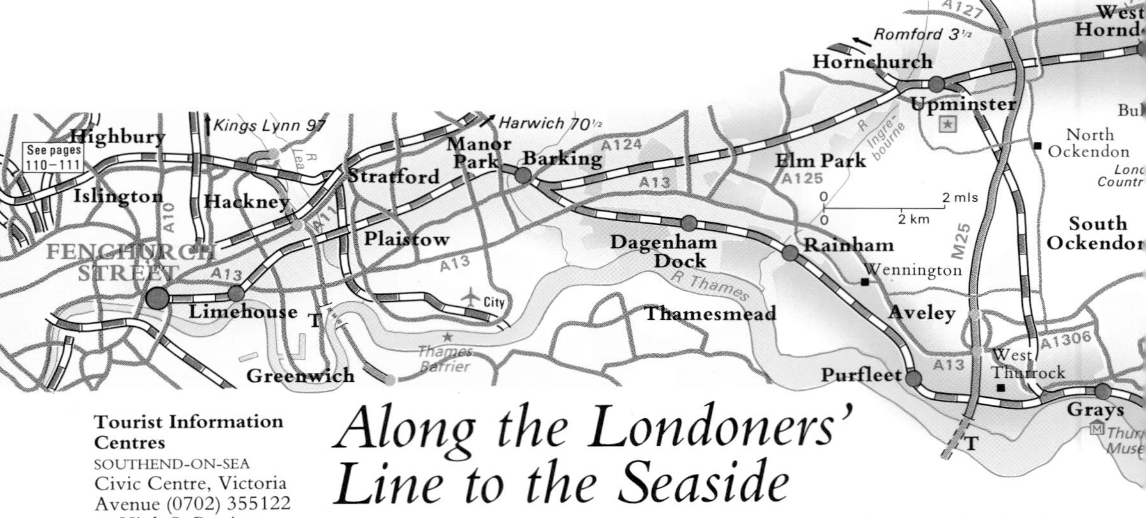

Along the Londoners' Line to the Seaside

FENCHURCH STREET – SHOEBURYNESS *via Southend*

Although predominantly a commuter line, the journey along the Essex shore of the Thames to its estuary at Shoeburyness is full of interest. All kinds of boats and ships, the distinctive marshland landscape of the tidal estuary, traditional seaside resorts, castles and churches and the legacy of Victorian industry and enterprise are all features of London's line to the sea.

The London, Tilbury & Southend Railway's monogram at Westcliff station

As far as Southend there are two routes from Fenchurch Street, the northern line that runs inland via Basildon, and a southern one that follows the Thames via Tilbury. Most trains for Shoeburyness take the northern route.

FENCHURCH STREET – SHOEBURYNESS *via Basildon*

39½ miles

Trains leaving or entering Fenchurch Street offer excellent views of the City, for the route is elevated all the way out of London. At Shadwell, with the church towers of Wapping to the south, the driverless trains of the Docklands Light Railway run alongside and there are views towards Docklands and the Canary Wharf development. The line then swings north-east away from the river towards West Ham, crossing over the River Lea, and then the Roding by its estuary at Barking Creek. From **Barking** to **Upminster** the train runs alongside London Regional Transport's District Line. Upminster's big smock windmill is clearly seen to the south and then the line is suddenly in open country, with undulating Essex hills to the north and to the south fine views towards the Thames and the distant cranes of Tilbury. The best section is east of **West Horndon**, with the Langdon Hills and Westley Heights to the south, and the spire of Dunton Church to the north. The next station is **Laindon**, whose bungalows and estates pave the way for **Basildon**.

At **Pitsea**, the junction with the Tilbury line, the houses give way, and there is a fine view south across a wide expanse of marshland towards distant Hole Haven and the towers of Shell Haven. The train takes an elevated route across the marshes, passing, right by the line, the isolated and charming church of Bowers Gifford. At **Benfleet** the train comes to the shore of Benfleet Creek, with boats of all kinds drawn up on the mudflats, and beyond is Canvey Island. The line now swings due east to cross the Hadleigh Marshes. High above on the hillside are the striking ruins of Hadleigh Castle, still looking as they do in Constable's painting. **Leigh-on-Sea**, formerly a little fishing village, is now a part of Southend, but the old village atmosphere survives in the cottages and boatyards between the railway and the river. The views now are excellent and there is a steady stream of large vessels bound in and out of Tilbury docks. Seaside houses and bungalows line the route past **Chalkwell** and **Westcliff**, many with elaborate balconies to make the most of the view and the sun. There are glimpses ahead of Southend pier. Westcliff station still has decorative ironwork incorporating the London, Tilbury & Southend Railway's monogram.

Southend Central is right in the heart of the town, but there is no view of the sea from the station. Southend, traditionally London's seaside resort,

Tourist Information Centres
SOUTHEND-ON-SEA Civic Centre, Victoria Avenue (0702) 355122 or High St Precinct (0702) 355120.

Walks
The London Countryway (see page 14). The path can be joined at Tilbury.

Places to Visit
BASILDON **Langdon Hills Country Park.** Former farmland with a variety of wildlife habitats.
GRAYS **Thurrock Museum,** Orsett Rd. Local history, agriculture, trade.
TILBURY TOWN **Thurrock Riverside Museum,** Civic Square. History of the local River Thames, its people, landscapes and fortifications.
TILBURY RIVERSIDE **Tilbury Fort.** Elizabeth I gathered an army here during threat of Spanish Armada.
BENFLEET **Hadleigh Castle.** Founded 1231 by Hubert de Burgh, rebuilt by Edward III in 14th century. Walls are of Kentish rag and the Castle retains two of its original towers.
SOUTHEND CENTRAL **Beecroft Art Gallery,** Station Rd, Westcliff-on-Sea. Contains municipal, Thorpe Smith and Beecroft collections. Monthly loan exhibitions. **Central Museum,** Victoria Ave. Human and natural history of SE Essex. **Prittlewell Priory Museum,** Priory Park. Former Cluniac monastery, housing local and natural history, with large collection of radios, TVs, gramophones and printing equipment. **Southchurch Hall,** Southchurch Hall Close. Early 14th-century moated, timber-framed manor house, with open hall furnished as medieval manor. Exhibition room.

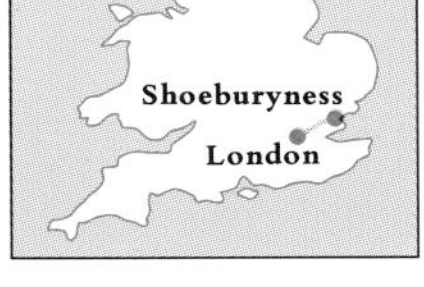

A replica of Sir Francis Drake's Golden Hind, *moored on the seafront at Southend*

Tilbury Fort, built by Henry VIII to guard the Thames estuary

was first developed in the late 18th century around the village of Prittlewell, whose 12th-century priory still survives as a ruin to the north of the town. Despite recent development and expansion, Southend still boasts some good 19th-century buildings, particularly big traditional hotels, a pretty bandstand, and other echoes of a more elegant seaside era. There is also a curious statue of Queen Victoria and a powerful war memorial by Edwin Lutyens, but the town's triumph has to be the pier, the longest in Britain, over a mile and with its own railway. Southend has another station, Victoria, served by trains from Liverpool Street which take an inland route via Romford.

Leaving Southend the train runs through suburbia to **Southend East** and **Thorpe Bay**, stations serving residential areas. The end of the line is **Shoeburyness**, a curiously isolated little town surrounded by military establishments and firing ranges, whose best features are the wonderful sea views. In the wooden station there is a touching memorial to Smokey the station cat.

FENCHURCH STREET – SHOEBURYNESS *via Tilbury*

45 ¼ miles

Trains for the Tilbury line from Fenchurch Street follow the same route through East London as far as Barking, and then they branch away to the south-east. **Dagenham Dock** is in the heart of the massive Ford car manufacturing complex, and then the train comes to **Rainham**. Just outside the station is the attractive village centre, made memorable by the fine Norman church, and the delightful formal brick façade of Rainham Hall, which dates from 1729. The train now runs through an area of isolated marshes and firing ranges to **Purfleet**, with Wennington Church to the north. From here eastwards to **Grays** and **Tilbury Town**, the surroundings are industrial, but views over Tilbury Dock's wharves, cranes and container ships add interest, and beyond are glimpses of Greenhithe and the Kent shore, soon to be linked by the new Thames bridge. Some trains take the branch line to **Tilbury Riverside** before reversing back to the main line and it is worth breaking the journey here to visit Tilbury Fort, built in 1682 to defend London from the Dutch and the French, with its splendid triumphal gateway. There are magnificent views of the Thames, busy with shipping, and across to Gravesend, whose old town centre is clustered around the church on the steeply rising southern shore. A ferry links Tilbury and Gravesend, making possible interesting round trips. The train now swings north-east to cross the marshes to **East Tilbury**, with distant views of the Thames to the south, and then passes close to Mucking's isolated church before reaching **Stanford-le-Hope**, whose big 1883 church tower is a clear landmark. With the A13 close by to the north, the line crosses a low-lying landscape to rejoin the main Shoeburyness route at **Pitsea**.

PIERS

A characteristic feature of the resorts that line the Essex shore of the Thames estuary are the seaside piers. Now rather overshadowed by larger, land-based leisure complexes, the pier may have passed its peak as a centre of popular seaside entertainment but it still has considerable appeal as part of the seaside landscape. Decorative details capture the flavour of forgotten eras, and bring back to life the Edwardian period, the 1920s and 1930s, and even the 1950s, that last great decade of the English seaside holiday. Piers were originally built, not for entertainment, but as landing stages for vessels visiting resorts without harbour facilities. Southend's pier, perhaps the greatest of them all, was constructed from 1889 and then rebuilt during the 1920s. However, its simpler predecessors date back to the 1830s and the early days of Southend's development. The growth of the Essex resorts was due to regular steam packet, and later, paddle steamer connections with London In 1848, for example, Southend pier received a daily steamer from London throughout the year, with five services a day during the summer.

Southend's pier runs out into the Thames for over one mile

1 *Wooded, rolling countryside characterises the route across the Kentish Weald to Hastings*

2 *A trip along the River Stour is a delightful way of seeing Canterbury's medieval buildings*

3 *River and railway make their way along the Arun valley, past Arundel Castle, to the coast*

4 *Tunbridge Ware, a form of wood mosaic using over 150 local woods, made in Tunbridge Wells*

5 *Onion domes and minarets lend Brighton Pavilion the incongruous look of an Indian palace*

2

1

3

4

ROUTES FROM

CHARING CROSS AND VICTORIA

5

The complex network of railways covering southern and south-eastern England was the result of fierce competition between three ambitious Victorian railway companies, the London, Brighton & South Coast, the London, Chatham & Dover and the South Eastern. Their battle for passenger and freight services and, in particular, for commuter traffic in and out of the capital left few parts of Sussex, Surrey and Kent isolated from the railway, and led to the building of a series of London termini from the 1860s. The most important of these were Victoria, Charing Cross, Cannon Street and London Bridge.

Victoria, built as two separate stations by rival companies which remained independent until the formation of the Southern Railway in 1923, is now the main London terminus for services to Sussex, Surrey and Kent, to the south coast and for most international connections via the Channel ports. Charing Cross, a station always limited by its size and its narrow approach across the Thames, now serves destinations in Kent and the east Sussex coast. Network SouthEast trains from these stations offer a range of journeys through the varied landscape of south-east England towards coastal destinations rarely more than an hour or two from London.

A TASTE OF LONDON

Buckingham Palace, the Queen's London home

IF ONE WENT TO LONDON EVERY day for a year there would still be something left to see – yet having said that there are several facets of the city that can easily be enjoyed in just one visit. The sample here aims to give some idea of the diversity of London's attractions, and to encourage visitors to plan further itineraries of their own.

LONDON'S RIVER

The Thames has witnessed London's development since Roman times and its banks carry the visible record of the city's history from Tudor Hampton Court to the 21st-century skyline of Canary Wharf. Anyone arriving at a London railway terminus from the south of England will have the Thames close at hand and a visit to the river makes a quick and easy introduction to a day in London.

The simplest way to do this is to walk along the embankment. A good route is to go from Waterloo westwards to Lambeth Bridge along the southern shore, passing the South Bank Centre and the Festival Hall, with views across to Somerset House, the Houses of Parliament and the government buildings of Whitehall, and then to return to Westminster Bridge along the northern shore. Also good is the northern embankment eastwards from Westminster Bridge to Blackfriars, passing gardens and statues, Cleopatra's Needle, and the ships moored in King's Reach, below the Strand.

With more time, you can take a boat trip on the river. For a short hop there is the regular river bus, or there are cruises westwards to Richmond and Hampton Court, or eastwards to Tower Pier and Greenwich. An excellent round trip is to take the Docklands Light Railway from Bank or Tower Bridge along its elevated route to Island Gardens, the southern tip of the Isle of Dogs, walk through the Thames tunnel to Greenwich for the Maritime Museum, the Queen's House, the *Cutty Sark* and the Observatory, and then take a river steamer back to central London.

ROYAL LONDON

A short walk from Victoria station leads to Buckingham Palace, the London home of the monarch since 1837. Here, the ceremony of The Changing of the Guard takes place at 11.30am, daily in summer, and on alternate days from October to March. Attached to the Palace, and the only parts open to the public, are the Queen's Gallery and the Royal Mews. The Mall runs from Buckingham Palace eastwards to Admiralty Arch and Trafalgar Square. To the north are the lesser-known Royal residences of St James's Palace, Clarence House, Lancaster House and Marlborough House, and to the south is St James's Park, a pleasant oasis of peace, originally laid out as a deer park by Henry VIII.

Another of Henry's deer parks was Hyde Park, opened to the public during the Stuart period. A good starting point is Hyde Park Corner, reached from Buckingham Palace by following Constitution Hill north-west through Green Park. Hyde Park runs north to Marble Arch and west to Kensington, merging imperceptibly with Kensington Gardens. At its heart is the Serpentine and at its western end is another Royal residence, Kensington Palace, whose state apartments are open to the public. London's other royal palaces are Hampton Court, by the Thames in Surrey but easily reached by train from Waterloo or boat from Charing Cross, Greenwich and the Tower of London, by Tower Bridge.

CULTURAL LONDON

It would take days to explore London's wealth of museums and galleries, but several are grouped conveniently together and so can form part of a day in London. South Kensington is the starting point for visits to the Natural History Museum, the Victoria & Albert Museum, the Geological Museum and the Science Museum. Another good centre is the Tower of London, with Tower Bridge near by and, moored in the Thames opposite the Tower, HMS *Belfast*. The nearest tube station is Tower Hill. Also close together are Madame Tussaud's and the London Planetarium, in Marylebone Road, and reached via Baker Street tube.

THE CITY AND ITS CHURCHES

The square mile of the City, London's financial heart, is well worth a day visit. At its centre is St Paul's Cathedral, one of London's most familiar landmarks, and easily approached on foot from Blackfriars or the new St Pauls Thameslink stations, or by tube. Near by is the Monument, commemorating the Great Fire of 1666. East of St Paul's is Bank, with the Bank of England and its museum, the Mansion House, the Royal Exchange and the Stock Exchange all close to hand, and to the north is the Museum of London – all within easy walking distance. Scattered throughout the City are the many churches designed by Sir Christopher Wren to replace those destroyed in the Great Fire.

SHOPPING

London is known throughout the world for its shops and markets, and many people will want to include shopping in a day trip. One good starting point is Piccadilly Circus. From here Regent Street, famous for Liberty's and Hamley's, runs north to Oxford Circus, where it meets Oxford Street. Oxford Street eastwards is mostly clothes shops, tourist shops and fast food shops. Westwards it leads to Bond Street, Selfridges and other department stores. For some of London's most exclusive shops, walk down Bond Street and through the Burlington Arcade to Piccadilly and Fortnum & Mason.

Another good centre is Knightsbridge, the famous home of Harrods. A short bus ride away is Kensington High Street. Alternatively, a walk down Sloane Street from Knightsbridge will lead to Sloane Square, and the start of Chelsea's Kings Road. Covent Garden is London's newest shopping centre, an entertaining mixture of boutiques, restaurants and open-air market stalls.

LONDON TRAVEL

All parts of central London can quickly be reached by tube or bus from all the main railway termini. Exploring chosen areas on foot can be rewarding, in terms of unexpected discoveries, and the distances are often less than expected. Individual journeys on public transport soon mount up, and so visitors should buy one-day Capitalcards, available from tube and British Rail stations. These give unrestricted travel (after 9.30am) on buses, tubes and some British Rail lines. See also page 7 for details of the One Day Travelcard which includes unlimited travel on tubes and buses.

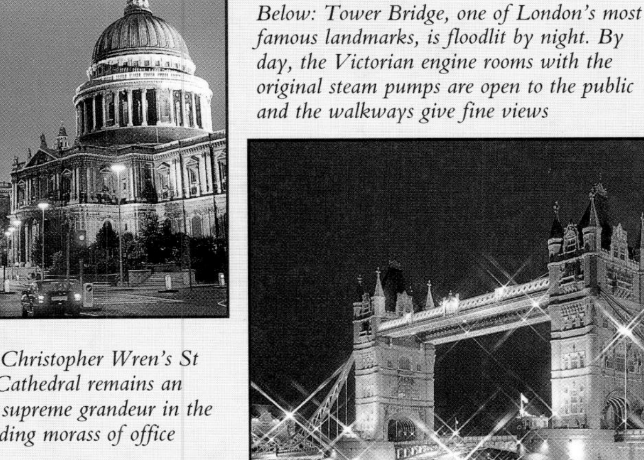

Above: Christopher Wren's St Paul's Cathedral remains an oasis of supreme grandeur in the surrounding morass of office blocks

Below: Tower Bridge, one of London's most famous landmarks, is floodlit by night. By day, the Victorian engine rooms with the original steam pumps are open to the public and the walkways give fine views

The British love pageantry and London has plenty. Above: The Life Guards in their distinctive plumed helmets and red tunics

Above: The graceful Cutty Sark, *the fastest tea clipper to be built, is preserved at Greenwich*

Left: The nation's time-keeper: the clock of St Stephen's tower, the Houses of Parliament – better known as Big Ben

Right: Nelson's column in Trafalgar Square, named to commemorate his victory over the French, dwarfs the fine statue of Charles I below

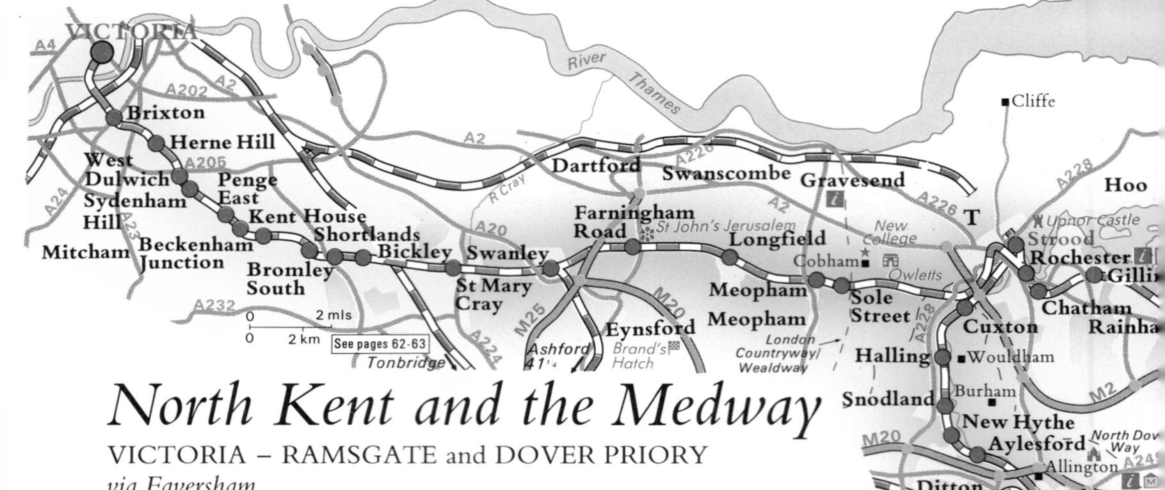

North Kent and the Medway

VICTORIA – RAMSGATE and DOVER PRIORY
via Faversham
and STROOD – PADDOCK WOOD

There are two routes from London to Ramsgate and Dover, one from Charing Cross via Tonbridge and Ashford, and the other from Victoria via Faversham. The Victoria route via Faversham is the more interesting of the two, offering as it does a tour of rural Kent, the Thames estuary, the Isle of Thanet and the north Kent coast. The journey from Strood to Paddock Wood is an exploration of the Medway, one of Britain's least-known river navigations, through a delightful landscape of orchards, hop fields, wooded hills and traditional farms.

Tourist Information Centres
ROCHESTER Eastgate Cottage, High St (0634) 843666
FAVERSHAM Fleur de Lis Heritage Centre, 13 Preston St (0795) 534542
WHITSTABLE The Horsebridge (0227) 275482
HERNE BAY Bandstand, Central Parade (0227) 361911
MARGATE Marine Terrace (0843) 220241
BROADSTAIRS 67 High St (0483) 68339
CANTERBURY 34 St Margaret's St (0227) 766567 or 455567
DOVER Townwall St (0304) 205108
MAIDSTONE The Gatehouse, Mill St (0622) 673581

Walks
The London Countryway (see page 14). The path can be joined at Sole Street.
The North Downs Way. Runs 140 miles along the North Downs and Kentish Weald. The path can be joined from Rochester.
The Saxon Shore Way. Runs 140 miles along the Kentish coastline. The path can be joined from Rochester, Sittingbourne, Whitstable, Faversham, Whitstable or Herne Bay (not shown on map).
The Wealdway. Runs 80 miles through the Kent and Sussex Weald. The path can be joined at Sole Street.

continued on page 57

Fast trains to Faversham do not stop at Rochester and so passengers wishing to visit Rochester have either to take the slow, stopping service, or to change at Chatham, the next stop, where there are connections back to Rochester and Strood. It is not far to walk back from Chatham to Rochester station. There is also a direct service to Rochester from Charing Cross, via Dartford and Gravesend.

VICTORIA – RAMSGATE
79¼ miles

Victoria – Faversham

Trains for the Ramsgate and Dover lines leave from the eastern side of Victoria station, entered via A W Blomfield's grand Edwardian baroque façade, completed in 1909 for the South Eastern & Chatham Railway. Sculpted mermaids and other maritime motifs on the façade hint at the seaside delights in store. Trains cross the Thames on the grand Grosvenor Bridge with good views westwards along the river to the decorative Chelsea and Albert Bridges, while to the east is the towering bulk of Gilbert Scott's former Battersea power station. The route across south London to Brixton is elevated, and then the line runs through Herne Hill, Dulwich, with the College and the Park to the east, and under Crystal Palace to Penge East, whose station and setting is now rather different from that painted by Pissarro in the early 1870s. The surroundings are suburban through Beckenham, Bromley South and Bickley and over the complex Chislehurst Junction to **St Mary Cray**, and then open country appears after the viaduct over the River Cray.

At Swanley the line south to Ashford via the heart of Kent's fruit-growing region branches away and then there are good views north towards the Thames and south to the Downs. There are stations at

Fruit fields are a feature of this route. Below, a pear orchard near Sittingbourne

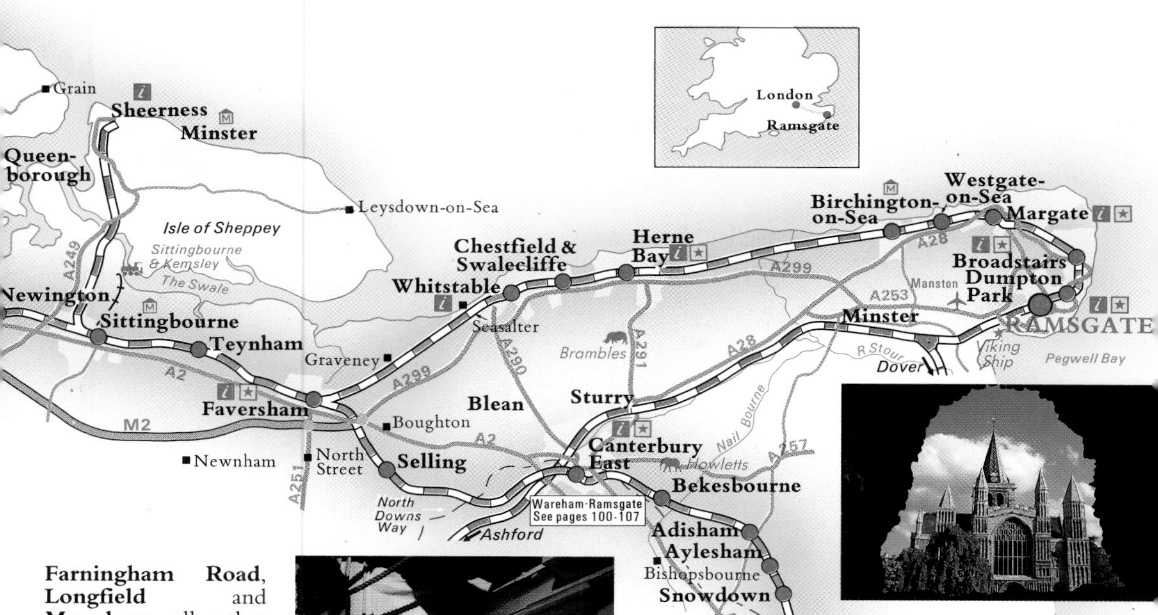

The squat outline of Rochester Cathedral

Farningham Road, **Longfield** and **Meopham**, all rather detached from their villages. Meopham's large 14th-century church lies to the north, while **Sole Street** is the nearest station for Cobham, with its fine church, the splendid 14th- and 15th-century college, and Owletts. To the east is Tudor Cobham Hall, set in its park by Repton. East of Sole Street there are fine views southwards and then the line drops down towards the Medway. The high M2 motorway bridge dominates and then beyond are splendid views along the broad Medway with its variety of moored boats towards Rochester's castle and cathedral. With Frindsbury Church high up on the chalk cliffs to the north and Strood station below, the train swings sharply south to cross the river.

Chatham Historic Dockyard: one of the displays which take visitors on a journey through time into British Naval history

Rochester is seen at its best from the line's elevated route through the city centre, with a backdrop of the castle and cathedral. Rochester is a splendid but little-known city and a powerful fortress from Roman times to the medieval period. The castle, with its great keep, is one of the finest Norman military buildings in England, while the cathedral was built between 1179 and 1240. The city's narrow streets, whose fine buildings reflect centuries of maritime wealth, have a particular atmosphere that was greatly attractive to Charles Dickens. To the north are the sharply curving river and the old quays.

Strood, Rochester, Chatham and Gillingham are, in effect, one large conurbation. The winding route, often elevated and in and out of tunnels, allows good views up the Medway towards **Chatham's** former naval dockyards, established by Queen Elizabeth I, and across to the war memorial obelisk. Leaving **Gillingham**, there are fine views to the north, across a foreground of fruit orchards, to the huge expanse of the Medway's estuary. From **Rainham** there is a view of Otterham Quay, and then the line continues through fruit and hop fields to **Newington**, whose church is in the woods to the north, and **Sittingbourne**, a centre for paper-making since the 1840s. Change here for the branch line north to the Isle of Sheppey and Sheerness, and for the steam trains of the Sittingbourne and Kemsley Light Railway (see page 58), whose terminus is a short walk from the station.

After Sittingbourne the fruit orchards continue and to the north across the Swale are the lowlands of Sheppey. Also to the north is Tonge's pretty barn-like church, while by the line to the south is the old castle mound and a big mill near by. **Teynham** is a village buried in fruit fields, and then the train reaches **Faversham**.

Faversham

A busy port since the Middle Ages, Faversham is also known for its beer and a big range of maltings stands by the station. It is an attractive town, easily explored from the big market square. Tudor buildings include the Guildhall and the Grammar School, while the large church, to the north, has medieval wall paintings inside. Colour-washed and redbrick cottages and terraces add to the appeal. Here, the lines divide, and trains for Ramsgate branch north-east.

Places to Visit
VICTORIA – RAMSGATE

FARNINGHAM ROAD **St John's Jerusalem Garden** (NT), Sutton at Hone, ¾m N. Large garden. 13th-century house (garden open Apr–Oct).

SOLE STREET **New College of Cobham**, 1½m NE. Almshouses (open Apr–Sep).
Owletts House (NT), 1m NE. 17th-century house (open Apr–Oct).

ROCHESTER **Cathedral**. Second oldest See in England.
Charles Dickens Centre, Eastgate House, High St. Display of Dickens characters.
Guildhall Museum, High St. Local collections.
Rochester Castle. Begun 1087.
Kenneth Bills Rochester Motor Cycle Museum, 144 High St. Over 100 British bikes.
Temple Manor. Built 1240 by Knights Templar (open Apr–Sep).

CHATHAM **Chatham Historic Dockyard**, Dock Rd. Museum and Visitor Centre.
Fort Amherst, Barrier Rd, off Dock Rd. Napoleonic fortress (open Apr–Oct).
Medway Heritage Centre, Dock Rd. Story of the Medway.

continued on page 58

GILLINGHAM
Gillingham Urban Heritage Centre, Napier Rd. History of the town.
SITTINGBOURNE
Dolphin Sailing Barge Museum, Crown Quay Lane (open Etr–Oct.)
FAVERSHAM **Fleur de Lis Heritage Centre**, Preston St. 1,000 years' history and architecture (open Etr–Sep, Suns only). **Maison Dieu** (God's House), Ospringe. Medieval hospital (open Mar–Oct).
HERNE BAY **Brambles Wildlife Park**, Herne Common, 2m S (open Etr–Nov).
Herne Bay Museum, High St. Story of Herne Bay.
BIRCHINGTON-ON-SEA
Quex House and the Powell-Cotton Museum. Regency mansion (open Apr–Sep).
MARGATE **Dreamland Theme Park.** Amusement park (open Apr–Nov).
Draper's Windmill, St Peter's Footpath, off College Rd. Restored windmill (open Suns, Etr–mid Sep).
Lifeboat House, Margate Harbour (open daily late May–late Sep).
Margate Caves, 1 Northdown Rd. 1,000 years old (open daily Etr–Sep).
Old Town Hall Local History Museum, Market Place. Local history (open May–Sep).

continued on page 59

Yachts and pleasure boats line the marina in Ramsgate's Royal Harbour (above), while work goes on (below) at the quayside of Whitstable harbour

Faversham – Ramsgate
The train runs straight across the low-lying marshland, with Graveney's delightfully decorative and unrestored church to the north. After the isolation of the saltmarshes, an outburst of caravans and bungalows announces Seasalter, before the line turns inland to pass to the south of **Whitstable**. The first steam-hauled railway in the south of England was opened between Canterbury and Whitstable in 1830, but little of that remains. The town, famous for its natives, or oysters, since Roman times, is to the north and is at its best around the old harbour, where there is plenty of old-fashioned seaside atmosphere. To west and to east are fine sandy beaches.

Chestfield & Swalecliffe is an extension of Whitstable, and this in turn spreads eastwards to **Herne Bay**. The big decorative station also reflects the holiday atmosphere. Herne Bay was developed as a resort from the 1830s, and the seafront terraces and the big clock tower still echo that period. Leaving Herne Bay, the line runs across saltmarshes again, with a fine view to the north towards Reculver's ruined Saxon abbey, destroyed in 1809, and the mound that was the Roman fort, with its ring of caravans. Crossing the network of rivers that makes Thanet an island, the train now comes to **Birchington-on-Sea**, the beginning of a spread of holiday and seaside development that extends all the way around the North Foreland to Ramsgate. To the south is Quex House, with its towers and the Powell-Cotton Museum.

Next is **Westgate-on-Sea** and then the train reaches **Margate**'s grand 1920s station. A short walk away is the little harbour and the attractive 18th-century terraces that reveal Margate's early development as a resort. Its popularity was ensured by the invention here of the bathing machine. It is a delightful resort, and the train is clearly the best way to arrive. East of the station the train passes Dreamland Theme Park and then runs inland across Thanet to **Broadstairs**. The harbour, beach and town centre are well to the east, below the cliffs.

SITTINGBOURNE AND KEMSLEY LIGHT RAILWAY

SITTINGBOURNE – KEMSLEY DOWN
2 miles

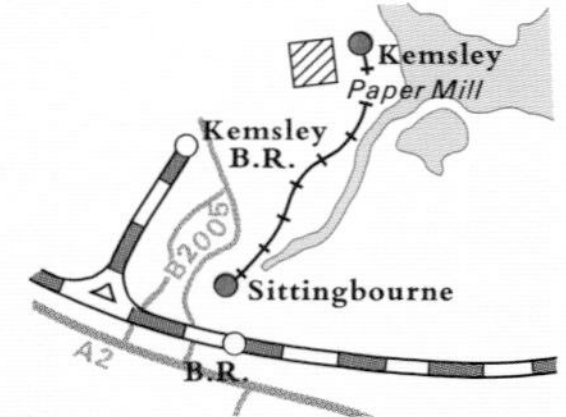

From 1906 an extensive narrow gauge railway was opened to connect papermills at Sittingbourne and Kemsley with Ridham Dock on the River Swale, and the network remained in regular use until the 1960s. Two miles of the 2ft 6ins gauge line is now maintained as a tourist railway with steam-hauled passenger services.
The terminus in Sittingbourne is five minutes' walk from the British Rail station and is well signposted. The route is through Milton Regis and then along the north bank of Milton Creek towards the Swale, through an interesting blend of marshland and industrial scenery. The first section of the route is on a twisting elevated viaduct, one of the first major structures in Britain to have been built from reinforced concrete.
Services: Sunday afternoons, Easter to October, Bank Holiday weekends, some Wednesday afternoons in summer, Christmas specials
For information: General enquiries (0634) 52672, talking timetable (0795) 424899
Note: There is no public access to Kemsley Down station, other than by train

Ramsgate
A cutting leads to **Dumpton Park** and then the train comes to the end of its journey at **Ramsgate**, another grand 1920s classical station, inconveniently placed high above the town and a long walk from the harbour, the beach and the centre of this popular resort. The Ramsgate area has been the landing place for many visitors from Europe, including Hengist, Horsa and St Augustine, and Sally Line's ferries keep the tradition alive. Development of the resort started in the late 18th century, and Ramsgate still has plenty of buildings that date from its early days, particularly in the harbour area. It is also a town noted for its Victorian churches, the best being St Augustine's, by the great A W N Pugin, who also built himself a house in Ramsgate. It is an enjoyable town to explore, full of seaside atmosphere, and a fitting end to the line.

VICTORIA – DOVER PRIORY
77¼ miles
There are direct services from Victoria to Dover Priory via Faversham. Alternatively, take a Ramsgate train as far as Faversham, where the change is very straightforward.

Canterbury Cathedral, the mother church of English Christianity

For Victoria – Faversham see pages 56–7.

Faversham – Canterbury
Trains for Canterbury and Dover branch away to the south-east soon after leaving Faversham station, pass under the M20, and enter a familiar landscape of orchards and rolling hills. Boughton Church can be seen on a hill to the east. The first station is **Selling**, well away from its scattered village, and then the line drops through woods towards the Stour valley. There are splendid views along the valley eastwards towards Canterbury, with the cathedral and its great central Bell Harry tower dominating the city. After crossing the Stour valley line to Ashford, and the river, the train enters **Canterbury East**, with the ruins of the Norman castle just to the north, commanding the river. The station is set just outside the city walls.

Canterbury
Canterbury is a city that encapsulates much of England's history. Its Roman origins are still to be seen, including the foundations of the largest theatre in Britain. However, it was the arrival of St Augustine in 597 that determined the city's subsequent development as a major centre of Christianity and learning. The remains of the abbey he founded still exist, but far more significant is the great Norman cathedral, whose construction was started in 1070. The martyrdom in 1170 of Thomas à Becket turned Canterbury into a major centre of pilgrimage, and the early Gothic elements of the cathedral were built as a shrine to the saint. The medieval period saw many additions to the cathedral, not least its collection of stained glass, and around the great church there grew a large medieval city, still contained within the Norman walls. Canterbury's core is still essentially medieval, full of the atmosphere of Chaucer and *The Canterbury Tales*. Narrow streets and timber-framed houses give it a particular flavour, best appreciated by explorations on foot.

Canterbury – Dover
The train takes a rather secret route out of the city through back gardens and cuttings to **Bekesbourne**. The church stands to the south, by the

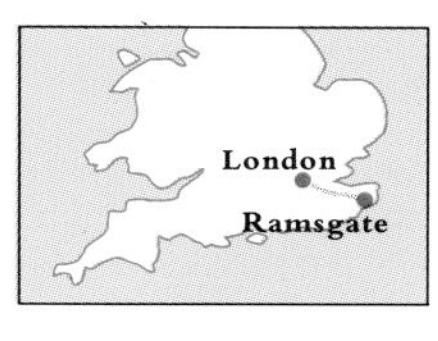

Salmestone Grange, Nash Rd (open Jun–Aug).
Shell Grotto, Grotto Hill. Ancient shell temple (open daily Etr–mid Oct).
Tudor House and Museum, King's St. History of Thanet (open May–Sep).
BROADSTAIRS **Bleak House Dickens**

A stained-glass panel of David Copperfield in Dickens' House, Broadstairs

Maritime and Smuggling Museum, Ford Rd. Favourite seaside residence of Charles Dickens (open Etr–mid Sep).
Crampton Tower Museum, High St. Commemorates Crampton, Victorian engineer (open May–Sep).

continued on page 60

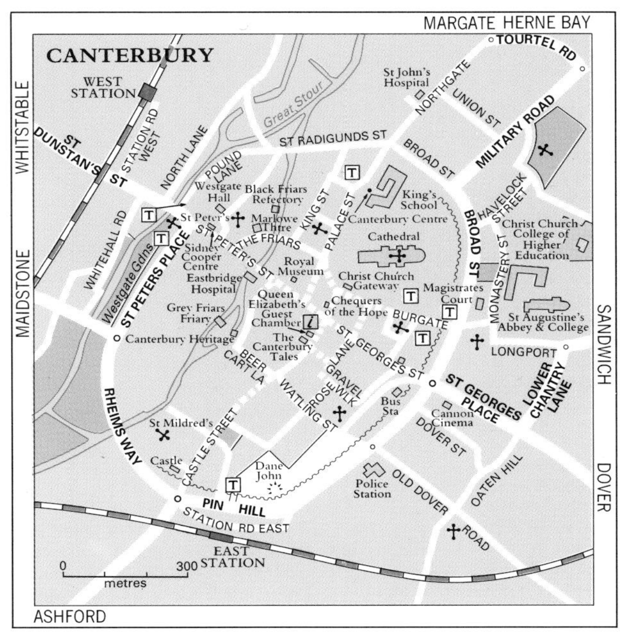

Dickens House Museum, Victoria Pde. Home of Betsy Trotwood in *David Copperfield* (open Apr–Oct).
Maritime Museum Complex, Pier Yard. Maritime history.
RAMSGATE **The Model Village**, West Cliff. England's countryside in miniature (open daily Etr–Oct).
Pegwell Bay picnic site. 70 acres of grassland and marsh.
Ramsgate Motor Museum, Westcliff Hall, The Paragon. Vintage cars and bikes (open Etr–Sep; winter, Suns only).
Ramsgate Museum, Library, Guildford Lawn. Local history.
Spitfire Memorial Pavilion, RAF Manston.
Viking Ship *Hugins,* Cliff top, Pegwell Bay. Replica Viking ship, rowed and sailed from Denmark to Thanet in 1949.

Figurehead of the Viking ship at Pegwell Bay

VICTORIA – DOVER PRIORY
CANTERBURY
Cathedral. Renowned for its stained glass.
Canterbury Centre, St Alphege Ln. Historical and contemporary exhibitions.
Canterbury Heritage, Time Walk Museum, Stour St. Tells story of the city.
The Canterbury Tales, St Margaret's St. Chaucerian characters telling their tales with authentic sights, sounds and smells of 14th-century life.
Royal Museum, Art Gallery and Buffs Regimental Museum, High St. Archaeology, porcelain, glass, clocks, local regiment.
St Augustine's Abbey. Ruins. Founded in 598.
Whitstable Museum, Oxford St. Social life of Canterbury.

continued on page 61

River Nail Bourne, with the remains of the Archbishop's old palace near by. The landscape is then more open to **Adisham** and **Aylesham**, with long views to the north across fields and orchards. Adisham's church and the Court, a 17th-century mansion, stand to the south just before the station. Aylesham is a planned village, laid out in the 1920s, to house the miners working in the Kent coalfield, and it is this, an unexpected presence in the garden of England, that dominates the line for a few miles. **Snowdown** was the first and the most important of the Kentish coal mines. It was opened in 1913, and others followed, along the line of the coal seam to the east. Today, Kent is no longer a major coal-producing region, and the great days of Snowdown have passed, leaving the station rather isolated in a setting of dramatic dereliction. The next station is **Shepherd's Well**, formerly the junction with the Kent & East Sussex Railway's trains to Wingham and Sandwich, part of whose rural route was later used by coal trains. A long tunnel now leaves industry behind and the train then drops down a steep-sided valley towards **Kearsney**, with Lydden Hill to the west, and then there is a fine view of Dover Castle to the east as the train approaches **Dover Priory**.

Dover
Set to the west of the town and hidden behind Western Heights, Dover Priory gives no sense of the town and its dramatic position in a narrow cleft in the white cliffs. It is worth walking down to the harbour, beneath the towering bulk of the castle, to appreciate that Dover's history is entirely bound up with the defence of the port. With Europe little over 20 miles away, Dover has been England's front door since the Iron Age, when the first defences were built. The Romans followed, and their lighthouse still stands on Castle Hill, near the Saxon church. Henry II built the first castle, from 1168. Expanded continuously until the 19th century, Dover Castle was an important garrison until 1958. Facing it across the town are the Western Heights, another clifftop fortress developed to

STROOD – PADDOCK WOOD
21¼ miles
Medway Valley line trains run specifically between Strood and Paddock Wood, but there are easy London connections at both ends. Strood is served by Kent Link trains from Charing Cross to Gillingham via Blackheath, Dartford and Gravesend. Alternatively, passengers can take a Faversham, Ramsgate or Dover train from Victoria as far as Rochester (see above), and then either walk back to Strood, about a mile, through Rochester, or take a local train.

From Paddock Wood there are regular connections to Tonbridge, which is on the Kent Coast route from Charing Cross to Ashford, Dover, Canterbury and Ramsgate (see pages 105–7) and on the Charing Cross–Hastings route (pages 62–3). Interesting round trips are therefore easy to plan, with a good selection of places to break the journey.

The route along the southern shore of the Thames from Charing Cross to Strood is full of interest and history, linking Blackheath, Greenwich and Woolwich with the once-great ports of Greenhithe and Gravesend.

Strood – Maidstone
Strood station is by the Medway, to the south of its town and all the interest is inevitably across the river. Leaving the station, there are wonderful views across the Medway to Rochester Castle and Cathedral and then the train runs along the river's shore and under the M2 motorway. The mudflats are dotted with little fishing boats and the hulks of old sailing barges, and over the river is the busy marina. The first stop is **Cuxton**, where the pretty Tudor-style station, with its little signal box and hand-operated crossing gates, faces out across the Medway to the Wouldham Marshes. The train follows the river's shore to **Halling**, a village dominated by industry. A better view is across the Medway to Wouldham, a pretty village clustered round its church. Between Halling and **Snodland**, the line passes the huge Holborough cement works with the meandering river to the east. Snodland is an estate village, but it has a fine ragstone church, set by the river and facing across the water its pair at Burham. With lakes and flooded gravel pits all around, the line continues to **New Hythe**, with its vast papermills, and then on to **Aylesford**, where there are good views of the Friars, the first Carmelite house in England, founded in 1240, and across the river to the church with its Norman tower. Aylesford station, dating from 1856, is an attractive, ragstone building, whose Tudor style may have been inspired by the nearby Friary. A long cutting takes the train into Maidstone.

Maidstone
The first of Maidstone's three stations is **Maidstone Barracks**, quickly followed by **Maidstone West**, and between the two there is a brief glimpse of the 14th-century Archbishop's Palace. Near by is the collegiate Church of All Saints, the grandest late 14th-century building in Kent. Both stations are well to the west of the centre of Kent's county town, and the most convenient is the third, Maidstone East, on the Victoria – Ashford line via Otford. Geographically well placed, Maidstone

Dover Castle's massive walls and keep stand on cliffs fortified since Iron Age times

counter the threat posed by Napoleon, but in this case most of the fortifications were hidden underground.

Another way to see the town is to take a train that continues to **Dover Western Docks**, burrowing on the way under Western Heights, and then walk back alongside the quays, the harbour and the beach, watching the continual comings and goings of the cross-Channel ferries.

BEKESBOURNE **Howletts Zoo Park**. Breeding groups of gorillas, tigers.
DOVER PRIORY **Crabble Mill**. Built to provide flour for soldiers in Napoleonic wars.
Dover Castle. Roman lighthouse near by.
Dover Museum, Ladywell. Local and natural history.
Dover Old Town Gaol, Biggins St. Victorian prison life (open summer only).
Roman Painted House, New St. Well-preserved wall paintings (open Apr–Oct).
Time-Ball Tower, Beach St. Museum of time (open late May–Sep).

has been Kent's main market town since the Middle Ages, and its chief industries were, initially, textiles and, later, paper-making and brewing. Medieval and later buildings reflect the wealth generated by these industries.

Maidstone – Paddock Wood

Leaving Maidstone West, the train rejoins the river with a view across to Tovil Church, and then the line runs along beside the water to **East Farleigh**, attractively set against a background of orchards. Orchards also surround Barming Church, seen ahead to the north as the line follows the winding river valley closely to Wateringbury. On the way the train passes another medieval bridge, at Teston, with a lock near by, and to the north 18th-century Barham Court with its 1736 church, also with a dominant spire. **Wateringbury** station, opened in 1844, is a delightful riot of Tudor detailing in brick and stone, decorative barge-boarding and cast-iron lozenge windows. The signal box, painted in Southern Railway green and cream, adds to the quiet, old-fashioned atmosphere, and beyond is the river, with its moored boats.

The line continues by the Medway to **Yalding**, whose village is well to the east but definitely worth the walk. There are two medieval bridges, over the Medway and the Beult, a large church, and a pleasant cluster of 17th- and 18th-century houses on the curving main street. The valley opens out into a broader landscape of fruit fields and hop poles, and the train crosses the Medway. **Beltring** is an isolated station, surrounded by fruit farms. A fine group of oast houses can be seen to the west, just after the station. The train soon joins the main line and enters **Paddock Wood**, an unexciting sprawl whose origins are revealed by the huge sheds near the line, built for the storage of fruit and hops.

Old Southern Railway colours at Wateringbury

STROOD – PADDOCK WOOD

STROOD **Upnor Castle.** Built in 1559, for Elizabeth I, to protect warships moored in the Medway (open Mar–Oct).
AYLESFORD **Aylesford Priory**, The Friars. Restored Carmelite house. Fine cloisters.
MAIDSTONE WEST **Museum and Art Gallery**, Chilington Manor, St Faith's St. Elizabethan manor. Outstanding collections of art, furniture, etc. Also contains the **Museum of the Queen's Own Royal West Kent Regiment.**
Tyrwhitt Drake Museum of Carriages, The Archbishop's Stables, Mill St. Museum of horse-drawn vehicles (open Apr–Sep).
BELTRING **Whitbread Hop Farm.** Home of famous Whitbread shire horses (open Etr–Oct).

Victorian oasthouses and galleried barns at the Whitbread Hop Farm, Beltring

Tourist Information Centres
(*summer only)
SEVENOAKS Buckhurst Ln (0732) 450305
TONBRIDGE Tonbridge Castle, Castle St (0732) 770929
TUNBRIDGE WELLS Monson House, Monson Way (0892) 515675
BATTLE 88 High St (04246) 3721
HASTINGS 4 Robertson Terrace (0424) 718888 or The Fishmarket*, Old Town (0424) 722022

Walks
The London Countryway (see page 14). The path can be joined from Sevenoaks.
The North Downs Way (see page 56). The path can be joined from Sevenoaks.
The Sussex Border Path. Runs 148 miles, from Thorney Island to Rye. The path can be joined from Wadhurst station.
The Weald Way (see page 56). The path can be joined from Tonbridge.

Places to Visit
SEVENOAKS **Knole House and Garden** (NT). Home of the Sackvilles (open Apr–Oct, gardens once a month, May–Sep).
TONBRIDGE **Tonbridge Castle.** Norman, with 13th-century gatehouse.
TUNBRIDGE WELLS **Municipal Museum and Art Gallery**, The Civic Centre. Local and natural history, Tunbridge ware.
FRANT **Bayham Abbey ruins**, 2m E. Dating back to 13th century (open Mar–Oct).
STONEGATE **Bateman's House** (NT), Burwash, 3m SE. Home of Rudyard Kipling (open Apr–Oct).
ETCHINGHAM **Haremere Hall**. Early 17th-century manor house with terraced gardens (gardens open Etr–Oct, house BH weekends only).
ROBERTSBRIDGE **Bodiam Castle.** Built 1385–9.
Robertsbridge Aeronautical Museum, Bush Barn (open last Sun of month, Apr–Oct).
BATTLE **Battle Abbey ruins.** Built by William the Conqueror on the Hastings battle site.
Battle Museum, Langton House.

continued on page 63

Into the Weald

CHARING CROSS – HASTINGS *62½ miles*

The journey to the traditional seaside at Hastings through the Weald of Kent and East Sussex, an attractive landscape of wooded, rolling hills, starts from Charing Cross, one of London's less familiar termini. Built by the South Eastern Railway in 1864, Charing Cross is marked by the replica of the Eleanor Cross and a generous courtyard backed by the Renaissance façade of E M Barry's hotel, but inside is a new station. Some trains start from Cannon Street station instead of Charing Cross.

The Pantiles, Tunbridge Wells, centre of the spa town

Charing Cross – Tonbridge
The train draws out from Charing Cross directly onto Hungerford Bridge and then follows an elevated route past **Waterloo East** to **London Bridge**, with glimpses of both St Paul's and Southwark Cathedrals to the north, and then onwards through south London via New Cross and Chislehurst to **Orpington**, whose station stands on the site of a Roman villa. Soon after, suburbia gives way to fields and woodland. Ahead now are the North Downs, great chalk hills through which the line cuts in long, deep cuttings and tunnels. Soon after the long tunnel under Polhill, there are fine, sweeping views westwards towards Chevening and east into the Darent valley, which the train enters as it approaches **Sevenoaks**. The town is a handsome one, with its range of tile-hung and timber-framed buildings, its battlemented church, and its famous school, founded in 1432. Just to the south-east is the grand Tudor mansion of Knole, linked with the Sackville family since 1566.

Another long tunnel carries the train away from Sevenoaks and into the Weald of Kent. A long, elevated stretch offers fine views and then the train runs through Hildenborough before it enters **Tonbridge**, with the powerful remains of the Norman castle standing guard over the River Medway crossing. Tonbridge is still a typical Kentish town with one main street and all its interesting buildings near by. Most feature local ragstone and sandstone. Tonbridge has another famous school, founded in 1553, whose most striking building is the chapel of 1902, sadly damaged by fire in 1988.

Tonbridge – Hastings
From Tonbridge to Tunbridge Wells, the route is rather suburban but there is a fine view of Southborough's Decimus Burton church from the high viaduct. Passing **High Brooms**, the train enters the tunnel that leads to **Tunbridge Wells**. Developed first in the 17th century, Royal Tunbridge Wells really grew up in the late 18th and early 19th centuries, a time when spas were at the peak of their popularity. The heart is around the Pantiles, an early and attractive version of a pedestrian precinct. Decimus Burton was responsible for the elegant expansion of the town in the 1830s. The curving station is a fine building, sandwiched between two tunnels. The up side is Italianate, and dates from 1846, but the grander down side was planned by Sir Reginald Blomfield in 1911.

South of Tunbridge Wells, views are limited by cuttings and woods. This little-known region along the valley of the Rother is served by stations at **Frant**, **Wadhurst**, **Stonegate** and **Etchingham**. Etchingham is a typical stone-built station in the Tudor style favoured by the South Eastern Railway's architect William Tress. A more open landscape accompanies the line to **Robertsbridge**, formerly the junction with the Kent & East Sussex Railway

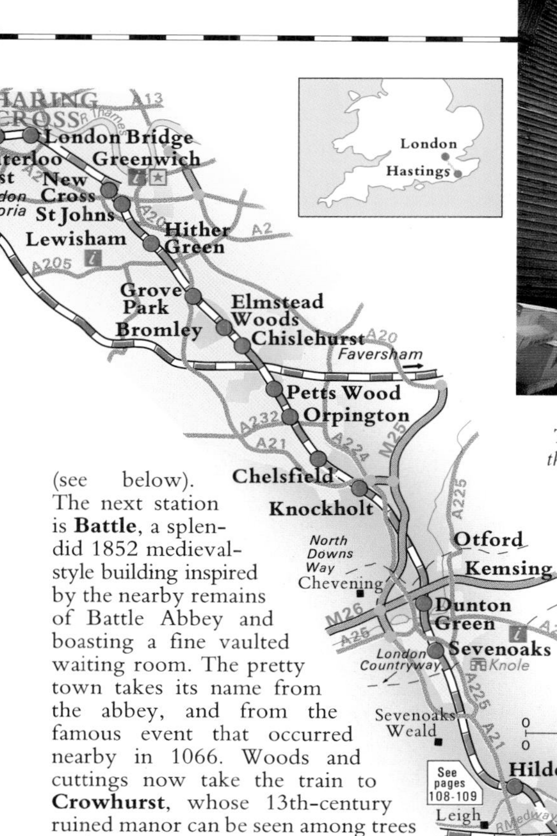

(see below). The next station is **Battle**, a splendid 1852 medieval-style building inspired by the nearby remains of Battle Abbey and boasting a fine vaulted waiting room. The pretty town takes its name from the abbey, and from the famous event that occurred nearby in 1066. Woods and cuttings now take the train to **Crowhurst**, whose 13th-century ruined manor can be seen among trees to the south.

A final series of cuttings takes the line down towards the sea. At **West St Leonards** the train joins the coastal line and then quickly reaches St Leonards main station, **Warrior Square**. Tunnels once again hide from view both the sea and the town, largely created from scratch by Decimus Burton from 1828.

Hastings
St Leonards spreads inseparably into **Hastings** and the journey ends with excellent views of Hastings' castle and old town. Not far away, on the beach, are the tall, wooden fishermen's net huts that give Hastings a quality all its own.

The three-storey wooden huts on the beach at Hastings. Known as 'deezes' and built for fishermen to dry nets and store tackle, they are unique to Hastings

Diorama of Battle of Hastings, reproduction of Bayeux Tapestry (open Etr–Oct). **Buckley's Museum of Shops and Social History**, 90 High St. HASTINGS **Fisherman's Museum**, Rock-a-Nore Rd. Former fisherman's church (open May–Sep). **Hastings Castle**, Castle Hill. Norman remains. **Hastings Embroidery**, Town Hall, Queen's Rd. Shows great events of British history. **Hastings Museum and Art Gallery**, Cambridge Rd. Local natural history, archaeology, art, craft. **Museum of Local History**, Old Town Hall, High St. Fishing, the Cinque Ports and smuggling. **St Clement's Caves**, West Hill. Used by smugglers. **Shipwreck Heritage Centre**, Rock-a-Nore Rd. Important local wrecks (open Mar–Oct).

Bodiam Castle's absolute symmetry makes it a classic toybox castle. Its round towers are at the corners of a perfect square and it stands in a perfect moat

KENT & EAST SUSSEX RAILWAY

TENTERDEN – NORTHIAM *7 miles*

One of a number of light railways built in the South East, the Kent & East Sussex ran originally from Robertsbridge to Headcorn, a typical rural line through attractive countryside, linking villages and towns relatively isolated before the coming of the motor car. After a long period of closure, the line has been progressively reopened westwards from Tenterden as a tourist steam railway. The attractive town of Tenterden is the headquarters of the railway at one end, while Northiam is the present terminus, re-opened in 1990, at the south-western end, and the line is now being extended towards Bodiam. With steam locomotives dating back to the 1870s and a large collection of vintage carriages and freight wagons, the railway recaptures the flavour of a rural line in the Edwardian era.

Services: Weekends April to October, Bank Holidays, Wednesdays and some other weekdays June to September, Sundays only in November, Christmas specials

For information: General enquiries (0580) 65155, talking timetable (0580) 62943

Access: Nearest British Rail stations Ashford or Robertsbridge. Bus connection from Ashford

Surrey and Sussex Landscapes

VICTORIA – EAST GRINSTEAD and UCKFIELD

The journeys to East Grinstead and across the Sussex Weald to Uckfield are all that remain of what was once an extensive network of country railways that crossed West Kent and East Sussex on their way to the south coast. The two journeys, one a main line and the other a long branch, both busy peak-time commuter routes, are pleasant ways to explore the varied landscape of Surrey and Sussex.

There are regular direct services from Victoria and London Bridge to East Grinstead. Direct services from London to Uckfield are limited, and so passengers will find it easier to change at Oxted and take the regular branch line shuttle.

VICTORIA – EAST GRINSTEAD
30¼ miles

Trains for East Grinstead follow the Brighton route from Victoria to **East Croydon**. South of the station the track branches southwards, to run parallel to the Brighton line through suburban surroundings to **Sanderstead**. With Purley Downs to the east, the train passes **Riddlesdown**, a station set in a wooded cutting, and then a tunnel takes it through the chalk Downs and into a wooded valley scattered with well-established suburban houses. High on the valley side, with old quarries to the east, the line continues to **Upper Warlingham**. By the station is a big 1950s brick church, with a distinctive pierced spire. South of Warlingham, London suburbia gives way to a landscape of wooded fields, with views to the east towards the Garden Village that precedes **Woldingham** station. Beyond the station, the train enters a long tunnel before passing under the M25 and reaching **Oxted**. The church, with its squat, 12th-century tower, stands to the west. Oxted has a new station, with an underpass tiled with a colourful mosaic completed in 1985. On either side of the station is new Oxted, a series of shopping arcades, while to the south is the old town.

Change at Oxted for Uckfield.

A metal viaduct carries the line high above the A25 and then the next station is **Hurst Green**. South of the station is the junction, and the East Grinstead line branches south-west, to run through a more open landscape with the spire of Crowhurst Church on the skyline to the west. After the rather unexpected sight of the brickworks by the line, the train comes to **Lingfield**. The town is at its best near the church, famous for its collection of carved misericords. South of the station is the racecourse, by the line to the west, and then the next station is **Dormans**, serving the Victorian estates of Dormansland and Dormans Park, mostly hidden from view by wooded cuttings. The train then suddenly emerges from the woods high on a viaduct above a lake.

East Grinstead

After this brief excitement, cuttings take the line into **East Grinstead**, spanned by high brick bridges. The station gives no sense of the town, but is quite well placed, for close at hand are the 18th-century church and the High Street, with its fine range of typical Sussex timber-framed buildings, dating from the 15th century onwards. Also striking is the 1619 Sackville College. To the south of the town is Standen, Philip Webb's finest house. Dating from the early 1890s, and full of William Morris wallpapers

Sackville College, East Grinstead, was founded as a home for twenty old people

Tourist Information Centres

As there are no TICs at the towns on this line, the nearest are listed

LEWES 32 High St (0273) 471600 or 483448 (accommodation)
TUNBRIDGE WELLS Monson House, Monson Way (0892) 515675

Walks

The Forest Way. Runs 9½ miles along a disused railway, from East Grinstead to Groombridge, 2½m NE of Eridge station.
The Worth Way. Runs 6 miles along the disused railway line from East Grinstead to Three Bridges (a station on the Victoria–Brighton route, pages 66–9).
The Greensand Way. Runs 55 miles, along the greensand escarpment of the Surrey Hills, from Haslemere to Limpsfield. The path can be joined at Oxted.
The London Countryway (see page 14). The path can be joined from Oxted.
The North Downs Way (see page 56). The path can be joined from Woldingham.
The Sussex Border Path (see page 16). The path can be joined at East Grinstead.
The Weald Way (see page 56). The path can be joined from Uckfield.

Places to Visit

VICTORIA – EAST GRINSTEAD
OXTED **De Tillens House,** Limpsfield, 1m E. 15th-century Weald house (open May–Sep).
LINGFIELD **Greathed Manor**, 2m SE. Victorian manor house (open May–Sep). **Lingfield Racecourse** (contact TIC). **Haxted Watermill Museum**, Working waterwheels, picture gallery (open Apr–Sep).
EAST GRINSTEAD **East Grinstead Town Museum.** Part of East Court Mansion (1769). **Sackville College**, High St. Jacobean almshouses (open May–Sep). **Standen House and Gardens**, (NT) 2m S. Built 1894 by Philip Webb, with William Morris wallpapers and textiles (open Apr–Oct).

continued on page 65

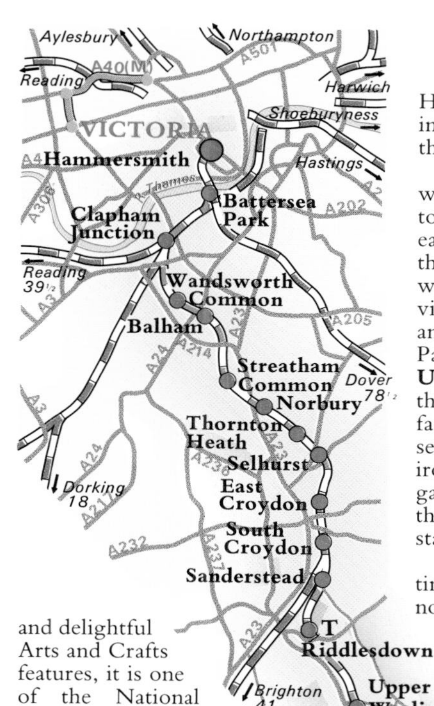

and delightful Arts and Crafts features, it is one of the National Trust's most important Victorian houses.

Formerly a busy railway junction with lines converging from four directions, East Grinstead is now the end of the line. To the south is the Bluebell Railway (see page 66). To west and to east the old lines are now official footpaths, the Worth Way to Three Bridges and the Forest Way to Groombridge.

OXTED – UCKFIELD *26 miles*

At Hurst Green junction, trains for Uckfield swing away to the south-east, with long views away to the Downs to the east, and across the Sussex Weald to the west. A short tunnel carves under the Reading–Tonbridge line and then the train curves round on an embankment to **Edenbridge Town**, with views to the south across the wide Eden valley. The station, its three colours of brickwork typical of the line, is well placed for the town, all of whose best features are ranged along the main street. Leaving the station, the line crosses the Eden, whose winding course is still guarded by World War II pillboxes, to cross a typical Wealden landscape dotted with tile-hung farms to **Hever**. The village, and the castle formerly owned by the family of Anne Boleyn, are well to the north-east. From here there are good views towards the Downs to the north and then woods, cuttings and tunnels take the line to **Cowden**, also a long way from its village. Crossing a rolling landscape, the train comes to **Ashurst**, and then it follows the headwaters of the Medway along a narrow, wooded valley. To the east, on the hillside, is Burrswood, a big Tudor-style Victorian house, and then the line winds past the dramatic outcrop of Harrison's Rocks to **Eridge**, a surprisingly large and decorative station in the middle of nowhere.

The line now criss-crosses a small, winding river along a wooded valley to **Crowborough** station, well to the east of the town. A short tunnel takes the train into a long, wooded valley, with good views from two high viaducts. The next station is **Buxted**, and then the line curves round Buxted Park to make an elevated approach to **Uckfield**. Crossing the River Uck, the line comes to its end at the old-fashioned station, with its signal box, semaphore signal perched on the cast-iron footbridge, and wooden crossing gates. The town spreads up the hill to the north, easily accessible from the station.

The track of the former line continues to the south. A section running north for 1½ miles from Isfield station has been reopened as a tourist steam railway. Known as the Lavender Line, this has services on Sundays from March to October.

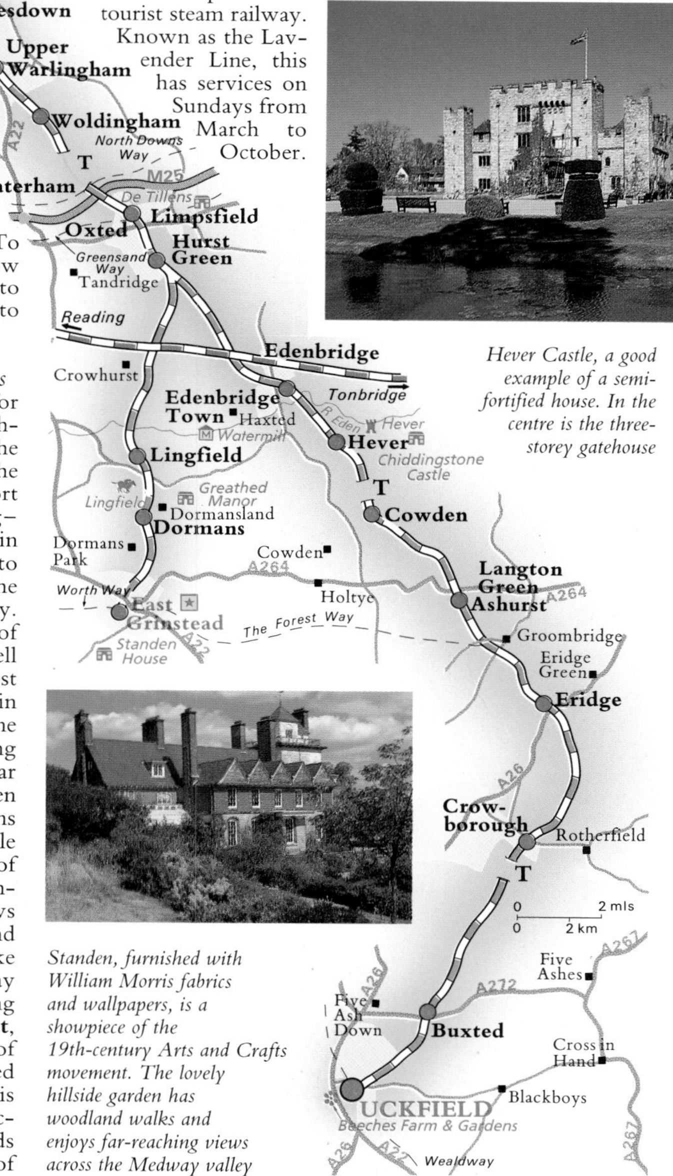

Hever Castle, a good example of a semi-fortified house. In the centre is the three-storey gatehouse

Standen, furnished with William Morris fabrics and wallpapers, is a showpiece of the 19th-century Arts and Crafts movement. The lovely hillside garden has woodland walks and enjoys far-reaching views across the Medway valley

London
East Grinstead
Uckfield

OXTED – UCKFIELD

HEVER **Hever Castle and Gardens**, 1½m NE. 13th-century double-moated castle. Italian gardens, lake, fine topiary and maze (open Mar–Nov). **Chiddingstone Castle**, 2½m E. 17th-century house with Royal Stewart and Jacobite paintings and relics (open Mar–Oct).

UCKFIELD **Beeches Farm and Gardens**, 2m W. Sunken garden, borders and yew trees (gardens open all year, house by appointment only).

The Sussex Coast

VICTORIA – BRIGHTON *and* VICTORIA – NEWHAVEN and SEAFORD

One of Britain's most famous train journeys is the Brighton line, and its history is an entertaining blend of fact, fiction, myth and tradition. Built by the London & Brighton Railway and their great engineer J U Rastrick, the line was opened in 1841 and from the outset was known for fast running. The Victoria–Newhaven line, a legacy of the days when the Newhaven–Dieppe ferry was the premier cross-Channel route between London and Paris, was established and run during its heyday from the 1890s to the early 1920s by the London, Brighton & South Coast Railway, with both trains and ships also being known for their speed.

VICTORIA – BRIGHTON
51 miles

The starting point for this railway classic is the 'Brighton side' of Victoria station, whose elaborate Edwardian baroque façade in brick and stone, topped by a grand clock, was completed in 1908 by the London, Brighton & South Coast Railway.

Victoria – Haywards Heath
Leaving Victoria, the train curves round to cross the Thames on the Grosvenor Bridge and then runs quickly to **Clapham Junction**. It cuts through Wandsworth Common and then takes an elevated route to Balham. Tooting Bec Common and Streatham Park flank the line and then the Crystal Palace television masts come into view on the skyline to the east. Through Norbury and Thornton Heath the surroundings are more suburban and then at Selhurst the train passes the huge BR depot, with the floodlights of Crystal Palace football ground in the distance. Tower blocks flank **East Croydon** and then suburbia accompanies the line to South Croydon, gradually yielding to gardens, parks and allotments. Raised high on its embankment, with good views of the Downs to east and west, the train passes **Purley**. The short Caterham branch, built by the independent Caterham Railway in 1856, swings away to the east, while to the west another branch leads to Tattenham Corner, opened in time for the Derby in 1901. As the train approaches **Coulsdon South**, the surroundings get greener and then, as it enters a long, steep-sided cutting, the line is duplicated for some miles, to allow expresses to bypass Merstham and Redhill.

BLUEBELL RAILWAY

SHEFFIELD PARK – HORSTED KEYNES *5 miles*

Originally part of the 1870s line from East Grinstead to Lewes, the Bluebell Railway was opened as a tourist steam line in 1960, the first standard gauge passenger route to be taken over by enthusiasts. It takes its name from the bluebell woods that flank the line. At present the restored line is being gradually extended northwards, the eventual aim being to run trains to East Grinstead. The Bluebell has a strong atmosphere of the railways of the Victorian era, with a fine collection of steam locomotives built between 1872 and 1959, many of which can be seen in the museum and depot at Sheffield Park. Near by are the 18th-century house and gardens (NT).

Services: Weekends March to November, Bank Holidays, Wednesdays and other occasional weekdays from May to October, Sundays only December to February, Christmas specials

For information: General enquiries (0825) 722370, talking timetable (0825) 723777

Access: Nearest British Rail station Haywards Heath, with bus connection

A Bluebell Railway signalman at work in Sheffield Park signal box

J U Rastrick's Balcombe Viaduct, railway architecture at its most powerful

After a long tunnel, trains on the slower line pass **Merstham**, an unexpectedly attractive town famous for its stone quarries since the Middle Ages. A railway, horse-drawn, was built in 1805 to carry stone and fuller's earth from here to Croydon. To the east is the vast multi-storey intersection that links the M25 with the M23, while to the west there are glimpses of Gatton Park, a mansion rebuilt in 1936 in a classical style. The next station is **Redhill**, serving Reigate's easterly extension. South of Redhill is **Earlswood**, with a big 1853 hospital by the line to the east, and beyond it views to Redhill airfield, famous for its 1930s Tiger Moths, and the backdrop of the Downs. The line now runs fast and straight to **Salfords** and **Horley**, with all the best views to the east. With a steady stream of planes low overhead, the train quickly reaches **Gatwick Airport**.

Lineside development spreads southwards from here to **Three Bridges**, where the line to Horsham, Arundel and Chichester swings away to the west. South of the station the houses are quickly left behind as the line runs through thick woodland, with Tilgate Forest to the west and Pottage Worth Forest to the east. A short tunnel is followed by cuttings that take the line to **Balcombe**. Further cuttings limit views south of the station, and so J U Rastrick's great viaduct over the Ouse valley is an unexpected excitement, railway theatre at its best. Completed in 1841, with 37 massive, brick arches and a splendid classical balustrade, the 1,475ft viaduct strides over the landscape. There are excellent views along the Ouse valley to east and to west, but they are hard to appreciate fully from the flying train. With the former Horsted Keynes line to the east, the line makes its way into **Haywards Heath**. Little of the town, which grew rapidly in the 19th century after the arrival of the railway, can be seen and a tunnel carries the line under the centre.

This is the station to change for the line to Lewes and Eastbourne.

Haywards Heath – Brighton

Cuttings take the line away from Haywards Heath and then the next station is **Wivelsfield**, with its original wooden buildings. Little of the village remains, buried in the sea of 19th-century and later housing that has spread northwards from **Burgess Hill**, typical railway-inspired development. To the south, an embanked section of the line allows brief views of the Downs ahead, towering above **Hassocks**, another indeterminate railway town. At both Burgess Hill and Hassocks parts of the original 1841 classical-style stations survive. It is a fine sight, with Wolstonbury hillfort to the west, Ditchling Beacon to the east and in the centre the Clayton windmills.

Another cutting now paves the way for the famous Clayton tunnel of 1841, with a cottage perched in the centre of the castellated north portal. Just above the tunnel mouth is Clayton Church, with its unique

Tourist Information Centres

BRIGHTON Marlborough House, 54 Old Steine (0273) 23755 or 27560 (accommodation)

LEWES 32 High St (0273) 471600 or 483448 (accommodation)

SEAFORD Station Approach (0323) 897426

Walks

The London Countryway (see page 14). The path can be joined from Merstham.

The North Downs Way (see page 56). The path can be joined from Merstham.

The South Downs Way. Runs 80 miles, along the South Downs, from Eastbourne to the Sussex/Hampshire border near Petersfield. The path can be joined from Southease.

The Sussex Border Path (see page 62). The path can be joined from Gatwick or Three Bridges stations.

The Worth Way (see page 64). The disused railway footpath starts at Three Bridges.

Places to Visit

VICTORIA – BRIGHTON

REDHILL **Royal Earlswood Hospital Museum.** Covering early history, finance, medicine/nursing, education and training.

BALCOMBE **Wakehurst Place**, ½m E. Woodland and lakes. Run by the Royal Botanic Gardens at Kew. **Nymans** (NT), Handcross, 3m W. Flowering shrubs and roses, sunken garden (open Apr–Oct).

SALFORDS **Outwood Old Mill.** Oldest working mill in England. Small museum with collection of old coaches (open Etr–Oct).

HAYWARDS HEATH **Borde Hill Garden**, 1½m N. Large garden with woods and parkland, rare trees and shrubs (open Mar–Oct).

continued on page 68

Outwood Old Mill, dating from 1665

Heaselands, 1½m SW. Over 30 acres of gardens, aviary and waterfowl (gardens only open, May–Jul).
HASSOCKS **Danny**, 1½m SE. E-shaped house, dating from 1593 (open May–Sep).
PRESTON PARK **Preston Manor.** Georgian house with Edwardian additions. Notable collection of fine furniture, silver, porcelain and pictures.
BRIGHTON **Aquarium and Dolphinarium,** Marine Pde and Madeira Dr. Britain's largest aquarium, with marine, tropical and freshwater fish. Underground galleries house seals, sealions and shark tanks. Dolphin show.
Booth Museum of Natural History, 194 Dyke Rd. Exhibits British birds mounted in natural settings. Also butterfly gallery, displays of vertebrate evolution and 'unnatural history'.
Museum and Art Gallery, Church St. Old Master paintings, watercolours, 20th-century art, musical instruments, archaeology and local history.
The Royal Pavilion, Old Steine. Marine palace of Prince Regent (George IV). Henry Hollands' neoclassical villa (1787) transformed by John Nash into Oriental style. Splendidly furnished.

continued on page 69

Clayton Tunnel: the cottage built in the centre of the north portal may have been for the person in charge of the gas used to light the tunnel

series of 12th-century wall paintings. The tunnel is followed by another deep cutting, carved through the chalk of the Downs and then a short tunnel beneath Patcham concludes the line's passage through the Downs. The dramatic quality of the engineering shows how Rastrick strove to create a fast, level route through undulating country for this early inter-city line.

Brighton

Leaving the Downs behind, the train reaches Brighton's outskirts and **Preston Park**. This was the depot where many famous Pullman carriages were built and maintained. The line is now elevated high above north Brighton. The viaduct carrying the Lewes line curves away to the east and then the journey comes to an end beneath the great iron and glass roof of **Brighton**'s 1883 trainshed. The station's classical façade of 1841 provides a suitably grand introduction to the town.

The best way to enter Brighton is by train, for the station is set high, and from it the visitor is drawn naturally downwards towards the Royal Pavilion, the Regency terraces, the sea front and the piers, the enticing pubs and antique shops. Brighton is England's most fashionable resort, and has been since 1783 when the Prince of Wales first came here to sample the beneficial effects of sea air and salt-water bathing. Brighton's royal associations continued through the Regency period, and resulted in the Royal Pavilion, Britain's most eccentric royal palace. Since then, the resort has maintained its particular appeal to all kinds of visitors, from politicians to playboys, and the town's slightly raffish air has always added to its attraction.

VICTORIA – NEWHAVEN and SEAFORD *59¼ miles*

The only services that run direct to Newhaven from Victoria are the few boat trains for the Dieppe ferry, so passengers should take an Eastbourne or Hastings train from Victoria, and change at Lewes for the connecting service to Newhaven and Seaford.

From Victoria, the train follows the Brighton line to **Wivelsfield**, and then at Keymer Junction the Eastbourne line swings away to the south-east. An embankment leads to **Plumpton**, with its delightfully decorative wooden station of 1863. To the north is the little church and to the south the racecourse, right by the track. It is a pretty setting, against the steep flanks

The Brighton Line

In 1991 the Brighton line, one of Britain's best-loved and most familiar routes, celebrated its 150th anniversary. Planned by the Northumberland engineer, John Urpeth Rastrick and constructed by the London & Brighton Railway Company, the line was splendidly engineered for fast running, with tunnels, cuttings, embankments and the magnificent Ouse viaduct at Balcombe creating a remarkably level route through the difficult terrain of the North and South Downs. Brighton's elegant classical station, designed by David Mocatta and completed in 1840, was a suitably grand terminus for the line, while at the London end, the London, Brighton & South Coast Railway, who had taken over the original company, constructed at Victoria an equally ambitious terminus.

Commuter services between London and Brighton were running as early as the mid 1840s, while, at the same time, the line was able to establish a reputation for style and elegance, helped by William Stroudley's handsome yellow engines and by the fast boat trains to the company's steamers on the Newhaven – Dieppe service. However, best known of all were the named trains, the first being the *Southern Belle*, introduced in 1908 and renamed the *Brighton Belle* in 1934, an all-electric, all-Pullman train that continued to run until its final demise in 1972. Equally famous at the time was the commuters' special, the *City Limited*, whose successors, now in Network SouthEast livery, maintain the fast and regular service that has been a feature of this line since its opening in 1841.

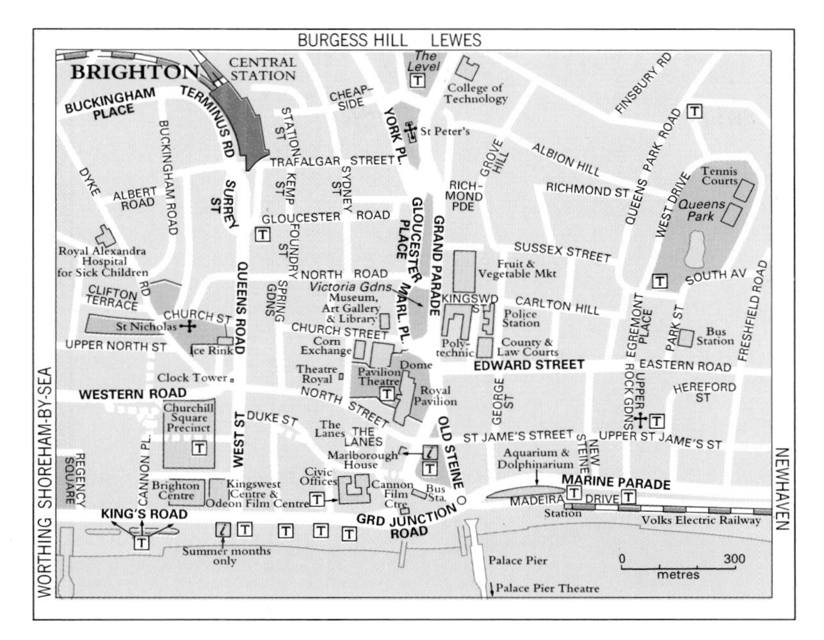

of the Downs in the far distance. The line now curves round towards the gap carved through the Downs by the Ouse, passing **Cooksbridge**, and makes its elevated way along the Ouse valley, with the river close by to the north. There are splendid views northwards along the Ouse watermeadows, with the isolated churches at Hamsey and South Malling in the foreground. To the east is steep Malling Hill, with its group of Neolithic barrows.

Ahead is **Lewes**, the county town, and a remarkably attractive and unspoilt one, with the river running through it, and its buildings clustered on the steep hillsides below the castle. The station, a grand and elegant affair of 1889 in decorative brick, reveals its former importance as the meeting point for six lines. The train continues southwards, with fine views back towards Lewes. It is a lovely journey along the broad flood plain of the river, with distant views of flint churches at Iford, Rodmell and Southease to the west against the backdrop of the Downs. **Southease** has a tiny station. With Tarring Neville and old chalk quarries to the east, and the round Norman tower of Piddinghoe's church to the west, the valley narrows as the train enters Newhaven.

Newhaven and Seaford

Newhaven Town is the first station, followed shortly by **Newhaven Harbour**, with the docks and ferry terminal close at hand. The line now swings east, to run along the shore to **Bishopstone**, which has an Art Deco station, to its terminus at **Seaford**. Once a Cinque port, Seaford is now a rather quiet resort known for its medieval church, its many schools and its Martello tower at the end of a rather tame esplanade.

WIVELSFIELD – SEAFORD

PLUMPTON **Racecourse** (contact TIC).

LEWES **Castle and Barbican House Museum of Sussex Archaeology**, High St. Norman castle with shell keep and 14th-century barbican. Prehistoric, Roman, Saxon and medieval antiquities (open Apr–Oct).

Museum of Local History, Anne of Cleves' House, Southover High St. 16th-century timber-framed building. Domestic equipment, Sussex ironwork and history gallery (open Feb–Nov).

Lewes History Centre, Barbican House, High St. Large scale model of historic Lewes with A/V programme (open Mar–Oct).

SOUTHEASE **Monk's House** (NT), Rodmell, 1¼m W. Home of Virginia and Leonard Woolf (open Apr–Oct).

SEAFORD **Seaford Museum of Local History**, Tower 74, Esplanade. Martello tower containing period shops, domestic appliances, photographs.

The Living World, Exceat, 2½m E. Exhibition of small creatures and marine life.

Brighton Pavilion, an architectural extravaganza for the Prince Regent

Tourist Information Centres
(*summer only)
ARUNDEL 61 High St (0903) 882268
HORSHAM The Museum, The Causeway (0403) 211661
BOGNOR REGIS Belmont St (0243) 823140 or 820435 (accommodation)
LITTLEHAMPTON* Windmill Complex, Coastguard Rd (0903) 713480

Walks
The South Downs Way (see page 67). The path can be joined from Amberley.

The Long Gallery, Parham House, near Amberley

The Wey South Path. Runs 35 miles, from Guildford to Amberley, connecting the North and South Downs Ways. Follows the Wey and Arun Canal for two-thirds of the distance. The path can be joined from Amberley, Billingshurst, or Pulborough stations.

Places to Visit
HORSHAM **Horsham Museum**, 9 The Causeway. 16th-century house with walled garden. Costumes and accessories, toys, early cycles, rural crafts and local history.
AMBERLEY **Amberley Chalk Pits Museum.** Situated in 36-acre former chalk quarry and limeworks. Working blacksmith, potter and printer. Narrow gauge railway (open Apr–Oct).
Parham House and Gardens. Grey-stone Elizabethan house with gardens and deer park (open Etr–Oct.)
continued on page 71

The Arun Valley

VICTORIA – BOGNOR REGIS and LITTLEHAMPTON

The journey to Bognor Regis links rural Surrey, the Sussex Weald and the Arun valley with the seaside, through a changing landscape that shows southern England at its most varied. Direct services to Bognor run from Victoria via Three Bridges, Horsham and Arundel. Passengers for Littlehampton change at Barnham or Ford or alternatively, there is a direct service from Victoria via Hove and Worthing.

VICTORIA – BOGNOR REGIS
63 miles

Trains from Victoria to Bognor follow the Brighton line to **Three Bridges** (see pages 66–7). Leaving Three Bridges, the train branches west and runs through a suburban landscape to **Crawley**, and then on to **Ifield** before finally escaping from domestic sprawl. The boundary is marked by the crossing of the Mole, with its related ponds, and then the line runs along a valley between gentle, wooded hills to **Faygate**, a station serving a region rather than a village. With St Leonard's Forest to the south, the train curves round Roffey, passing **Littlehaven**, to join the line from Dorking just north of **Horsham** station. Well placed for the town centre, the station offers few views of Horsham. This traditional market town is rather dominated by traffic and has never really come to terms with its potential. The most bizarre building is the Town Hall, and behind it is Horsham's best street, the Causeway, lined with timber-framed cottages and later brick terraces, with the atmosphere of a Wealden village hidden in the heart of the town. The earliest building now houses the museum. As the train approaches **Christ's Hospital**, the Edwardian buildings of the famous Blue Coat School can be seen to the east. Founded in 1553, the school moved here from the City of London late in the 19th century. At one time Christ's Hospital was a busy junction, with lines running south to Shoreham and north-west to Guildford, but little trace remains today, although parts of both routes are now official walkways.

From Christ's Hospital, the line runs through a pleasant, domestic landscape to **Billingshurst**. The town, set to the north, is rather hidden from the station, but the powerful church tower is a useful landmark. Built along one main street, Billingshurst has preserved the atmosphere of an old coaching town. Curving southwards, the train enters the more open landscape of the Arun valley. Beside the line is Roman Stane Street, now the A29. On a wooded hilltop to the east are the battlemented towers of Victorian Beedings House. The next station is **Pulborough**, serving a town that grew up around its transport links. River, railway and road are all close together, but it was the Arun that was the key to its development. Pulborough was once a busy port, where boats that had sailed up the Arun from its mouth at Littlehampton transferred their cargoes to the barges of the Wey and Arun Canal, a long-lost link between London and the south coast well worth exploring on foot. The best parts of the town are still by the river.

Amberley

There are excellent views southwards as the train follows the meandering

Arundel's fairytale castle looks down from its hilltop on to the River Arun

river with the valley narrowing steadily ahead as it approaches **Amberley** and the dramatic gap through the chalk hills of the Downs. Amberley Castle comes into view, a magnificent sight that dominates the Arun valley from its eastern flank. Hidden behind its wall is the pretty village it protects. This is one of the most dramatic views in southern England, seen at its best from the train, and the panorama continues as the train and the river wind closely together through the gap in the towering white cliffs. Amberley is the stop for the Chalk Pits Museum with its displays of the working life of the past, and for walking the South Downs Way.

Leaving Amberley, the line criss-crosses the Arun, with South Stoke to the west and, to the east, the hilltop village of Burpham.

Arundel

Arundel now comes into sight to the west, and its romantic skyline of towers and pinnacles dominates the valley from here southwards to Ford. Set in the watermeadows below the town is the Wildfowl and Wetlands Centre. Arundel station, set half a mile away from the town, is a simple classical building with delicate iron-work, and it forms an ideal introduction to a hilltop town whose dramatic qualities are unexpected in southern England. The castle has been the seat of the Dukes of Norfolk and their ancestors for over 700 years. Close by are the picturesque streets of the town, all dependent upon the castle, and a short walk away is the 14th-century church with its Norfolk monuments.

Arundel – Bognor Regis

With this spectacular backdrop to the west, the line continues along the Arun valley, now a wide, open landscape, passing isolated Lyminster

Climping sand dunes at Littlehampton are easily accessible from the station

Church to the east. With the sea ahead and the river a wide tidal waterway, the train now joins the Portsmouth–Brighton line, crosses the Arun for the last time and reaches **Ford**. Near by is the pretty church with its bellcote, one of the best in Sussex.

Change at Ford or Barnham for Littlehampton.

The next station is **Barnham**, and then the train branches southwards for the short journey to **Bognor Regis**. With its pier, its beach and its 19th-century terraces, Bognor has plenty of traditional seaside atmosphere. Early in its history it was a very select resort, probably the model for Jane Austen's Sanditon, but popular holiday-making later took over. The 'Regis' dates from 1929, following a period of convalescence spent here by George V.

FORD–LITTLEHAMPTON

4¾ miles

The short line to **Littlehampton** runs beside the Arun to its estuary. The station is well placed for the port, the old heart of the town and its *raison d'être* before it was developed as a resort early in the 19th century. Since then, Littlehampton has spread into Rustington and Angmering, villages now absorbed into the general seaside growth.

A different way to see the Arun valley is by boat, and from Easter to October the River Arun Trust runs daily river trips between Littlehampton, Arundel and Amberley in traditional wooden launches.

ARUNDEL **Arundel Castle**, Mill Rd. Norman stronghold restored in 18th and 19th centuries. Fine portraits by Van Dyck, Gainsborough and Reynolds, and furniture from 16th century (open Apr–Oct).
Arundel Toy and Military Museum, 23 High St. Private collection of old toys, games and militaria from around the world.
Museum and Heritage Centre, 61 High St. Old Arundel on view (open Etr–Oct).
Wildfowl and Wetlands Trust, Mill Rd. 55 acres with ducks, geese and swans from all over the world.

LITTLEHAMPTON
Littlehampton Museum. Sea captain's house, containing maritime paintings, local archaeology and history.

1 A sunset silhouette of Salisbury Cathedral's spire, the tallest in England

2 A train from Exeter passes through the Wiltshire countryside west of Tisbury

3 The River Thames at Hampton Court, where rowing boats may be hired

4 The Houses of Parliament, Westminster, forming a backdrop to the railway line

5 The clock on the Victory Arch which forms the main entrance to Waterloo station

6 Admiral Lord Nelson at Portsmouth, a naval base since the days of Henry VIII

7 The line near Brockenhurst, as it passes through the heart of the New Forest

1

2

ROUTES FROM

WATERLOO

Waterloo, London's grandest station and an important monument to Edwardian elegance, was built by the London & South Western Railway, the Great Western's main rival for West Country passenger and freight traffic. In its heyday, Waterloo was the starting point for main line journeys to Hampshire, Wiltshire, Somerset, Dorset, Devon and Cornwall, as well as a host of Home Counties commuter services.

Today, Waterloo trains serve a smaller region, from Surrey and West Sussex to Hampshire, Wiltshire, Dorset and Devon, but a legacy of the station's important place in railway history is the two longest Network SouthEast journeys, to Exeter and Weymouth. With routes to the south coast ports and the resorts of the South West, as well as its future role as the International terminus for the Channel Tunnel trains, Waterloo probably offers a greater variety of destinations and landscape to the Network SouthEast traveller than any other London station.

3

4

5

6

7

RAILWAY ART

FROM THEIR EARLY DAYS, RAILways have attracted artists. The creation of many main lines and their major engineering features were recorded by J C Bourne and other engravers, while major painters such as J M W Turner and the watercolourist David Cox were quick to depict the impact of the new railways on Britain's landscape. In the Victorian era train travel was a constant source of interest and social comment, and many of the narrative painters of the day such as Augustus Egg, George Earl and John O'Connor illustrated railway life. The best-known example of this genre is probably W P Frith's great painting of Paddington station. Later in the 19th century French Impressionists working in Britain were drawn to railway subjects. Camille Pissarro painted Penge East station in a series of subjects around Crystal Palace, where he was staying in the 1870s, and later Hungerford Bridge featured among Monet's Thames views. Early in this century, English artists of the Camden Town school, such as S F Gore, sometimes used the theme of trains and railway architecture in both rural and urban settings.

Another popular area of railway art is the poster. The first pictorial railway posters appeared in the 1890s, and from then on designers and illustrators had a field-day producing striking and decorative images to promote the idea of travel by train. The 1920s and the 1930s were probably the heyday of the colourful poster, as rival companies battled to gain their share of the growing holiday traffic. Particularly notable were those published to promote the many cross-Channel services, for this was the era of high-speed ferries and competing ports, as well as the famous, named trains such as the *Golden Arrow*, running between London and Paris.

Letchworth Garden City, in the heart of Hertfordshire's countryside, was built from 1903. The first simple timber station, built by the Great Northern Railway for the new commuters, is shown in this colourful view painted in 1912 by the Camden Town artist, Spencer Frederick Gore. The present brick station was built a year later

The pleasures, and the pitfalls, of railway travel in the Victorian age are well depicted by several leading 19th-century artists, notably William Powell Frith and Augustus Egg, painters who specialised in narrative themes. Their love of detail, combined with a lively eye for social comment, gives their pictures great interest and appeal today, for interwoven on to the surface of the canvas is a remarkable panorama of Victorian life.

A marvellous but little-known example of this genre, rediscovered in 1990 after decades of oblivion, is George Earl's Going North: Kings Cross Station, *painted in 1893. This shows a Great Northern Railway express being prepared for departure to Scotland, and on the platform are gathered all the passengers who are travelling north for the start of the shooting season on August 12th. Few paintings are so revealing about railway travel in general, or give so fascinating an insight into the social strata and mores of late Victorian Britain. Every inch is filled with intriguing detail, from the piles of luggage and shooting equipment to the dogs, the children with their nannies, the parting lovers, the boy selling paperback books and all the railway staff, including the man busy placing lamps into the carriage roof*

J M W Turner's famous 1844 painting, Rain, Steam and Speed, *shows a Great Western broad-gauge express thundering across Brunel's Maidenhead Bridge. Apparently the artist leaned far out of the carriage window into the wind and rain to experience fully the excitement and atmosphere of this new form of travel*

Eric Ravilious's watercolour is a delightful evocation of rural railway travel in southern England in the 1930s

This modernist poster was designed by Edmund Vaughan in the 1930s for the Southern Railway to promote out of season travel to the West Country

The Fringes of Surrey

WATERLOO – SURBITON and DORKING

with The Chessington and Hampton Court Branches

Waterloo is the gateway to an extensive network of suburban services to south-west London and the Home Counties, some of which reflect old route rivalries between formerly independent companies. Most of these services branch off the broad, high-speed main line and are served by stopping trains.

Tudor gardens at Hampton Court Palace. Elizabeth I added plants from the New World

Chessington World of Adventures – fun for all the family

The Chessington Branch

RAYNES PARK – CHESSINGTON *5¼ miles*

Passengers from Waterloo can take either a direct train or a stopping service and change at **Raynes Park** or **Motspur Park**. The short journey through suburbia is a curiosity, a complete 1930s railway with only the modern trains to give the game away. All the stations, **Malden Manor, Tolworth, Chessington North** and **Chessington South**, have dramatic cast-concrete Art Deco canopies and other period details, along with block-like modernist buildings. All the bridges are also cast concrete and in the same style, and there are even the original gradient posts. Trains terminate at Chessington South – a long walk, or a short taxi ride, to Chessington World of Adventures.

Tourist Information Centres

As there are no TICs at the towns on this line, the nearest are listed

GUILDFORD Guildford House Gallery, 155 High St (0483) 444007

WALTON-ON-THAMES Town Hall, New Zealand Ave (0932) 228844

Walks

Epsom Downs. The Downs, and Epsom Racecourse, lie 2 miles south of Epsom station.

The North Downs Way (see page 56). The path can be joined from Boxhill & Westhumble or Dorking. See also Walk 5 on page 97.

The London Countryway (see page 14). The path can be joined from Dorking station at Box Hill, 1 mile north-east.

Places to Visit

HAMPTON COURT

Hampton Court Palace. Begun in 1514 by Cardinal Wolsey. Henry enlarged the palace by adding the great hall and kitchens, William and Mary rebuilt the eastern portion to the design of Sir Christopher Wren. (State apartments and gardens open all year. Great kitchens and Tudor tennis courts open Apr–Sep; Maze open Mar–Oct).

EPSOM **Epsom Racecourse.** Contact Walton-on-Thames TIC.

BOXHILL & WESTHUMBLE

Box Hill Country Park, 1m E.

Polesden Lacey (NT), Great Bookham, 2¼m W. Regency villa housing Greville collection. 18th-century gardens (house

continued on page 77

The view westwards near Mickleham, across Norbury Park

WATERLOO – SURBITON
12 miles
The train leaves Waterloo's curving platforms, then runs parallel to the Thames to Clapham Junction. From the elevated route there are glimpses of the Houses of Parliament, Lambeth Palace, the Tate Gallery and the river, and the train then passes the new Covent Garden market at Nine Elms. As the train approaches Battersea, the skyline to the north is dominated by the 337ft, 1930s chimneys of Gilbert Scott's former power station, and then the train runs into **Clapham Junction**. A cutting carries the line past Wandsworth Common, and then the route is elevated once again as it crosses the River Wandle on its way to **Wimbledon**, where the station is shared with London Regional Transport's District Line. At **Raynes Park**, the Dorking line swings away to the south, while just after **New Malden** trains for Shepperton branch to the north. The train crosses the River Hogsmill and then enters the long cutting that leads to **Surbiton**. The Thames and the ferry to Hampton Court Park are only a short walk away from J R Scott's excellent 1937 station, whose Art Deco clock tower and modernist façade make it unique in Britain.

WATERLOO – DORKING
22 miles
From Waterloo, Dorking trains follow the main line west to Wimbledon and then swing south at **Raynes Park**. The route is predominantly suburban at first, with plenty of opportunity to study the architectural styles exploited by builders during the 1930s. The first stop is **Motspur Park**, the station to change at for the Chessington branch. At **Stoneleigh**, Nonsuch Park can be seen to the east, the site of Henry VIII's last great palace, and then the train comes to **Ewell West**. Ewell has managed to retain some individuality in the great suburban sprawl.

Equally independent in feeling is **Epsom**, with plenty of buildings that still reveal its development as a smart suburb in the 18th century. Epsom's popularity, and its smartness, were due to two things, Epsom Salts, and the Races. The salt well was discovered in 1618 and the Derby was first run in 1780. Epsom's wooden signal box, built on a bridge over the tracks, allowed the signalman a good view of the junction. From Epsom the route is now more rural, and a pleasant green interlude leads to **Ashtead**, and then the line swings south into the Mole valley. **Leatherhead** has another good station, French gothic this time, with plenty of decorative coloured brickwork and complete with a tower.

Crossing the Mole, the train enters the best part of the journey, a delightful run along the wooded valley, with views ahead over the rolling farmland towards the Downs. The river is never far away as the line passes Mickleham, with good views westwards towards Polesden Lacey. **Boxhill & Westhumble** station is another 1867 French gothic delight. From here it is a pleasant two-mile walk to Polesden Lacey. The steep wooded flanks of Box Hill now dominate the line to the east as it runs into **Dorking**. The station is set to the north of the town, whose best feature is its undulating main street which retains a strong country town flavour. There is also an excellent Victorian church, by Woodyer, that dominates the skyline. However, Dorking is best as a starting point for walks through the wooded hills that surround it.

The Hampton Court Branch

SURBITON – HAMPTON COURT *3 miles*

Trains for Hampton Court follow the main line west from **Surbiton** then swing over the main line to the north. The route is elevated to **Thames Ditton**, with views over suburban gardens, parks and playing fields, and then the train comes slowly into the terminus at **Hampton Court**, having crossed the River Mole on its way to join the Thames. Designed by Sir William Tite and built in 1849 in a decorative Tudor style inspired by English domestic architecture of the Renaissance, the station is an enjoyable and entirely suitable way to arrive at Hampton Court. Hampton Court Palace is just a short walk away across the Thames. Visitors wishing to return to London by a different route have a number of attractive choices: a walk through the park and a ferry across the Thames to Surbiton, a walk eastwards across the park to Hampton Wick, or northwards past the Diana Fountain to Teddington.

open Mar–Nov, gardens all year).
CHESSINGTON
Chessington World of Adventures. 65 acres. Rides for all the family. Zoological gardens (gardens open all year, park Apr–Oct only).

Polesden Lacey's glittering drawing room

SPORTING LINKS
Stations with sporting associations have long been a feature of the British railway network, and there are plenty in Network SouthEast. Trains on the Banbury line from Marylebone call at Wembley Stadium and Denham Golf Club, but more commonly it is racecourses that are directly linked to stations. The long-standing popularity of the Derby at Epsom encouraged two rival companies to open stations to serve the course. The London, Brighton & South Coast Railway got there first at Epsom Downs, but the South Eastern & Chatham followed with Tattenham Corner, opened in 1901 in time for the Derby meeting. This simple, weather-boarded building is typical of racecourse stations, and similar examples can be seen at Newbury Racecourse and at Plumpton, the latter a particularly pretty one with decorative barge-boarding, dating from 1863. There are other stations near racecourses, but not built specifically for them, even though the course is by the track, for example, Ascot, Lingfield and Esher (for Sandown Park).

Tourist Information Centres
(* summer only)
ESHER/WEYBRIDGE Contact Walton-on-Thames TIC, Town Hall, New Zealand Avenue (0932) 228844
GUILDFORD Guildford House Gallery, 155 High St (0483) 444007
PETERSFIELD County Library, 27 The Square (0730) 68829
HAVANT 1 Park Road South (0705) 480024
PORTSMOUTH Clarence Esplanade (0705) 832464 or Continental Ferryport*, Rudmore Roundabout (0705) 698111
SANDOWN The Esplanade (0983) 403886
SHANKLIN 67 High St (0983) 862942

Walks
The Greensand Way (see page 64). The path can be joined from Haslemere.
The London Countryway (see page 14). The path can be joined from

continued on page 79

South to the Solent

WATERLOO – PORTSMOUTH and THE ISLE OF WIGHT

There are two main routes from London to Portsmouth. The slower of the two starts from Victoria and then goes via Horsham and the Arun Valley line (see pages 70–1), and along the coast via Chichester. The scenic appeal of this route is considerable, particularly from Horsham southwards, but the direct route from Waterloo via Woking and Guildford is far quicker, and also attractive. For days out, this is a more practical proposition. The recently introduced alternative, via Basingstoke, Winchester and Fareham, makes possible a varied round trip.

WATERLOO – PORTSMOUTH *74½ miles*
For the route from Waterloo to Surbiton, see page 77.

Surbiton – Guildford
Leaving Surbiton, the line is elevated again, and remains so for some distance, offering good views over suburbia and, to the south, the distant line of the North Downs. **Esher** is the station for Sandown Park, with the racecourse right by the line. To the south of the town is the recently restored 18th-century garden at Claremont. The train crosses the Mole, with its reservoirs to the north, and then a long, wooded cutting takes it to **Weybridge**. After the station, there is a glimpse of the River Wey Navigation and its junction with the newly re-

Claremont Landscape Garden, near Esher, was laid out in 1720

The Isle of Wight Railway has recreated a Victorian atmosphere

ISLE OF WIGHT RAILWAY

WOOTTON – HAVEN STREET/SMALLBROOK *1½/5 mile*

From 1862 an extensive railway network was created in the Isle of Wight, whose rural charm and Victorian atmosphere survived well into the 20th century, thanks in part to the system's isolation from the mainland. With the exception of the line from Ryde to Shanklin, operated by British Rail, the network virtually vanished after the 1950s, but a short section has been reopened as a tourist steam railway. The rural line, from Haven Street north-west through woodland to Wootton, is part of the original route built to connect Newport with the Ryde–Shanklin line at Smallbrook. The line is to be extended eastwards to Smallbro in 1991. Some of the steam locomotives date from the 1870s and are typical of those used a century ago.

Services: March to October Sundays and various weekdays, Bank Holidays. Christmas speci
For information: (0983) 88220
Access: Bus services to Wootto from Ryde and Newport. Direct connection at Smallbrook with British Rail from 1991.

opened Basingstoke Canal, while to the south is the airfield built on the site of the famous Brooklands motor-racing circuit. Part of the legendary, steeply banked track can be seen from the train. The line runs now straight to **Woking**, with a glimpse of the decorative 1889 Shah Jehan mosque in woods to the south, just before the station.

Soon after leaving Woking, the train branches away to the south and enters a pleasant landscape of woods and farmland. **Worplesdon** station is a long way from its village and then the line runs straight to **Guildford**, with a good view of the cathedral and the university as it approaches the station. There is a junction here with the line from Reading to Tonbridge (see pages 108–9).

Guildford

Guildford is a fine town, and the newly rebuilt station is not far from its heart. Built over the steep sides of the Wey valley, it is a visually dramatic town, best explored on foot, and the remains of the 12th-century castle show how it grew up around the river bridge. The High Street runs steeply through the centre from the Wey, and is lined with 18th-century buildings. Particularly impressive is the earlier Guildhall, with its 1683 clock projecting out over the street. The Royal Grammar School, at the top of the High Street, was founded in 1507 and still has a library of chained books. Near by is Abbot's Hospital, of 1622. There are several interesting churches, but it is the cathedral whose presence on its high hill dominates the town. Designed by Sir Edward Maufe and built betweeen 1936 and the mid-1960s, it is one of only two Anglican cathedrals built in Britain this century. It is a powerful brick structure, in a simplified gothic style with Art Deco overtones, but the interior is much more exciting than the rather bland exterior.

Guildford – Portsmouth

On leaving Guildford station, the train enters a tunnel that hides from view the castle and the southern part of the town. The line follows the Wey to **Farncombe** and **Godalming**, but the woods limit views of the river, which then swings away to the west. Between **Milford** and **Witley**, the train passes a series of ponds and lakes. Relics of the iron industry that dominated the region until the late 17th century, these were dug to store water to power the water-wheels that drove the bellows and hammers of the forges. Witley is a particularly attractive village, with many tile-hung and half-timbered houses, typical of the area. From here the line winds its way through thickly wooded hills, with occasional views to the south and a glimpse of Grayswood Church with its wooden bell-turret. The hilly, rather romantic landscape continues to **Haslemere**, famous for the Dolmetsch music workshops. The town is folded into the surrounding hills and looks good from the train, with plenty of the handsome, late Victorian country houses that abound in this part of Surrey.

Guildford: the Guildhall clock projects over the elegant High Street

From Haslemere, the landscape opens out and then the line crosses into Hampshire shortly before **Liphook**, one of whose best features is Sir William Tite's classical station of 1859, a Palladian villa in miniature. The next station is **Liss**, serving a village divided by the railway, with a church in each half. Shortly before the station is the site of the junction with the old Longmoor Military Railway that used to serve the camps at Longmoor and Bordon before joining the Alton line near Bentley. It was also on this railway that generations of soldiers were taught to drive trains. From Liss, the line follows the River Rother to **Petersfield**, a handsome town with a fine Norman church and a main square made memorable by the lead equestrian statue of William III, made in 1757. The station is also attractive, with delicate Tudor details. Leaving Petersfield, the line swings to the south, giving good views of the great flat top of Butser Hill, to the west. The Downs now form a long

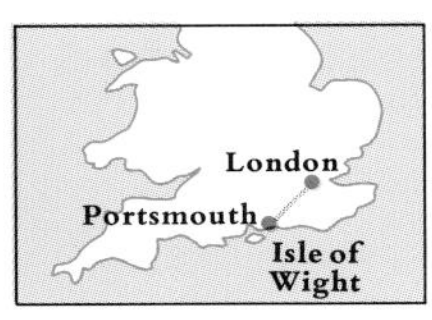

Byfleet, or Woking at Horsell.

The North Downs Way (see page 56). The path can be joined from Guildford.

The Solent Way. Runs 58 miles along Solent and Spithead coastline. Involves 4 ferry crossings. The path can be joined from Portsmouth or Rowland's Castle stations.

The South Wessex Way. 117 miles from Petersfield to Poole, linking South Downs Way to South-West Peninsula Coast Path. The path can be joined from Petersfield.

The Sussex Border Path (see page 62). The path can be joined from Liphook.

The Wayfarer's Walk. 70 miles through Hampshire to Berkshire. Can be joined from Bedhampton.

The Wey Navigation Towpath. The path can be joined from Weybridge, Guildford, Farncombe or Godalming (not shown on map).

The Wey South Path (see page 70). The path can be joined at Guildford.

The Isle of Wight Coastal Path. 60 miles round the coastline. The path can be joined from Ryde, Sandown, Lake or Shanklin.

Places to Visit

WATERLOO – PORTSMOUTH

ESHER **Sandown Racecourse** (contact TIC). **Claremont Landscape Garden** (NT). Earliest surviving landscape garden.

WEYBRIDGE **Weybridge Museum**, Church St. Local collections.

GUILDFORD **Guildford Castle**, Castle St. 12th-century, 3-storeyed keep (keep open Apr–Sep).

Guildford Cathedral. Consecrated 1961.

Guildford House Gallery, 155 High St. Temporary art exhibitions.

Guildford Museum, Castle Arch, Quarry St. Local history, archaeology, needlework.

continued on page 80

FARNCOMBE **Loseley House and Park Farm**, 2m N. Elizabethan house. Farm famous for its dairy produce. Farm tours (open end May–Sept).
Watts' Picture Gallery, Compton, 2m NE. 150 paintings by G F Watts.
GODALMING
Godalming Museum, 109A High St. Local history, Jekyll and Lutyens style garden.
Winkworth Arboretum (NT), Hascombe, 2m SE. 100-acre hillside, shrubs and rare trees.
HASLEMERE **Haslemere Education Museum**, High St. British flora and fauna, local industries.
LIPHOOK **Bohunt Manor**. Woodland and water gardens, birds.
Hollycombe Steam Collection, 1½m SE. Steam-driven 2ft-gauge railway, saw mill etc (open Apr–Oct).
ROWLAND'S CASTLE
Stansted Park, 2m E. Neo-Wren house, walled gardens, arboretum, theatre (open Etr–Sep).
HAVANT **Museum and Art Centre**, East St. Local history, firearms, gallery.
PORTSMOUTH & SOUTHSEA **Charles Dickens' Birthplace Museum**, 393 Old Commercial Rd (open Mar–Oct).
City Museum and Art Gallery, Museum Rd. Furniture, decorative art, local history.
Cumberland House Natural Science Museum and Butterfly House, Eastern Pde. Natural history, aquaria and butterfly house (open all year, butterfly house Mar–Oct).
D-Day Museum and Overlord Embroidery, Clarence Esplanade. Story of D-Day with A/V presentations.
Eastney Pumping Station, Henderson Rd, Eastney. Boulton and Watt beam engines (open Apr–Sep).
Round Tower, Broad St, Old Portsmouth. 15th-century defensive work.
Royal Marines Museum, Eastney. History of Royal Marines since 1664.
Southsea Castle and Museum, Clarence Esplanade. Fort built by Henry VIII.

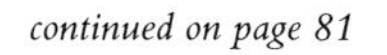

continued on page 81

'England expects . . .' is HMS Victory*'s signal on Trafalgar Day*

barrier ahead, and as the train begins to carve its way through them in a tunnel and deep cuttings, there is a view of Buriton's pretty church to the east. The landscape is a mixture of forest plantation and bare downland, and to the west is the village of Chalton, seemingly unchanged since the Middle Ages, and beyond, high on top of a hill, a windmill. **Rowland's Castle** is the next station. There is no castle, but the village has an attractive, curving green and some good houses around it. Leaving the Downs behind, the train now comes to **Havant**, joining the coastal line from Chichester to Portsmouth shortly before the station.

With Hayling Island to the south, which once had its own branch line from Havant, the train passes through suburbia to **Bedhampton**. From here there are views northwards to Portsdown, with its succession of 19th-century forts. Built to defend Portsmouth harbour with the support of Lord Palmerston and named 'Palmerston's Follies' by Gladstone, some are now open to the public. To the south are the marshes and mudflats of Langstone Harbour, much of which has been reclaimed. The train swings south away from the main line and on to Portsea Island, crossing the Broom Channel. The next station is **Hilsea** and then the line runs through

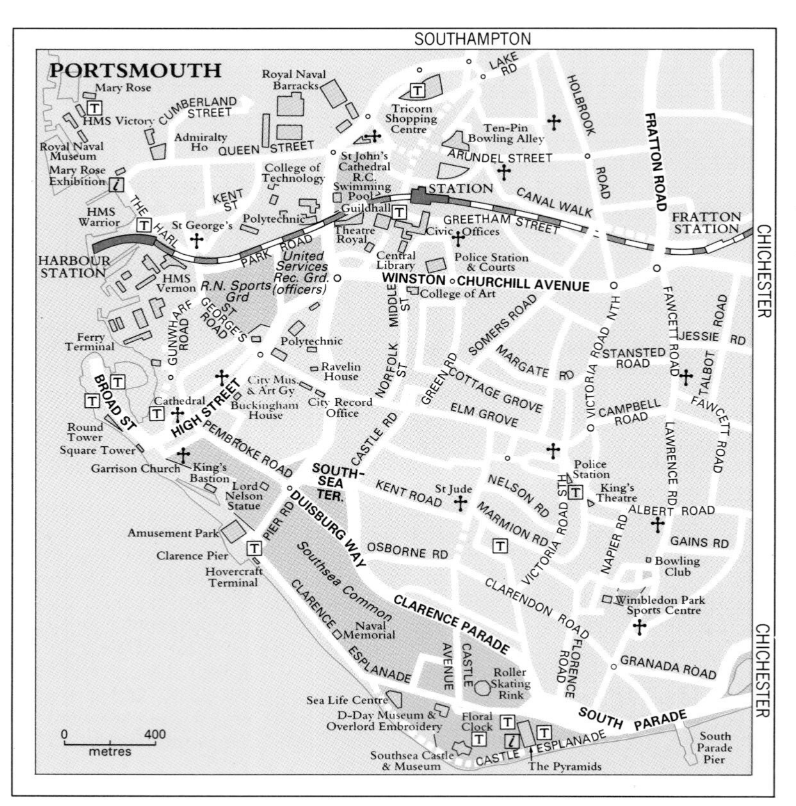

an urban landscape to **Fratton**, with sea views disappointingly absent. Here the train turns west and makes an elevated entry into **Portsmouth & Southsea**, both a terminus and a through station. The façade, best seen from trains continuing to Portsmouth Harbour, is a splendid affair in the style of a French château. This is the station for the city centre, its shops and the grand civic square, with its interesting blend of Edwardian baroque and modern architecture. Queen Victoria's statue stands at the heart of the square, while at its northern corner is Jagger's powerful war memorial, its crouching gunners well seen from the train.

Portsmouth

Portsmouth is an excellent and greatly undervalued city, offering visitors the best of many worlds. There is the seaside, with all its attendant pleasures, at Southsea; there is the fine architecture of the dockyard, which dates back to the reign of Henry VII; there is the old town with, at its heart, the magnificent, medieval church which was made into Portsmouth's cathedral in 1927, its nave still unfinished; and there is the continual coming and going in the harbour of ships and boats of every kind. Henry VIII made Portsmouth the first royal naval base, and it has been the navy's major city ever since. The story of the navy is represented by its ships, from Henry's *Mary Rose* to the latest guided missile destroyer, and in between are Nelson's *Victory* and HMS *Warrior*, the great Victorian ironclad that lies proudly beside the railway pier.

Portsmouth Harbour station is high on its pier above the sea, and from where the train stops, it is only a short walk to the sea and the passenger ferry to Ryde on the Isle of Wight. The ferry, now a high-speed catamaran, offers a quick and regular service. Straight across from the railway pier is Gosport, and the passenger ferries ply constantly to and fro.

THE ISLE OF WIGHT

Ryde – Shanklin *8½ miles*

Until the 1960s, the Isle of Wight had its own railway network which served almost every corner of the island, linking Freshwater and Yarmouth in the west with Newport, Cowes, Bembridge, Ryde and Ventnor in the south. The first line was opened in 1864, from Ryde to Shanklin, and for some reason that was also allowed to be the last, and continues to survive today. It is a delightful and rather eccentric journey that starts at **Ryde Pier Head** station, half a mile out to sea at the end of the pretty, cast-iron pier. Visitors stepping off the ferry will find waiting for them a train of former London Transport tube carriages, resplendent in Network SouthEast livery and enjoying a new lease of life after years of service underground. The train rumbles slowly along the pier and then stops at **Ryde Esplanade**, the best station for this smart, Victorian seaside resort with its elegant houses and its surprising number of 19th-century churches. A short tunnel leads the train round the town to **Ryde St Johns Road**, and then it runs into an open landscape of fields broken by clumps of woodland and little streams to **Brading**, where there is a Roman villa.

The line now follows the Yar valley to **Sandown**, with views to the east towards Culver Cliff. Sandown and Shanklin are now inseparable, but both started life as little villages, developed into seaside resorts in the 19th century and have continued to develop ever since. The railway played its part in this, and it still runs through the centre, pausing at **Lake** station by the golf links. The journey now ends rather abruptly at **Shanklin** station, but it used to continue southwards to Ventnor.

Queen Victoria's wax effigy in the Wax Museum, Brading. She died on the Isle of Wight, in her much-loved home, Osborne House

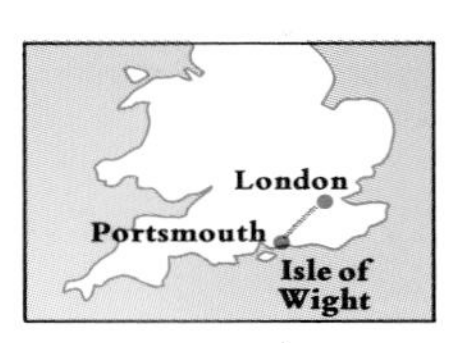

PORTSMOUTH HARBOUR
HMS *Victory*, HM Naval Base. Nelson's flagship.
HMS *Warrior* (1860), HM Naval Base. World's first iron-hulled warship.
The *Mary Rose*, HM Naval Base. Henry VIII's warship raised from the Solent.
Royal Naval Museum, HM Naval Base. Naval history.
Spitbank Fort. Napoleonic defence. Ferry connection (open Etr–Oct, weather permitting).

Spitbank Fort, one mile out to sea in the Solent

ISLE OF WIGHT
RYDE **Flamingo Park**, Seaview. Water gardens and birds (open Apr–Oct).
BRADING **Bembridge Windmill**, 3m E. Built *c.*1700 (open Apr–Sep).
Lilliput Doll and Toy Museum, High St.
Maritime Museum, Sherbourne St, Bembridge, 3m E. Shipwreck items (open Mar–Oct).
Morton Manor. Built 1680, landscaped gardens, turf maze (open Etr–Oct).
Nunwell House and Gardens. Fine furniture, militaria collections (open Jul–Sep).
Osborn Smith's Wax Museum. Includes Chamber of Horrors.
Osborn Smith's Animal World. Preserved animals, birds, reptiles.
Roman Villa. Fine mosaics (open Apr–Sep).
SANDOWN **Museum of IOW Geology**, Library, High St.
SHANKLIN **Shanklin Chine**. Gorge with waterfall. Nature trail (open Mar–Sep).

Tourist Information Centres
(* summer only)
FARNBOROUGH The Library, Pinehurst (0252) 513838
BASINGSTOKE Willis Museum, Old Town Hall, Market Place (0256) 817618
WINCHESTER The Guildhall, The Broadway (0962) 840500 or 67871 (accommodation)
EASTLEIGH Town Hall Centre, Leigh Rd (0703) 614646
SOUTHAMPTON Above Bar Precinct (0703) 221106
CHRISTCHURCH 30 Saxon Square (0202) 471780
BOURNEMOUTH Westover Rd (0202) 291715
POOLE The Quay (0202) 673322 Dolphin Shopping Centre
WAREHAM* Town Hall, East Street (0929) 552740
DORCHESTER 7 Acland Rd (0305) 67992
WEYMOUTH Pavilion Theatre Complex, The Esplanade (0305) 772444
ALDERSHOT Military Museum, Queens Ave (0252) 20968
FARNHAM Locality Office, South St (0252) 861111
LYMINGTON* St Thomas St Car Park (0590) 672422

Walks
The Clarendon Way. 35 miles from Winchester to Salisbury. The path can be joined at Winchester.
The Dorset Coast Path. Part of South-West Peninsula Coast Path. The path can be joined from Bournemouth, Poole or Weymouth.
The London Countryway (see page 14). The path can be joined from Byfleet, or Woking at Horsell.

continued on page 83

Down to Dorset

WATERLOO – WEYMOUTH

with Woking – Alton and The Lymington Branch

This journey, one of the longest and the most varied in Network SouthEast, links rural Surrey and Hampshire with the New Forest and the Dorset coastline, a cathedral city with modern centres of industry, a busy international port with old-fashioned harbours, and 18th- and 19th-century resorts with the contemporary seaside. The line to Alton connects with the Mid Hants Steam Railway.

Spacious lawns surround Winchester Cathedral's west front

WATERLOO – WEYMOUTH
142¾ miles
For the route from Waterloo to Surbiton and Woking, see pages 76–7 and 78–9.

Woking – Winchester
From Woking the main line westwards is remarkably straight and built for high-speed running. **Brookwood** station was built originally in the 1850s to serve the huge cemetery being laid out by the London Necropolis Company. For many years the London & South Western Railway ran special funeral trains from Waterloo. There are also British, American and Canadian military cemeteries here, mostly dating from World War I. For this is primarily a military region, with the garrison and ranges of Pirbright to the south and Bisley to the north. After Brookwood, the Basingstoke Canal runs beside the track to the north, crossing the railway on an aqueduct shortly before **Farnborough**. The station is set well to the north of the town, which has grown up around the famous airfield. After **Fleet** there are open views southwards towards the Downs. **Winchfield** is a station with no real village, but more substantial is **Hook**, with its coaching inn and 1930s church by Sir Edward Maufe,

Mid Hants Railway's 'N' class locomotive, built in 1925

the architect of Guildford Cathedral. A long, elevated stretch then leads to Old Basing, a delightfully attractive village set below the line to the south. At the centre is the big 16th-century church, and all around are fine timber-framed and tile-hung houses and barns. To the south is the site of Basing Castle and House, destroyed in 1645. The train now enters **Basingstoke**, whose galaxy of glass towers fills the skyline.

Leaving Basingstoke, the train passes the ruins of two chapels, Holy Ghost and Trinity, visible in the cemetery to the north, and runs through Basingstoke's expanding suburbs. At Worting Junction, the line continues to the south-west, and is carried through the rolling hills by a series of embankments and deep cuttings whose scale underlines the massive engineering required to build the railway to Southampton. **Micheldever's** handsome 1840 flint-built station, designed by Sir William Tite in a simple, classical style, is miles from its village, but further south there is a glimpse of the unusual church, with its powerful, brick octagon. Cuttings and a tunnel take the line into **Winchester**, with only limited glimpses of the Itchen valley and the Worthys.

Winchester
Winchester is easily reached from the station. Already a substantial town in the Roman period, Winchester's fame was established in the 9th century when King Alfred made it England's first capital city, a position it continued to enjoy until well after the Norman Conquest. The cathedral, built over three centuries from 1087 on the site of Alfred's Saxon church, is one of the longest in Europe. Near its grand Close are the famous public school, the Bishop's Palace, the two arms of the River Itchen and many of the city's most interesting streets. Near the Guildhall, King Alfred stands in

(continued on page 84)

London
Weymouth

The New Forest. Details of forest walks from Lyndhurst Information Centre (042128 2269). The Forest can be reached from Brockenhurst, Beaulieu Road or Lyndhurst Road.
The North Downs Way (see page 56).

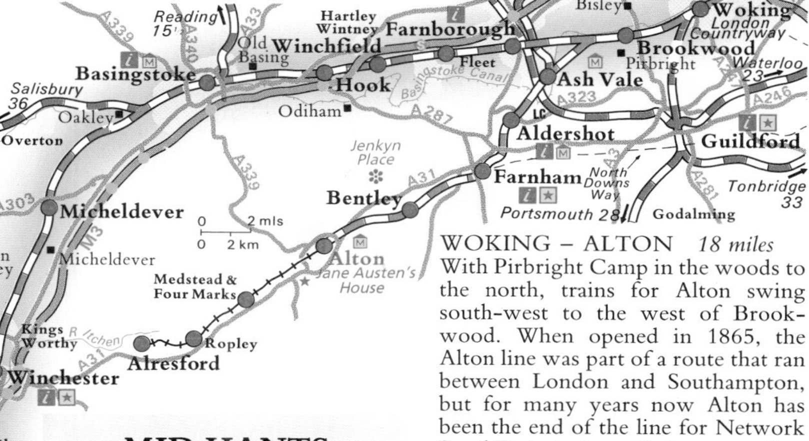

The 1645 siege of Basing House is re-enacted

MID HANTS RAILWAY

ALTON – ALRESFORD *10 miles*

Originally part of a line opened in the 1860s to connect King's Worthy, north of Winchester, with Guildford and Woking via Alton, and thus provide an alternative route from Southampton to London, the Mid Hants Railway, or Watercress Line, as it is popularly known, is the longest main line tourist steam railway in the South East. From Alton, where there is a direct connection with British Rail, with the two railways using adjacent platforms in the same station, the line climbs steeply, forcing hard work from the large and powerful locomotives which are a feature of the railway. The two market towns of Alton and Alresford are at either end of a pleasant journey through a varied Hampshire landscape.

Services: Sundays January to October, Saturdays and Bank Holiday weekends April to October, Tuesdays, Wednesdays, Thursdays May to mid July, daily mid July to early September, Christmas specials
For information: (0962) 733810/734200
Access: Direct connection at Alton British Rail station, with through-ticketing available. For Alresford, bus connection from Winchester

WOKING – ALTON *18 miles*

With Pirbright Camp in the woods to the north, trains for Alton swing south-west to the west of Brookwood. When opened in 1865, the Alton line was part of a route that ran between London and Southampton, but for many years now Alton has been the end of the line for Network SouthEast trains. Trains run first through woodland and then enter a region dominated by the military. With barracks to the north, the line crosses the Basingstoke Canal and its associated lakes. The first stop is **Ash Vale** and then the train makes its elevated way to **Aldershot**, an army town since 1854. **Farnham** is the next station, set to the south of the town whose Georgian heart is enclosed between the River Wey and the castle. The line now follows the course of the Wey and runs along the northern edge of Alice Holt Forest to **Bentley**, a little station well south of its village. **Alton** station is unexpectedly painted in the old Southern Railway colours of cream and green, and it must be one of the very few Network SouthEast stations not in the house colours of red, blue and grey. The reason for this eccentricity is that Alton is also the terminus of the Mid Hants Railway, the Watercress Line to Alresford. Alton is a pleasant market town whose Curtis Museum & Allen Gallery has, among collections of toys and material of local interest, a good display of pottery and porcelain.

The path can be joined from Farnham.
The Solent Way (see page 79). The path can be joined from Lymington or Southampton.
The South Wessex Way (see page 79). The path can be joined from Poole.
The Test Way. Runs 60 miles along the River Test. The path can be joined from Totton station.

Places to Visit

For information on Esher, see page 79

BASINGSTOKE – WEYMOUTH
BASINGSTOKE **Willis Museum and Art Gallery**, Old Town Hall, Market Place. Local collection, Basingstoke Canal.

continued on page 84

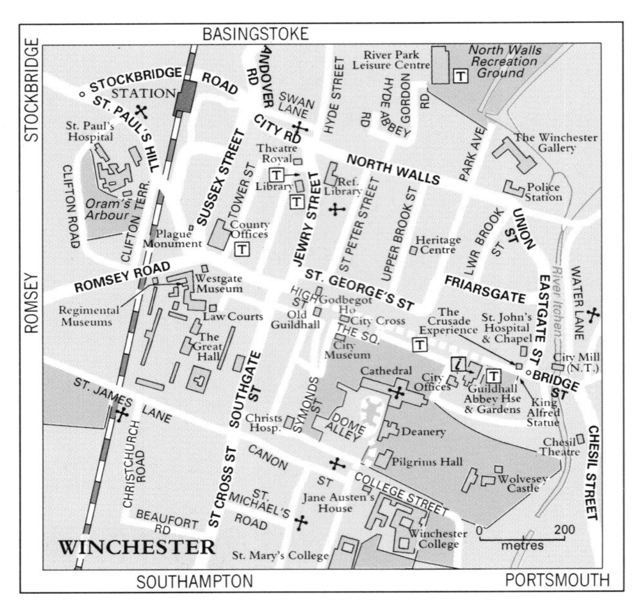

WINCHESTER **Cathedral and Close**. Begun in 1079. **City Mill**, Bridge St. Built on site of medieval mill in 1774. **The Crusade Experience**, The Broadway. Richard I's Crusade, A/V displays. **Heritage Centre**, Upper Brook St. 200 years of Winchester (open Mar–Oct). **Hospital of St Cross**, St Cross Rd. Founded in 1136, gives Wayfarers' Dole. **Regimental Museums**, Romsey Rd. **Royal Hampshire Regiment Museum. Serle's House**, Southgate St. **The Great Hall** of Winchester Castle, off High St. King Arthur's legendary Round Table. **Westgate Museum**, High St. Arms, armour etc. Fine rooftop views. **Winchester City Museum**, The Square. History of the city and central Hampshire. **Winchester College**, College St. Founded by William of Wykeham in 1382. **The Winchester Gallery**, Winchester School of Art, Park Ave (open during term times).
EASTLEIGH **Eastleigh Museum and Art Gallery**, High St. Local collections.
SOUTHAMPTON **Bargate Guildhall Museum**, High St. Local history, changing exhibitions. **God's House Tower Museum**, Town Quay. Early 14th-century fortification, local archaeology.

continued on page 85

bronze, surveying his capital city. Buried in the cathedral, among others, are King Canute, St Swithun, William Rufus, Izaak Walton and Jane Austen.

Winchester – Bournemouth

As the train leaves Winchester, there are good views to the east across the river and the former navigation. A fine 17th-century mansion can be seen standing by the river at **Shawford**. **Eastleigh** station was built in open country in 1839 to serve the junction with the lines to Gosport and, later, to Salisbury. Eastleigh only came into its own from the 1890s, when the London & South Western Railway progressively moved its carriage and locomotive works here, and it quickly grew up as a distinctive railway town. South of Eastleigh is Southampton airport, right by the line and served by **Southampton Parkway**. Passing the Ford works to the east, the train runs through the decorative stations at **Swaythling** and **St Denys** and then alongside the estuary of the Itchen.

Turning sharply to the west, the train enters **Southampton** via a short tunnel, with the line to the docks straight ahead. Boat trains still use this occasionally, but in the heyday of the transatlantic liner it was busy with Pullmans and other special services. Southampton's quays have witnessed many major moments in Britain's history. The Crusaders sailed from here, Edward III embarked here with the army that was to rout the French at Crécy in 1346 and in 1944 Southampton played a major role in another invasion of France. The town's buildings range from medieval churches and defensive towers to the massive 1920s civic centre, and modern shopping precincts. The port is still busy and there are good views of the container ships and Southampton Water beyond as the train runs westwards.

The Tudor House Museum, Southampton

Between **Redbridge** and **Totton** stations, the Salisbury line branches away to the north, and the train crosses the estuary of the Test, with a

The Lymington Branch

BROCKENHURST – LYMINGTON *5 ¼ miles*

An enjoyable journey to an exciting terminus, the short line to Lymington represents branch-line travel at its best. After Brockenhurst the train branches south to cross Setley Plain, typical New Forest countryside of heath broken by clumps of woodland. The woods increase, partly hiding from view Buckland Rings, an Iron Age earthwork. To the east lies Boldre, whose rector in the late 18th century was the picturesque author William Gilpin. The train then follows the river down into **Lymington Town** station, a short walk from the handsome main street. At the far end is the church, with its unusual cupola, and to the south the network of narrow streets leads down to the harbour. For the best view of the

Where the New Forest meets the sea: Lymington is a busy haven for yachts

harbour and the estuary, stay on the train as it makes its way across the river to its terminus at the **Pier** station, where the Isle of Wight ferry to Yarmouth should be waiting.

A Wessex Electric crosses an open stretch of New Forest countryside

view across the marshland towards Eling's 18th-century tidemill, still operational. Southampton suburbs end suddenly as the line enters the New Forest. **Lyndhurst Road** and **Beaulieu Road** are isolated stations, but their setting is convenient for visits to the Forest. The train's route through the Forest is enjoyably private and remote from civilisation and there is plenty of time to look out for the wild ponies. **Brockenhurst** is the changing point for the branch to Lymington and Isle of Wight ferries (see left). The redbrick villas of Brockenhurst, **Sway** and **New Milton** reflect the development that the railway inspired in the latter part of the 19th century. At **Hinton Admiral**, the New Forest is left behind and a long embankment carries the line over the flat plateau formed by the estuaries of the Mude, the Avon and the Stour into **Christchurch**. There are fine views of Christchurch Priory and the castle ruins to the south. The little town is pleasantly enclosed by the Avon and the Stour and it is easily reached from the station.

Bournemouth

Leaving Christchurch, the line is quickly surrounded by Bournemouth's suburbs, and the train runs through **Pokesdown** before entering **Bournemouth's** grand station, with its glazed roof, well to the east of the town centre. Bournemouth is essentially a 19th-century resort, and the Winter Gardens, the Pavilion and the town's attractive parks give the resort a particular appeal, with the brasher aspects of the English seaside successfully kept at bay. The splendid Russell-Cotes museum adds greatly to its charms.

A view over Bournemouth's beaches and its pier, towards the Isle of Purbeck

London
Weymouth

Southampton Hall of Aviation, Albert Rd South. Historic aircraft. **Southampton Maritime Museum**, The Wool House, Town Quay. Shipping museum. **Tudor House Museum**, St Michael's Sq. Social and domestic history, Tudor garden. TOTTON **Eling Tide Mill**. Uses tidal energy to grind wheat into flour.

Veteran cars in the Motor Museum at Beaulieu

LYNDHURST ROAD **New Forest Butterfly Farm**, Ashurst. Free-flying butterflies. Worldwide and British species (open daily Mar–Oct). BEAULIEU ROAD **The National Motor Museum and 'Wheels', Palace House and Gardens, Beaulieu Abbey and Exhibition of Monastic Life.** CHRISTCHURCH **Christchurch Castle and Norman House**. Ruined Norman House (1160). **Tricycle Museum**, Quay Rd (open Etr–Oct). **Red House Museum and Art Gallery**, Quay Rd. Local collections. BOURNEMOUTH **Russell-Cotes Art Gallery and Museum**, East Cliff. Period rooms, Oriental art, theatrical collection. PARKSTONE **Compton Acres Gardens**, Canford Cliffs Rd. Rock and water gardens (open daily Apr–Oct). POOLE **Brownsea Island** (NT). 500 acres of heath, woodland, beach (open Apr–Oct). **Guildhall Museum**, Market St. History of town. **Waterfront Museum**, Paradise St, The Quay. Poole's

continued on page 86

maritime history. **The Old Lifeboat House** (open Etr–Sep). **Great Poole Model Railway**. 'Life in Space', 'Smugglers and Pirates' and model railway. **Poole Park Zoo**. Small but well equipped. **Poole Pottery**, The Quay. Pottery manufacture. **Scaplen's Court**, High St. Medieval merchant's house.
WAREHAM **Wareham Town Museum**. Local collections (open Etr–mid Oct).
WOOL **Clouds Hill** (NT), Bovington Camp, 3m NW. Home of T E Lawrence. **The Tank Museum** (Royal Armoured Corps and Royal Tank Regiment), Bovington Camp, 2½m NW. Armoured fighting vehicles.
DORCHESTER SOUTH **Dinosaur Museum**, Icen Way. Actual size reconstructions, audio-visual displays. **Dorset County Museum**, High St. Local history etc. **Dorset Military Museum**, The Keep. 300 years of military history. **Old Crown Court**, Old Shire Hall. Scene of Tolpuddle martyrs' trial, 1834. **Maiden Castle**, 1m SW. Huge prehistoric earthworks. **The Tutankhamun Exhibition**, High West St. Reconstructed tomb. **Wolfeton House**, 1½m NW. Medieval and Elizabethan manor house (open May–Sep).
WEYMOUTH **Sea Life Centre**, Lodmoor Country Park. **Deep Sea Adventure**, Custom House Quay. Diving for treasure brought to life. **Tudor House**, 3 Trinity St.

continued on page 87

The harbour has been vital to Poole's history: above, the Custom House

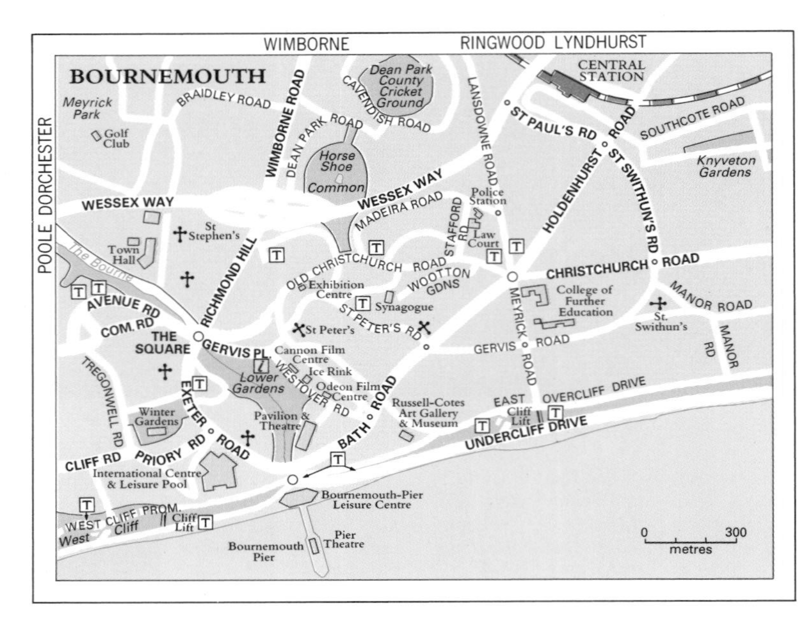

Bournemouth – Weymouth
Bournemouth now spreads westwards into Poole, with **Branksome** and **Parkstone** stations serving leafy suburbs. The train runs past Parkstone Bay, with wonderful views across the vast expanse of Poole Harbour to the south, often dotted with sailing boats, and in the distance Brownsea Island. The line cuts through the heart of **Poole** and enters the new station after crossing the shopping precinct. The narrow streets of the town and the old quays with their warehouses, Custom House and the Poole Pottery are to the south, easily reached from the station.

Views of Poole Harbour continue to dominate the line as the train crosses Holes Bay on a long causeway and passes through the junction at **Hamworthy**. From here the line follows the shore of the Wareham Channel and then runs inland to **Holton Heath** and **Wareham**. Wareham station, with its tall gables and Flemish detailing, dates from 1889. Facing it is a pub with an excellent tile panel of a steam train. Wareham, which still has its earth ramparts, is at its best around the old priory and the harbour on the Frome. West of the station, the train crosses the Piddle and passes the old branch line across the Isle of Purbeck to Swanage, and then runs through a landscape of heath and woodland. East Stoke Church is by the line, which follows the Frome towards Wool, with the ruins of Bindon Abbey to the south. Approaching Wool, there is a view of Woolbridge Manor to the north. **Wool** is the station for Bovington Camp, the Tank Museum and, four and a half miles to the south, Lulworth Castle and Cove. Leaving Wool, the train passes the Winfrith Heath nuclear research station and then crosses a rolling landscape to **Moreton**. The village is 1½ miles to the north-east, but it is worth the walk

The effigy of T E Lawrence ('of Arabia') in St Martin's Church, Wareham

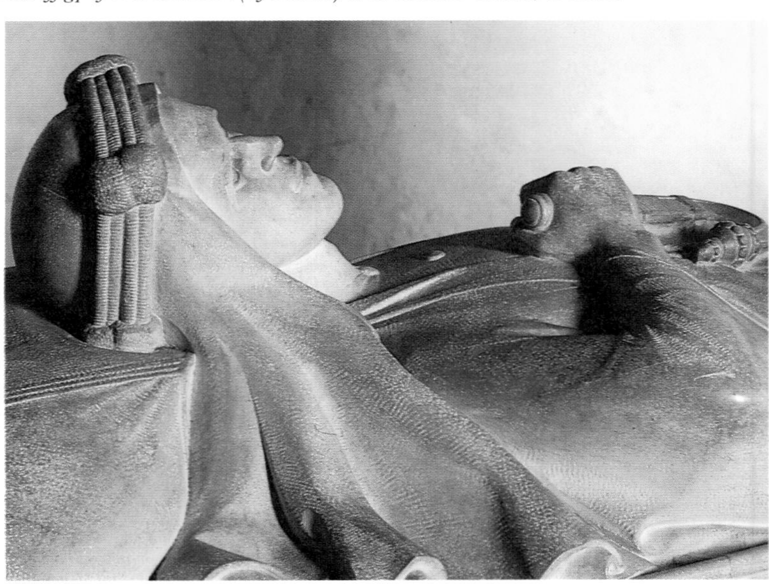

A mosaic from Durnovaria, Roman Dorchester, on display in the County Museum

to see the church with its unique Laurence Whistler windows. Lawrence of Arabia is buried here, and his cottage at Clouds Hill is one and a half miles on to the north.

The line now follows the course of the Frome towards Dorchester, passing pretty churches at West Stafford and Stinsford to the north, and to the south a group of barrows and earthworks. **Dorchester South** was rebuilt in 1989 and the handsome, stone town, Thomas Hardy's Casterbridge, is just to the north. Important since prehistory, Dorchester was a major Roman town, a Saxon mint and a Cromwellian stronghold. It was also the setting for two notorious trials, one Judge Jeffreys' 'bloody assizes' in 1685, and the other the six Tolpuddle Martyrs' trial in 1834. Notable is the County Museum, with its Victorian cast-iron interior.

From Dorchester to Weymouth, the landscape is rich in prehistory. To the west is the massive Stone Age earthwork of Maiden Castle, a hillfort that housed 5,000 people at the time the Romans overran it, and to the east Maumbury Rings, another Stone Age settlement, which was later used by the Romans as an amphitheatre. The line then burrows under Ridgeway Hill, passes another hillfort, Chalbury, to the east and then reaches Weymouth's outer suburbs at **Upwey**. The train runs along beside the marshland of Radipole Lake, and then the journey ends at **Weymouth's** station.

Weymouth

Built on a narrow spit of land, Weymouth is one of Britain's most distinctive resorts. A fine, sandy beach runs along the curve of Weymouth Bay, and behind it are elegant, Regency terraces. George III made Weymouth popular, and his colourful statue stands on the esplanade. The enclosed harbour is busy with fishing boats and yachts and a hydrofoil service links Weymouth with the Channel Islands. With its old-fashioned atmosphere, Weymouth is a resort for all seasons, and all tastes.

A cartoonist's view of George III at Weymouth

The coming of the railway in 1857 established Weymouth as a ferry port and until recently boat trains used to run down to the harbour

SWANAGE RAILWAY

SWANAGE – HARMAN'S CROSS *3 miles*

In 1885 a branch line across the Isle of Purbeck from Wareham to Swanage was completed and for many years this was a popular holiday route. Although long closed to passenger traffic, part of the route to Furzebrook had remained open as a freight line. This prompted the reopening of the southern part of the line as a tourist steam railway, and the route is now being restored through Corfe Castle to join the present British Rail line, with the aim of running steam services back to Wareham. Crossing the distinctive open landscape of Purbeck, with distant views over Poole Harbour, the line is at its most impressive as it circles the powerful ruins of Corfe Castle. The trains reflect the atmosphere of the Purbeck line during its Southern Railway period.

Services: weekends all year, Fridays and Mondays April, May and October, daily June to September, Christmas and other specials
For information: General enquiries (0929) 425800; talking timetable (0929) 424276
Access: Bus connections to Swanage from Poole and Wareham, nearest British Rail stations

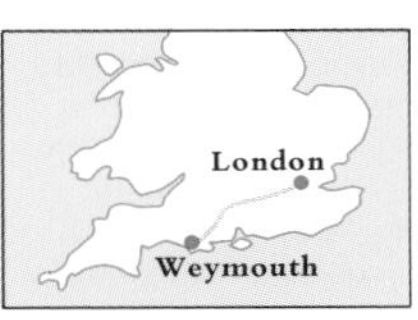

17th-century middle-class, harbourside house (open Jun–Sep). **Weymouth Museum**, Westham Rd. History of the town and area.

WOKING – ALTON

ASHVALE **RAMC Historic Museum**, Keogh Barracks. 2,500 items.
ALDERSHOT **Airborne Forces Museum**, Browning Barracks, Queen's Ave. Includes briefing models from World War II, Falklands War. **Aldershot Military Museum**, Queen's Ave. Story of the home of the British Army. **Royal Corps of Transport Museum**, Buller Barracks. Models and photographs.
FARNHAM **Farnham Castle Keep.** Ruined 12th-century keep. **Farnham Museum**, 38 West St. Local collections.
BENTLEY **Jenkyn Place Garden**. Rare plants, roses, herbaceous borders (open Apr–Sep).
ALTON **Curtis Museum & Allen Gallery**, High St. Local collections, ceramics, temporary exhibitions. **Jane Austen's House,** Chawton, 1½m SW. The novelist's home. **Mid Hants Railway** (Watercress Line). See page 83.

BROCKENHURST – LYMINGTON

LYMINGTON **Spinners**, School Ln, Boldre, 2m N. Azaleas, rhododendrons, etc (open Apr–Sep, by appointment only).

The West of England Line

WATERLOO – EXETER *172½ miles*

This journey, the longest within the Network SouthEast region, is a legacy of 19th-century competition between the Great Western and the London & South Western companies for West Country traffic. In its heyday, the route was used by Waterloo's most famous trains, the *Atlantic Coast Express* and the *Devon Belle*, but today it is a more leisurely exploration of a countryside that is quintessentially English – a journey of two cathedrals and a wealth of churches, castles, country houses, farms, cottages and quiet rivers. Some trains do not stop at every station.

Tourist Information Centres
(* summer only)
BASINGSTOKE Willis Museum, Old Town Hall, Market Square (0256) 817618
ANDOVER Town Mill Car Park, Bridge St (0264) 24320
SALISBURY Fish Row (0722) 334956 or 27269 (accommodation)
SHERBORNE Hound St (0935) 815341
AXMINSTER* The Old Courthouse, Church St (0297) 34386
HONITON* Angel Hotel Car Park, High St (0404) 43716
EXETER Civic Centre, Paris St (0392) 72434

Walks
The Clarendon Way (see page 82). The path can be joined from Salisbury.
The London Countryway (see page 14). The path can be joined from Woking at Horsell.
Old Sarum. A 4½-mile walk from Salisbury to the original site of the town.
The South Wessex Way (see page 79). The path can be joined from Salisbury.

Places to Visit

For Basingstoke, see page 83.

ANDOVER **Andover Museum**, Church Close. Locally manufactured agricultural machinery. Local fish aquarium.
Finkley Down Farm and Country Park. Farm animals and countryside museum (open Apr–Oct).
SALISBURY **Malmesbury House**, The Close. 13th-century origins. Rococo plasterwork (open Apr–Sep).
Mompesson House (NT), Cathedral Close. Built 1701, with fine plasterwork, 18th-century glasses. Walled garden.
Museum of the Duke of Edinburgh's Royal Regiment, 58 The Close. Militaria, medals.

continued on page 89

Waterloo – Basingstoke
For the route from Waterloo to Basingstoke, see pages 82–3.

Salisbury Cathedral: the Early English style perfectly expressed

Basingstoke – Salisbury
Soon after leaving Basingstoke, look out, on the north side, for a trackside garden full of old station name plates. The Exeter line then swings away to the west. The train runs through an open, rolling landscape, with Oakley's 1869 church to the south, towards **Overton**. East of the station, which is dominated by the government paper mill where bank note paper is produced, is the source of the River Test and the line now follows the north side of the Test valley for some miles. Westwards from Overton, cuttings limit the view and at **Whitchurch**, too, little of the town, famous for its silk mill on the Test, can be seen. Leaving Whitchurch, the train passes over the remains of the former Great Western line to Winchester, and then over the River Bourne, with its watercress beds. After a long cutting, the line approaches **Andover** on an embankment. Clearly visible is the early Victorian church which was inspired by Salisbury Cathedral.

From Andover westwards the landscape becomes more open and approaching **Grateley** there are long views to north and south. The village, with its 13th-century church, which contains some fine stained glass, is well to the east of the station. Crossing into Wiltshire, the train makes its way across the edge of Salisbury Plain, a countryside dotted with tumuli, barrows and other earthworks, along with military establishments. With Boscombe Down to the north and Porton Down to the south, the line crosses through the Winterbournes, along the valley of the Bourne. The hillfort at Figsbury Ring stands to the south. On the hillside to the east are the faint remains of badges carved into the chalk and then a tunnel carries the line under north **Salisbury**. The train crosses the Avon, with a view south towards the cathedral and then enters the station.

Mompesson House, one of the most elegant buildings in Salisbury's Cathedral Close

A warp threaded up on a loom at the Wilton Royal Carpet Factory

Salisbury

Salisbury's most famous feature is the spire of the cathedral, which rises to a height of 404ft. Constructed over the relatively short period of 38 years, Salisbury has a unity of style that makes it distinctive among English cathedrals. Several rivers meet in Salisbury – the Avon, the Nadder and the Bourne – and their waters and backwaters give the city a particular quality that has appealed to many painters, notably Constable. Salisbury was laid out in the 13th century, a new town to serve the cathedral after the move from the fortified hill of Old Sarum to the north. It is still full of medieval buildings, including the Deanery and Bishop's Palace, the gateways to the handsome, walled Close, the Poultry Cross and a selection of timber-framed houses. Later periods are also well represented in a city whose scale makes exploration on foot easy.

Salisbury – Sherborne

Leaving Salisbury, the train follows the valley of the Nadder with, to the south, Inigo Jones's Wilton House of 1647 and the 18th-century landscaped park, largely hidden by trees. Wilton, famous for its carpets, once boasted 12 parish churches but only two survive, one of which is a colourful Victorian mixture of mosaics, marble and stained glass.

The Nadder valley, with its oxbow bends and pockets of woodland, is a delightful landscape and set in it are a series of traditional stone villages. Burcombe, to the south, has a fine, arched bridge, and to the north is Dinton, with the church and 18th-century Hyde House forming an attractive group. Just to the west is classical Philipps House. With the wooded Castle Ditches hillfort to the south, the train follows the river closely to **Tisbury**, passing close to England's largest thatched tithe barn. Also near the station is Tisbury Church, whose waggon roof is supported by lively 15th-century carved angels. With the river now little more than a stream, the train winds through the hills, with the classical façade of Pythouse dominating the hillside to the north.

The landscape is now more open and rather remote as far as **Gillingham**, a typical stone-built country town, with a large church and a mid-18th-century silk mill. Just east of the station mounds mark the site of King John's hunting lodge. Leaving Gillingham, the line crosses the Stour, with good views along the valley.

The river curves away to the south and the encroaching hills give warning of Buckhorn Weston tunnel. The line then runs straight to **Templecombe**. Named after a former preceptory of the Knights Templars, the town is dominated by its church. The attractive station, recently reopened

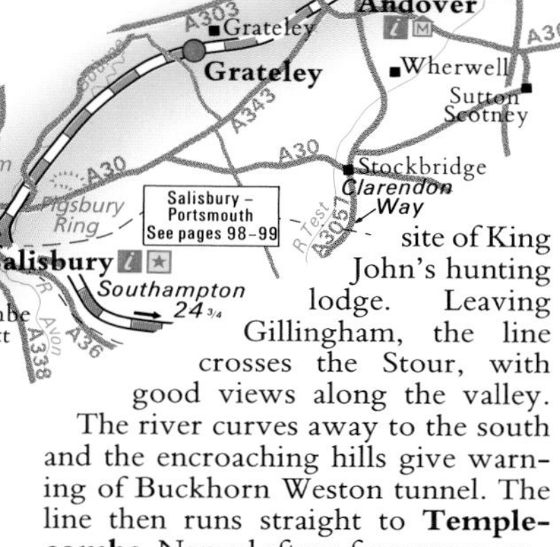

Old Sarum, 2m N on A345. Iron Age camp, later Roman Sorbiodunum and site of Norman castle and cathedral town. **Salisbury Cathedral**. Highest spire in England. **Salisbury Library**, Market Place. Three art galleries. **Salisbury and South Wiltshire Museum**, 65 The Close. Displays include Stonehenge, Early Man, Old Sarum and Salisbury, Pitt Rivers collection. **Wilton House**, 2½m W. 16th- to 17th-century house by Inigo Jones, Holbein and James Wyatt. World-famous paintings, model soldier exhibition (open Mar–Oct). TISBURY **Pythouse**, 2½m W. Palladian style Georgian mansion (open May–Sep).

continued on page 90

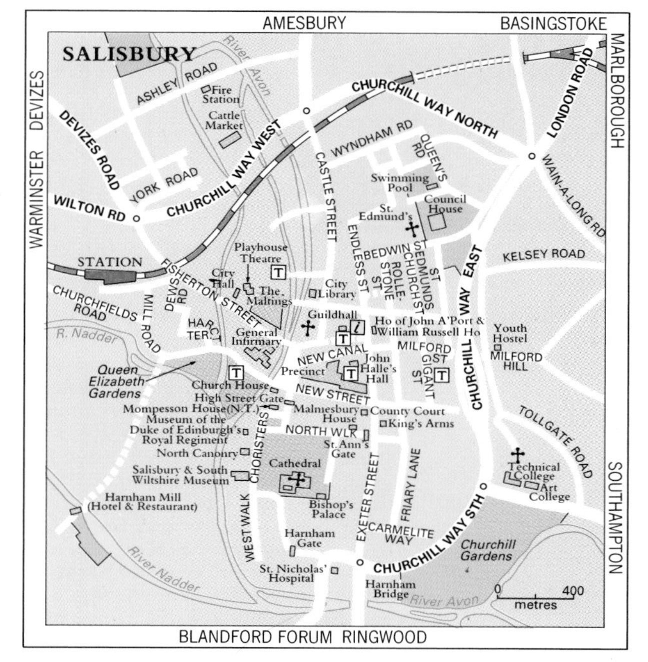

Old Wardour Castle. Built 1392. Damaged after Civil War. Substantial 60ft walls can be climbed.
SHERBORNE **Sherborne Abbey**. Founded in 8th century as a cathedral but largely rebuilt in 15th century.
Sherborne Castle. Sir Walter Raleigh's 16th-century house; Capability Brown grounds (open Etr–Sep).
Sherborne Museum, Abbey Gate House, Church Ln. Domestic and agricultural bygones, plus items of local geological, natural history and archaeological interest.
Sherborne Old Castle, ½m E. Ruined Norman castle.
Worldwide Butterflies and Lullingstone Silk Farm, Compton House, 3m W. Butterfly and silk farm (open Apr–Oct).
YEOVIL **Yeovil Museum**, Hendford Manor Hall. Local history, etc.
CREWKERNE **Clapton Court Garden**, 3m S on B3165. Rare and unusual plants in 10-acre formal and woodland settings (open Feb–Nov).
HONITON **All Hallows Museum**, High St. Display of Honiton lace. Demonstrations Jun–Aug. Also local history (open Etr–Oct).

Honiton is famous for lace and the museum has a fine collection

FENITON **Cadhay House**, Ottery St Mary, 3m S. Elizabethan manor (open certain days spring and summer).
EXETER ST DAVID'S **The Devonshire Regiment Museum**, Wyvern Barracks, Barrack Rd. Regiment's history.
Exeter Cathedral. Longest stretch of

continued on page 91

The ancient town of Sherborne has two castles, one Norman, the other (above), built for Sir Walter Raleigh in the 16th century

after some years of closure, marks the position of the former junction where the Somerset & Dorset line from Bath to Bournemouth used to connect with West Country services from London. Now, it is hard to imagine famous trains such as the *Pines Express* thundering through. Westwards from Templecombe, the line runs through a more undulating landscape towards Sherborne.

Sherborne

Approaching **Sherborne**, there is a fine view across the watermeadow of the infant River Yeo to the powerful ruins of the 12th-century castle. Beyond, across the other side of the lake that is part of the landscape garden created by Capability Brown in the 18th century, are the distant pinnacles of the 'new' castle, built for Sir Walter Raleigh in the 1590s. Sherborne is the most attractive town on the route, and the natural place for a break of journey. Honey-coloured buildings spread over the low hills to the north and within easy reach of the station are the abbey, the public school, Roman remains, the museum and plenty of shops and restaurants.

Sherborne – Exeter

Leaving Sherborne, the line follows the Yeo valley through a typically English scene, with foxes and deer sometimes to be seen. The magnificent tower of Bradford Abbas Church stands right by the line just east of Yeovil Junction. **Yeovil Junction** itself is a grand station with an attractive old, tiled buffet. Its turntable was built to serve the formerly busy intersection between the West Country route from Waterloo and the old Great Western line to Weymouth from Bath and Bristol. The town of Yeovil itself is well to the north, served by Pen Mill station on the Weymouth line. A shuttle bus service connects the two stations, and the town centre.

On leaving the station, there is a glimpse of the famous folly Jack the Treacle Eater, above the trees to the north, one of four surrounding Barwock House. West of Yeovil the train passes Sutton Bingham reservoir, a man-made lake used for water sports. To the north is East Coker, the burial place of the poet T S Eliot. Pendomer Church and Manor stand isolated on a hill to the north and then the line makes its elevated way into **Crewkerne**. Sir William Tite's tall, 1860 station in golden Ham stone is a mile south of the town, worth a visit for its handsome market square, old coaching inns and fine 15th-century church. Formerly Crewkerne was famous for sailmaking, and the sails for Nelson's *Victory* were made here. From Crewkerne, the train follows the twisting valley of the Axe passing, to the south, Clapton Court and Forde Abbey. The remote, but attractive landscape of rolling farmland accompanies the train into Devon, and the carpet-making town of Axminster. The 18th-century market town is the nearest point on the route for the Dorset and Devon coast and the traditional resorts of Lyme Regis and Seaton. Both can be reached by regular bus services replacing the long-closed branch lines.

After Axminster, with Kilmington Church to the north, the line stays close to the Axe, until, with a glimpse of the sea, the river swings towards its estuary at Seaton. The next station is **Honiton**, a town enclosed by the railway and the River Otter. Following a major fire in 1765, Honiton was largely rebuilt, and it is still a predominantly 18th-century town. Open-air markets add to the traditional atmosphere, and there are plenty of cafés and restaurants, along with a surprising number of antique shops. The museum has a fine display of Honiton lace.

The train now follows the Otter and the A30 westwards to **Feniton**, formerly the junction for the holiday line south to Sidmouth and Budleigh Salterton. After **Whimple**, the extensive Whiteway cider orchards stand beside the line, and then, leaving the hills behind, the trains runs straight towards Exeter, passing the airport, the M5 and the suburban station at **Pinhoe. Exeter Central** is the next station, the best placed for the cathedral and city centre, and then the train descends to its terminus at **Exeter St David's**, with a good view of the station's imposing classical façade and the Exe valley stretching away to north and south. St David's, with its old, tiled platform indicators and traditional, panelled waiting room, is a busy stopping point on the former Great Western main line from Paddington to the West Country. In the heyday of the Waterloo – Exeter line, Southern Railway expresses also used the station on their way to the north coast resorts and to Plymouth. The slightly unexpected presence of Network SouthEast trains in Exeter St David's is a legacy of those days.

Mol's Coffee House, Exeter, patronised by Drake. The town's links with the sea are illustrated in the Maritime Museum, where the barge below has found a home

Exeter

Exeter was a fortified town, and a busy port, from the Roman period on, but it was the Normans who developed the city as it stands today, and their legacy is the cathedral with its flanking Norman towers. Greatly expanded during the Middle Ages, the cathedral is also known for its vaulting and its 14th-century sculpture on the west front. It was the River Exe and its port that made Exeter a wealthy city in the Middle Ages and the surviving timber-framed buildings reflect this. In order to maintain this wealth, the city built its ship canal to the sea, from 1564. Little traffic uses the 5½-mile waterway now, but its warehouses and quays house the Maritime Museum, with its unique collection of ships and boats from all over the world. Pleasure trips around the harbour and along the ship canal are a good introduction to a thriving city with an exciting past.

Gothic vaulting in the world. **Guildhall**, High St. Dating from 1330. Oil paintings and civic regalia.

Maritime Museum, Town Quay and Canal Basin. Over 130 vessels afloat, ashore and under cover.
Rougemont House Museum, Castle St. Lace and costume.
Royal Albert Memorial Museum, Queen St. Local and natural history, Exeter silver, glass and lace. **St Nicholas's Priory**, Mint Ln. Remains of 11th- to 16th-century Benedictine priory. 15th-century kitchen.
Tucker's Hall, Fore St. Ancient Hall of the Weavers, Fullers and Shearmen.
Underground Passages, Princesshay. Medieval aqueducts.

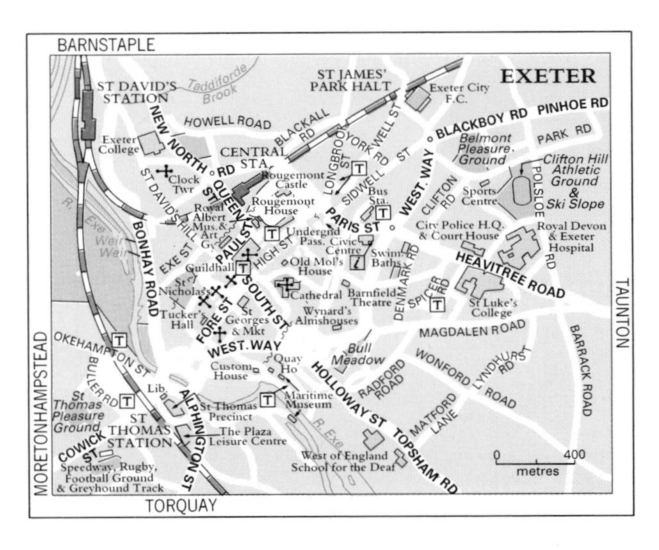

Royal Berkshire

WATERLOO – READING
and Staines – Windsor & Eton Riverside

The two routes to Reading, from Paddington and from Waterloo, are in reality completely different. The quicker by far is the old Great Western main line from Paddington, but the more meandering route created by the London & South Western Railway and its associated companies has a quality of its own.

Windsor has been a castle since the days of William the Conqueror, holding a commanding position over the River Thames

Tourist Information Centres
BRACKNELL Central Library, Town Square (0344) 423149
READING Town Hall, Blagrave St (0734) 566226
WINDSOR Central Station, Thames St (0753) 852010

Walks
The Kennet and Avon Canal (see page 14). The towpath can be joined from Reading.
The London Countryway (see page 14). The path can be joined from Windsor or Sunningdale stations.
Windsor Great Park. Once the hunting grounds of kings, it covers 4,800 acres, stretching from the Thames to Virginia Water. The Park can be reached from Windsor or Virginia Water stations.

Places to Visit

For information on Reading, see pages 14–15. For Windsor, see pages 20–1.

STAINES **Thorpe Park**, Staines Rd, Chertsey. 500-acre theme park with over 50 attractions, including 'Space Station Zero' roller-coaster ride,

continued on page 93

A genuine totem pole stands unexpectedly by Virginia Water

WATERLOO – READING
43½ miles

Waterloo – Staines
From Waterloo trains quickly reach **Clapham Junction** and then run parallel to the Thames through **Wandsworth Town** and **Putney**. They cross the old dock that marks the mouth of the River Wandle and then pass through the smart, leafy suburbs of **Barnes** and **Mortlake** to **Richmond**. Mortlake boasts a particularly flowery station. London Regional Transport's District Line runs alongside, to their terminus at Richmond. Just to the north is the Old Deer Park and Kew Gardens, and there are views across the park as the trains cross the Thames. **St Margarets** is the station for Marble Hill House, but not all trains stop here. There is a ferry link across the Thames to Ham House near by.

After **Twickenham** the line crosses the River Crane and then from **Whitton** the suburban landscape is replaced by scrub and heathland. **Feltham's** 1880 parish church stands right by the station. To the north is the first of the many huge reservoirs that characterise the region. From **Ashford** to **Staines** suburbia returns, and the train crosses the Thames again, with good views of the river-front to the south.

Change at Staines for the Windsor branch (see below).

Staines – Reading
The next station is **Egham**, with Runnymede Park to the north. Soon, rising above wooded hills, can be seen the astonishing spires and towers of Royal Holloway College. This, the most exuberant Victorian building in the home counties, was designed in 1879 by W H Crossland, and created out of the fortune made from Thomas Holloway's pills. The landscape of wood, parkland and farms continues to **Virginia Water**, little of whose grander suburbia can be seen from the station. Passing **Longcross** station,

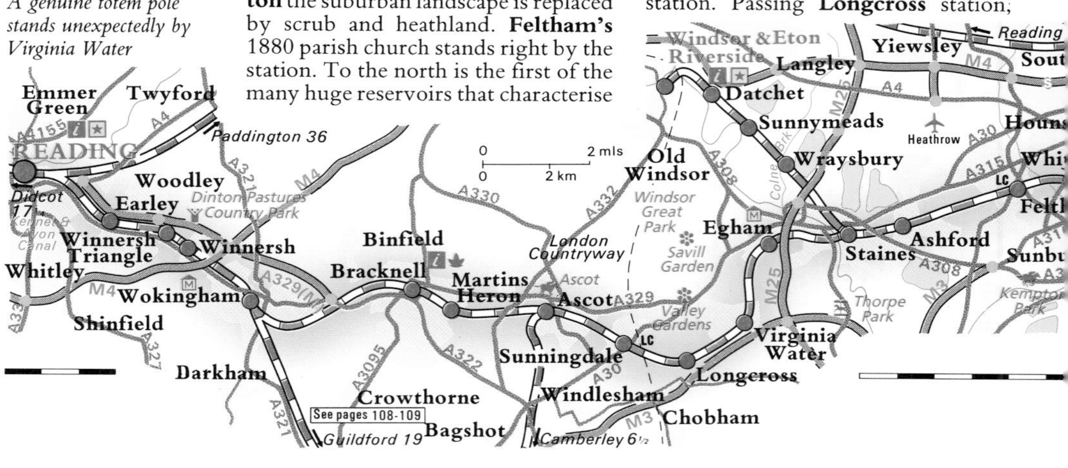

the train crosses the heathland of Chobham Common to **Sunningdale**. Smart houses are buried in woodland as the train goes through cuttings to **Ascot**. Distinctive are the handsome brick bridges, a feature of the line. Little of Ascot can be seen, and the racecourse lies to the north. **Martins Heron** is the next station, newly built to serve a Legoland dormitory suburb, and then the route is elevated into **Bracknell**, with plenty of new-town views.

Leaving Bracknell, the line runs beside the A329 through open farmland, as far as Wokingham's outskirts. **Wokingham**'s centre still has some quality, and the dramatic spire of Woodyer's 1864 church dominates the skyline to the north. The landscape is suburban now to **Winnersh**. **Winnersh Triangle** is the next station, apparently surrounded by busy roads, and then the train crosses the Loddon to enter Reading's outskirts at **Earley**.

Reading

With the university and Whiteknights Park to the west, the line drops down into the Thames valley. Caversham House crowns the hills to the north and then the train crosses the Kennet and runs into **Reading** station. There are good views of Reading's spires and towers, and the gaol, with its Oscar Wilde associations. The huge new Brunel arcade rather dwarfs the classical façade of the old station and, outside, Edward VII's statue stands on guard with a slightly disapproving air.

STAINES – WINDSOR & ETON RIVERSIDE *6¾ miles*

Trains from Waterloo to Windsor follow the Reading route to Staines, and then branch away to the north-west. All around are reservoirs and flooded gravel pits, giving the landscape a distinctive rural quality that belies its proximity to London. Stations are isolated, away from their villages. The first is **Wraysbury**, just after the line crosses the Colne Brook, and the church and village can be seen across the water to the west. Magna Carta Island and Runnymede lie across the Thames to the south. Even more isolated is **Sunnymeads**, and then the line runs briefly beside the Thames before crossing open common land to **Datchet** station, in the centre of its pretty Thames-side village. From here the train runs beside a golf course, with the Thames and Windsor Great Park beyond, to the south. The line crosses the river and the castle comes into view. There is soon a brief glimpse of Eton College Chapel, seen through the trees that line the river bank. Being at low level, the line's approach to Windsor lacks the drama and excitement of the Paddington route (see page 20). However, the journey is certainly worthwhile for its climax in the splendid Tudor-style station. **Windsor & Eton Riverside** was opened in 1849, a decorative confection in coloured brick and stone by Sir William Tite, designed to please the royal patrons. It is a spacious station, with old gas lamps and plenty of carved monograms: VR, PA (Prince Albert), LSWR, WC (William Chaplin, the railway's chairman), and WT (Tite himself).

One of Reading's best buildings, the Victorian gothic Old Town Hall

'Phantom Fantasia' ghost ride, and Thorpe Farm (open Etr–Sep).
ST MARGARETS Ferry crossing to **Ham House** (NT). Excellent Stuart house, 17th-century furniture. 17th-century garden. **Marble Hill House**. Complete example of English Palladian villa. Early Georgian paintings and furniture.
EGHAM **The Egham Museum**, Literary Institute, High St. Local history and archaeology. **Savill Garden**, Windsor Great Park. Woodland garden at its peak in spring, but producing a wealth of colour and interest all year.
VIRGINIA WATER **Valley Gardens**, Windsor Great Park. 300 acres with outstanding range of woodland trees and shrubs.
ASCOT **Ascot Racecourse** (contact TIC).
WOKINGHAM **Royal Electrical and Mechanical Engineers (REME) Museum**, Isaac Newton Rd, Arborfield, 2m SW. Life-size tableaux, models, photos and artefacts telling the story of REME.
WINNERSH **Dinton Pastures Country Park**.

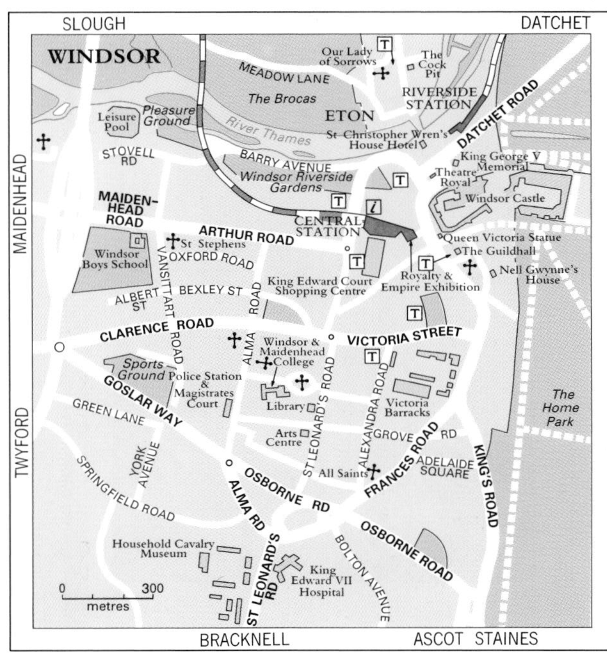

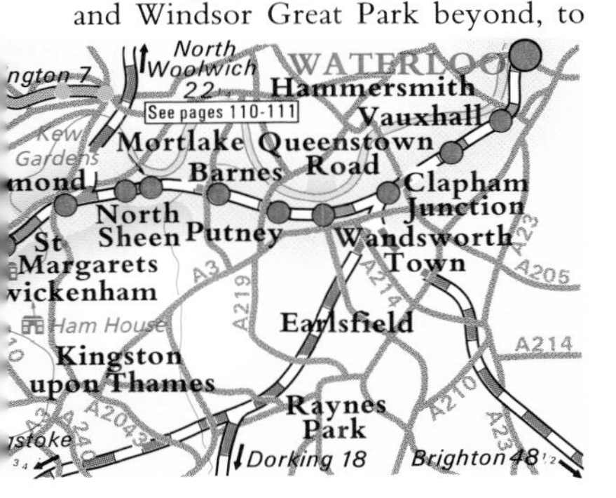

1 Shortly after leaving Salisbury the line to Portsmouth runs through open arable land

2 Eastbourne – a seaside resort that owes its existence to the arrival of the railway

3 Glorious spring colour at the Hillier Arboretum, three miles from Romsey

4 Dover's Roman lighthouse, the Pharos

5 Brighton station's famous clock: its delicate wrought-ironwork bears the arms of the London, Brighton & South Coast Railway

6 The castle ruins at Tonbridge overlook the Medway flowing through the town

7 Thameslink, a new service connecting places north of the Thames with those to the south

1

2

3

4

CROSS COUNTRY ROUTES

Cross-country journeys are a particular feature of Network South-East and the timetable includes a number of direct services that link together interesting and varied parts of southern England. Historically, cross-country travel was complex and time-consuming, involving long waits at obscure junctions to connect routes operated by independent companies. Now that traditional regional boundaries have been put aside, cross-country journeys have become a particularly relaxing way to see the changing landscape of southern England.

Included in this section are some of the most attractive of these routes, the best of which is without doubt the leisurely exploration of the south coast from Dorset to east Kent, made possible by a series of well-coordinated interconnecting services. At the other end of the spectrum is the North London Line's tour of London north of the Thames from Richmond to Woolwich.

5

6

7

WALKING BY TRAIN

FROM THE EARLY YEARS OF THIS CENTURY AND THROUGH THE 1920s and 1930s many independent railway companies, notably the Great Western and the Southern, published books of country walks accessible from their stations. Today, Network SouthEast is the ideal starting point for walks all over southern England. Walks by train can either be circular, starting and finishing at the same station, or go cross country from one station to another. The examples below, selected for variety of landscape, are short walks, generally taking from two to four hours, but some are parts of major long distance footpaths, such as the Ridge Way, the North Downs Way and the Test Way. Other sections of long distance footpaths accessible from Network SouthEast stations include the Ridge Way from Goring to near Salisbury, and the South Coast Path from south of Exeter to Poole.

Walking along disused railways is also increasingly popular and many have now been converted into official walkways. Those easily reached from Network SouthEast stations include Shalford south towards Shoreham (the Downs Link), Mottisfont to Fullerton Junction, Brockenhurst to Burbush Hill, and Shanklin to Wroxall.

1 Along the Kennet & Avon Canal

This is an easy, level walk along the towpath of the Kennet & Avon Canal, from the village of Great Bedwyn eastwards to Hungerford and Kintbury through the Wiltshire Downs. Pretty villages, fine churches, canal locks and bridges and the market town of Hungerford add to the attractions.

Great Bedwyn to Hungerford
5¼ miles
Hungerford to Kintbury *3 miles*
Take the train to Bedwyn from Paddington or Reading. From the station, turn left, cross the line and the canal and turn left down on to the towpath. Follow the well-maintained towpath alongside the canal with its series of steadily descending locks past Little Bedwyn to Hungerford. For Hungerford town centre, turn right from the old wharf on to the main street. For Kintbury, continue eastwards beside the canal. Note that the towpath crosses on to the northern bank of the canal just beyond the first lock after leaving Hungerford. Kintbury station is adjacent to the towpath.

An alternative is to turn left from Bedwyn and follow the canal westwards to the steam pumping station at Crofton, cross the canal and then follow a signposted path along by Wilton Water to the village of Wilton. Continue through the village towards the windmill, and turn left on to a path that passes through Wilton Brail, or wood, passes Brail Farm, and rejoins the canal just before Great Bedwyn. *4½ miles*

2 Along the Ridge Way through the Chilterns

This is a pleasant walk from Tring westwards along the Ridge Way Path to Wendover. The going is easy along the well-signposted route, marked by white acorns and yellow arrows or Ridge Way signs, and the hills are relatively gentle. The route is initially through beech woods, with magnificent views northwards and then through open farmland round Hastoe. The path flanks beech woods again, with fine views over the Vale of Aylesbury, and then descends quite steeply through dense woodland and into Wendover.

Tring to Wendover *8 miles*
Take the train to Tring from Euston. From the station turn left, follow the road across the canal, turn left at the junction, and soon turn right on to the signposted Ridge Way Path. Keep straight along the marked path to the A41. Turn right, cross the road and take first path on the left. Follow the signs carefully as the path skirts Wigginton and turn right after the village along a broad track that passes Wick Farm. Go straight across a minor road towards Hastoe, and straight on again at Hastoe crossroads, keeping to the road. The path then branches right away into Paris Wood. Follow the path along the crest of the hill, at the edge of the woods, to a minor road. Turn left and immediately right at the signpost. Cross the centre of the field and do not be put off by the lack of a defined track, for a stile by a small copse soon comes into view. Cross the next field, keeping the hedge on the left, to a minor road, and go straight across into the woods again. Follow the track along the top edge of the wood, turn right and immediately left at a minor road, and then follow the path down through Hale Wood, looking out for the yellow markers. Keep always straight ahead, on the main path, until there is a major junction in the woods. Turn right, as indicated by the acorn marker and the path now descends steadily, leaving the woods as it joins a broad track past farms towards Wendover. At the main road go straight on to the church, then turn right and follow Ridge Way signs to the town centre.

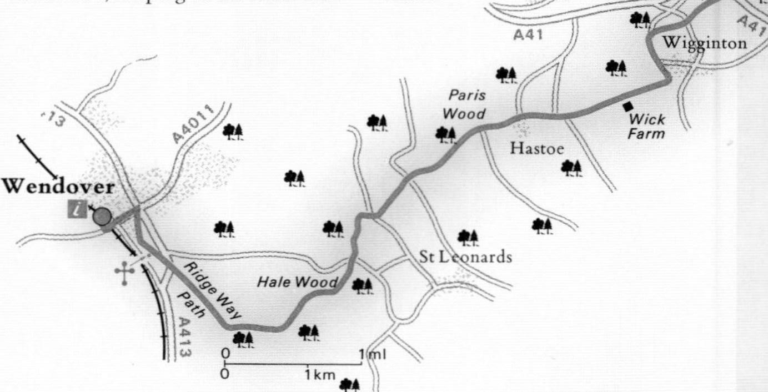

3 Rye, Winchelsea and the Marshes

This walk, between the old Cinque ports of Rye and Winchelsea, centres on the Rye marshes and the Rother estuary. The going is level. A shorter walk *(3 ¾ miles)* direct from Rye to Winchelsea is also possible.

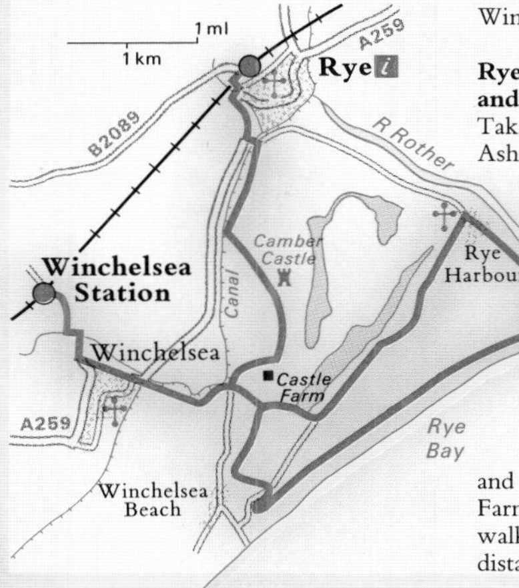

Rye to Winchelsea via Camber and the Rye marshes *9 ¾ miles*
Take the train from Hastings or Ashford to Rye. From the station turn right, then left at the level crossing and right at the junction with the A259. Cross the river and follow the road to its junction with the road to Rye Harbour. Turn left over the canal and right on to the path along the canal. Head straight towards Camber Castle. The path runs by the castle and then curves right through Castle Farm to rejoin the canal. Turn left and walk beside the canal for a short distance. (Those wanting to go straight to Winchelsea should now turn right along a track and join the road that leads straight on to Winchelsea.) To continue on the marshland walk, take a signposted path that runs across a field away from the canal. Continue towards the sea, to a flooded gravel pit. At a junction with a broad track turn left, and go along by the flooded pits for about 1½ miles to Rye Harbour. At the main road turn right, past the harbour and follow a track beside the Rother towards the sea. At a junction, turn right and walk along the raised sea wall until a colony of railway carriage houses can be seen across the marsh. Turn right along a path, pass between the carriages, over the shingle beds and across a field, and then turn right along a broad track past a series of houses. This leads back to a point passed earlier. Turn left here and then follow the main road to Winchelsea.

4 Along the Test Way

This is a gentle walk beside the River Test, linking the two abbey towns of Romsey and Mottisfont. The meandering path is well marked with TW signs, as part of the longer Test Way, and progress is limited only by the large number of stiles. For a longer walk, follow the Test Way northwards along the river passing near to Whitchurch station.

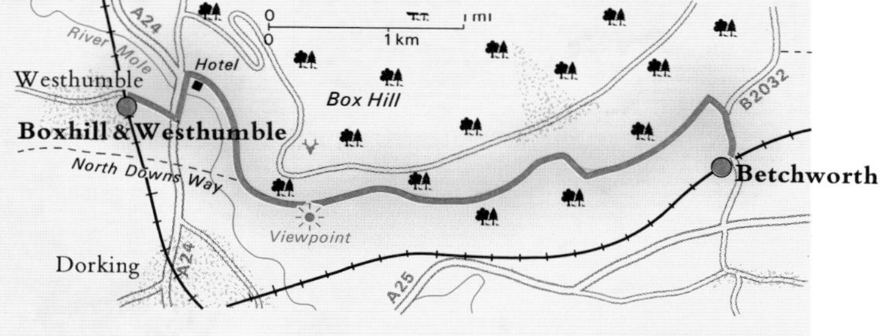

Romsey to Mottisfont Dunbridge
6 ¼ miles
Take the train to Romsey from Salisbury, Southampton or Portsmouth. From the station follow the pedestrian sign that leads down Station Road. Continue straight on. Turn right into The Hundred, bear right at Barclays Bank and then left through the abbey gateway. Keep straight on, cross the river and, keeping the park on the left, cross another stream and follow signs to Squabb Wood. Cross another branch of the river, wind through the houses and turn right along the marked Test Way. Follow the TW path through Squabb Wood, and turn left on leaving it and continue on the path across the fields. Go across one road, following the marked path through Awbridge, cross another road and walk along past a vineyard. At the junction with the B3084 turn right, by Awbridge House, and follow the road until the marked path branches away to the right. Continue past a pond and at the main road turn right and left on to the marked path just before the level crossing. The path crosses the railway and the Test and then leads straight to Mottisfont village. For the station bear left, and then left along the first signed footpath. Turn left at the road to reach the station.

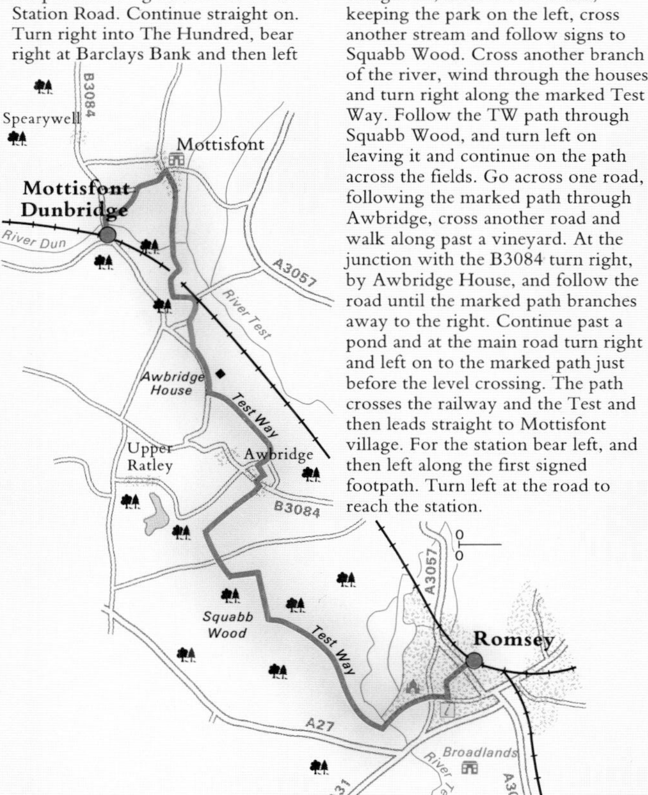

5 Along the Crest of the North Downs

This is a dramatic walk along the crest of the Downs, in and out of the woods, with magnificent views to the south. The North Downs Way is well marked by acorn signs but the going is at times quite hard, with some steep climbs.

Boxhill & Westhumble to Betchworth *3 ¾ miles*
Take the train from Waterloo to Boxhill & Westhumble. From the station turn right. At the main road, the A24, turn left, cross using the subway, turn left again and at the roundabout take the minor road to the Burford Bridge Hotel. Pass the hotel and turn right on to a track that leads steeply up the side of Box Hill. At the top, follow the chalk path that leads into the woods, passing the monument to a local eccentric. Take the left fork and at a minor road turn right, and follow it to the viewpoint. Join the signposted North Downs Way. Keep a watch for the signs, for the path rarely runs straight, at times climbing steeply up and down the flanks of the Downs. Coming out of the woods, the path skirts the top edge of the old quarry workings and then drops steadily down into the quarry itself. Now a well defined track, the path crosses an old bridge, passes some old cottages and then comes to an end at the B2032. For Betchworth station turn right. The station is on the Reading–Tonbridge line but not all trains stop at Betchworth. To continue along the North Downs Way towards Reigate, turn left at the B2032, and rejoin the path on the left side of the road, after ¼ mile.

Hampshire Estuaries

SALISBURY – PORTSMOUTH *50½ miles*

This journey, an excellent way to see the varied landscape and coastline of southern Hampshire, is part of a much longer cross-country route from South Wales to Portsmouth. A major feature is the rivers it connects, the Test, the Itchen and the Hamble, with their harbours and estuaries, but other highlights include cathedrals, abbeys, country houses, castles and some unusual museums.

Tourist Information Centres (* summer only)
SALISBURY Fish Row (0722) 334956 or 27269 (accommodation)
ROMSEY* Bus Station Car Park, Broadwater Rd (0794) 512987
SOUTHAMPTON Above Bar Precinct (0703) 221106
FAREHAM Ferneham Hall, Osborn Rd (0329) 221342
PORTSMOUTH Clarence Esplanade (0705) 832464 or Continental Ferryport*, Rudmore Roundabout (0705) 698111

Walks
The Clarendon Way (see page 82). The path can be joined from Salisbury.
The Solent Way (see page 79). The path can be joined from stations between Southampton and Portsmouth.
The South Wessex Way (see page 79). May be joined from Salisbury.
The Test Way (see page 83). The path can be joined from Mottisfont, Romsey or Southampton stations (see Walk 4 on page 97).

Salisbury – Romsey

Leaving Salisbury (see page 89), the train crosses the Avon, with the cathedral visible to the south, passes through a short tunnel, and then swings south at the junction with the line from Basingstoke. Salisbury suburbs accompany the line down to the Avon valley and then the city is left behind. Look back for a good view of the cathedral spire standing high above the city. The squat tower of Britford Church can be seen across the valley and then the line runs beside the A36 before turning eastwards away from the river. To the north are woodlands, to the south long views to Dean Hill and the open flanks of the Downs. The first station is **Dean**, and the village of West Dean, with its two churches and pretty walled gardens, is right by the line. From here, the train follows the rather remote valley of the Dun, with Lockerley's Victorian church to the north, to **Mottisfont Dunbridge**. The village of Mottisfont is half a mile to the north, and well worth the walk for the church, with its Norman details and 15th-century glass, and the old abbey, which stands by the Test. Originally an Augustinian priory founded in 1201, Mottisfont Abbey has been a private house since the Dissolution, and much of what stands today is 18th- and 20th-century. A major feature of the 20th century is Rex Whistler's gothic drawing room, painted in the late 1930s.

Romsey

The line now joins the Test valley, and follows the river southwards to its estuary. After crossing the Test, the train enters **Romsey**'s classical station, which is set well to the east of the town. There is a good view of the abbey from the elevated track as it approaches the station, its powerful and chunky Norman outline dominating the town. Founded first in 907, the abbey that stands today, overlooking the Test, was built largely between 1120 and 1230, with additions during later medieval periods. It is an exciting building, full of unusual details, such as the Romsey Rood, an 11th-century over life-size sculpture of Christ, and its presence fills the little market town, with its pleasant 18th- and 19th-century architecture. To the south is Broadlands House, the 18th-century mansion that was the home of the late Louis Mountbatten. Leaving Romsey, the line flanks the park but the house is hidden.

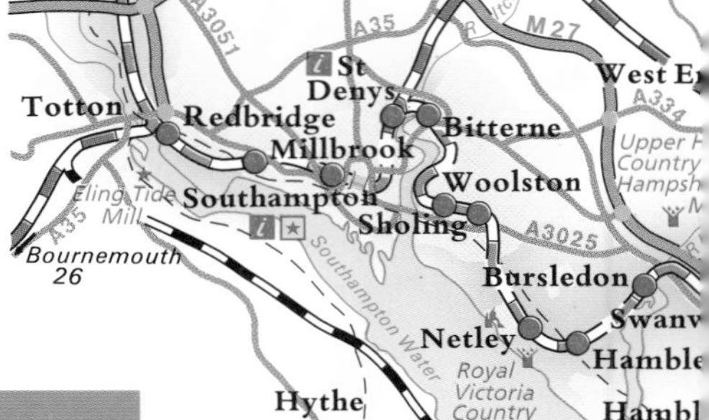

Places to Visit

For information on Salisbury, see pages 88–91; for Southampton, see pages 82–7; for Portsmouth, see pages 78–81.
†*To stop at stations marked thus, change at Southampton.*

MOTTISFONT DUNBRIDGE **Mottisfont Abbey** (NT). Mansion with sections of former Augustinian priory. Drawing room contains fine Rex Whistler painting. Walled rose garden (open Apr–Sep).
ROMSEY **Broadlands**. Home of Lord and Lady Mountbatten. Contains The Mountbatten

continued on page 99

Broadlands: the 18th-century house is set in 400 acres of grounds landscaped by Capability Brown

Southampton – Portsmouth
The train now continues along the steadily widening river valley, with good views westwards towards the wooded valley side. The M27 marks the barrier between open country and Southampton's outer suburbs, but these stay well away to the east as the train drops down to join the main line at **Redbridge**. Eling's tide mill is across the marshlands of the estuary. The train now follows the main line along by the docks into **Southampton**.

Between Southampton and Portsmouth, Salisbury – Portsmouth trains stop only at Fareham, Cosham and Fratton. To stop at other stations, passengers should change at Southampton and take a Wareham – Portsmouth train.

At **St Denys**, the line to Portsmouth branches eastwards. Opened from the 1860s as a more direct link between Southampton and Portsmouth, the line is marked by its series of simple but elegant classical-style stations, several of which survive in fairly original condition. After leaving St Denys, the train soon crosses the Itchen, with splendid views south along the river, and reaches **Bitterne**. The line now follows the curving east shore of the Itchen, elevated above the boatyards, quays and marinas, and turns eastwards and away from the river to **Woolston**. A long cutting leads to the next station, **Sholing**, with its suburban surroundings, and then a stretch of wooded country takes the train to **Netley**.

The ruins of 13th-century Netley Abbey stand to the south-west, overlooking Southampton Water, and near by is the castle, built originally as a Solent fort in 1542 and converted into a house in the 17th century. A short walk southwards along the shore leads to the Royal Victoria Country Park, whose fine, open riverside site contains the chapel of the Royal Victoria Hospital, all that remains of Britain's main military hospital. Inspired by the work of Florence Nightingale in the Crimea, it was built between 1856 and 1863 and was served by its own pier, where the hospital ships unloaded the wounded from various Victorian campaigns, including the Boer War. It also saw sterling service in both World Wars, but in recent times it became increasingly a white elephant, and was demolished from 1966.

The next station is **Hamble**, some way from Hamble village and the River Hamble, and then the line runs through woodland to **Bursledon**, where there are fine river views of the Hamble and its yachts. Crossing the river, the train now runs in and out of woodland to **Swanwick**. Long cuttings take the line to **Fareham**, interrupted by an elevated crossing of the valley of the Meon. Fareham is the junction with the Eastleigh line, and was formerly the junction with the long-closed Meon Valley line that ran northwards to Alton. In 1944 the line achieved lasting fame when Eisenhower's mobile command unit for the Normandy landings was hidden in a siding at Droxford.

From Fareham, the train runs parallel to Portsmouth Harbour, with good views southwards across Portchester, while to the north is Ports

View from Portchester Castle's Norman keep across the Roman walls towards Portsmouth

Down Hill, crowned by a line of 19th-century forts. Leaving **Portchester** station, there is a clear view of the castle, originally a Roman fortress and later a medieval castle. **Cosham** station is buried in Portsmouth's outer suburbia, and then the train joins the main line across Portsea Island to **Portsmouth & Southsea** and its terminus at **Portsmouth Harbour** station.

Wareham – Ramsgate See pages 100-107
Southwick
Ports Down
Waterlooville
Fareham
Portchester
Portchester Castle
Havant
Cosham
Hilsea
Solent Way
Lee-on-Solent
PORTSMOUTH HARBOUR
Gosport
Fratton
Portsmouth & Southsea
SPITHEAD

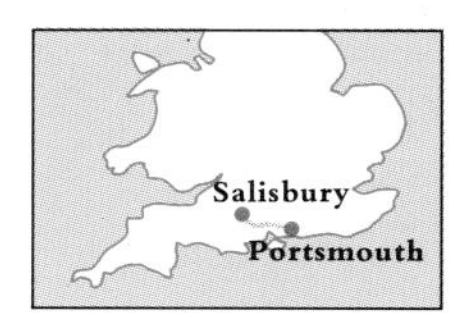

Exhibition and The Imperial Collection of Crown Jewels of the World (open Apr–Sep).
The Hillier Arboretum, Ampfield, 3m NE. Largest collection of trees and shrubs in Britain.
Paultons Park and Bird Gardens, Ower, 3m NW. 100 acres of parkland and gardens at edge of New Forest. Over 200 species of animals, birds and wildfowl. Contains Village Life Museum, Romany Museum, 10-acre lake and working waterwheel (open Mar–Oct).
Romsey Abbey. Norman abbey church. Contains Romsey Psalter, 15th-century illuminated manuscript.

Naval heritage at Portsmouth: HMS Warrior

NETLEY† **Netley Abbey ruins**. Extensive ruins of Cistercian abbey founded 1239 (open summer season and winter wknds only).
Royal Victoria Country Park. Grounds of former Royal Victoria Hospital.
BURSLEDON† **Upper Hamble Country Park and Hampshire Farm Museum**, 1½ m N. Illustrates development of agriculture in Hampshire over last 150 years.
SWANWICK† **Titchfield Abbey**, Titchfield. Surviving gatehouse of 13th-century abbey, converted into a mansion during 16th century (open summer only).
PORTCHESTER† **Portchester Castle**. Roman fortress with 12th-century keep.

Along the South Coast

WAREHAM – RAMSGATE

Tourist Information Centres (★ summer only)
WAREHAM★ Town Hall, East Street (0929) 552740
POOLE Dolphin Shopping Centre or The Quay (0202) 673322
BOURNEMOUTH Westover Rd (0202) 291715
CHRISTCHURCH 30 Saxon Square (0202) 471780
SOUTHAMPTON Above Bar Precinct (0703) 221106
FAREHAM Ferneham Hall, Osborn Rd (0329) 221342
PORTSMOUTH Clarence Esplanade (0705) 832464 or Continental Ferryport★, Rudmore Roundabout (0705) 698111
HAVANT 1 Park Road South (0705) 480024
CHICHESTER St Peter's Market, West St (0243) 775888
WORTHING★ Marine Parade (east of pier) (0903) 210022
HOVE King Alfred Leisure Centre, Kingsway (0273) 720371
BRIGHTON Marlborough House, 54 Old Steine (0273) 23755
LEWES 32 High St (0273) 471600 or 483448 (accommodation)
EASTBOURNE 3 Cornfield Rd (0323) 411400 or 27432 (accommodation)

continued on page 101

Connecting services make it possible to travel for over 220 miles along the coast, from Wareham in Dorset to Ramsgate in east Kent, via Bournemouth, Southampton, Portsmouth, Brighton, Eastbourne and Hastings. Throughout the journey the train is rarely more than a couple of miles from the sea, making this the ideal way to enjoy the landscape, harbours and resorts of the south coast.

The journey is composed of five sections, but interconnecting services make through travel quite practicable, and the changes are always straightforward. The five sections are: Wareham – Portsmouth Harbour, Portsmouth Harbour – Brighton, Brighton – Hastings, Hastings – Ashford, and Ashford – Ramsgate via Dover *or* Ashford – Ramsgate via Canterbury.

Ponies and people refresh themselves in a New Forest stream at Brockenhurst

A cannon at Tudor House, Southampton, presented to the town by Henry VIII

WAREHAM – PORTSMOUTH HARBOUR *67¼ miles*

This journey, via Poole Harbour, Bournemouth, the New Forest, Southampton, and the Solent to Portsmouth Harbour, is fully described on pages 84–6 (for Wareham–Southampton), and pages 98–9 (for Southampton–Portsmouth). (NB Wareham–Portsmouth trains do not stop at all the stations described on pages 84–7.)

Other links to the coast from the main line include the bus connection to the steam railway across the Isle of Purbeck at Swanage (see page 87), the bus connection from Poole to Poole Harbour, the Lymington branch and the Isle of Wight ferry to Yarmouth (see page 84), the bus connection from Southampton to the Royal Pier, for the Isle of Wight ferry to Cowes, and the ferry from Portsmouth Harbour to Ryde Pierhead and the connecting Isle of Wight line to Shanklin (see page 81).

PORTSMOUTH HARBOUR – BRIGHTON *45½ miles*

Portsmouth – Chichester

From Portsmouth Harbour, the train follows the main line to London as far as **Havant**, and then swings east to run parallel to the coast. **Warblington** is on the outer fringes of Havant but the surrounding suburbs are worth penetrating for the ruined castle and pretty 13th-century church set in a delightfully remote and wooded spot on the water's edge, about three quarters of a mile south from the station. There are fine views out across Hayling and Thorney Islands. The next station is **Emsworth**, whose 18th-century port is now a popular sailing centre. Although never far from the coast, the line from here eastwards offers only occasional glimpses of the sea and the tide marshes of Chichester Harbour. This is frustrating, for all the coastal villages, sailing centres and remote moorings are close at hand and easily reached from the extensive network of estuarial footpaths that are accessible from most stations. For example, a short walk south from **Southbourne**, a station apparently serving a residential area, leads directly to the moorings at Prinsted and the Sussex Border Path around Thorney Island. After Southbourne, the train shortly reaches **Nutbourne** and then **Bosham**, where again the station is well to the north of the famous sailing village whose picturesque cottages are clustered round the church. Near **Fishbourne** station is one of Britain's best Roman remains, the palace excavated in the 1960s and famous for its mosaics. From here the great spire of Chichester Cathedral is clearly in view and the train comes into the station passing the remaining section of the former Lavant Valley line that ran northwards to Midhurst.

Mid-2nd-century mosaic at Fishbourne

Chichester

The cathedral, which dates largely from the 11th century, dominates the town and the surrounding flat landscape for miles around and makes an impressive heart for a city that is full of interest. Chichester was a major Roman town but its main attractions today belong to later periods, the medieval hospital, the early 16th-century market cross, the good variety of 18th-century buildings, particularly around the Pallant, and the Festival Theatre. Exploring is made easy by the compact centre and the grid pattern of the streets. Never really a port, despite its coastal position, Chichester was linked to the sea by its canal which arrived in the 1820s, to flourish briefly before becoming the pleasant rural backwater it is now. To the south, are remote villages, little quays and sailing centres in the estuaries of Chichester Harbour and the resorts that line the beaches of Bracklesham Bay and Selsey Bill.

Chichester–Brighton

Leaving Chichester, the train continues straight across the flat coastal plain to **Barnham**, passing to the north the former airfield at Tangmere, a famous front-line RAF station in the Battle of Britain in 1940.

Change at Barnham, or the next station, Ford, for the branches to Bognor Regis and Littlehampton respectively (see page 71).

East of **Ford**, the train crosses the Arun, with a splendid view north up the river valley to Arundel, with its castle, and then reaches the junction with the Arun Valley line that runs north to Horsham and London (see pages 70–1). To the north is the remote and unspoilt flint village of Lyminster, with its fine church that was once part of a Benedictine nunnery. It is one of a number of outstanding churches along this route. Arundel's dramatic skyline is still in view as a backdrop to the first of the many huge greenhouses that line the route eastwards, but views to the south are now limited by the bungalows and salubrious seaside estates of Rustington, West and East Preston and Angmering, served by **Angmering** station. These increasingly dominate the landscape as the train approaches Worthing, pausing briefly at **Goring-by-Sea** and **Durrington-on-Sea** – misnomers, as

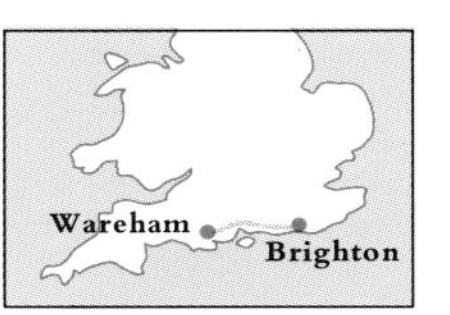

PEVENSEY* Castle Car Park (0323) 761444
BEXHILL-ON-SEA De La Warr Pavilion, Marina (0424) 212023
HASTINGS 4 Robertson Terrace (0424) 718888 or The Fishmarket, Old Town (0424) 722022
RYE 48 Cinque Ports St (0797) 222293
ASHFORD Lower High St (0233) 37311
RAMSGATE Argyle Centre, Queen St (0843) 591086
DOVER Townwall St (0304) 205108
DEAL Town Hall, High St (0304) 369576
SANDWICH* St Peter's Church, Market St (0304) 613565

John Piper's tapestry, Chichester Cathedral

Walks

For Wareham – Portsmouth, see pages 84–6, 98–9.

The North Downs Way (see page 56). The path can be joined at Dover.
The Saxon Shore Way (see page 56). May be joined from Rye, Dover, Deal or Sandwich.
The Solent Way (see page 79). May be joined from Portsmouth.
The South Downs Way (see page 67). The path can be joined from Eastbourne or Falmer stations.

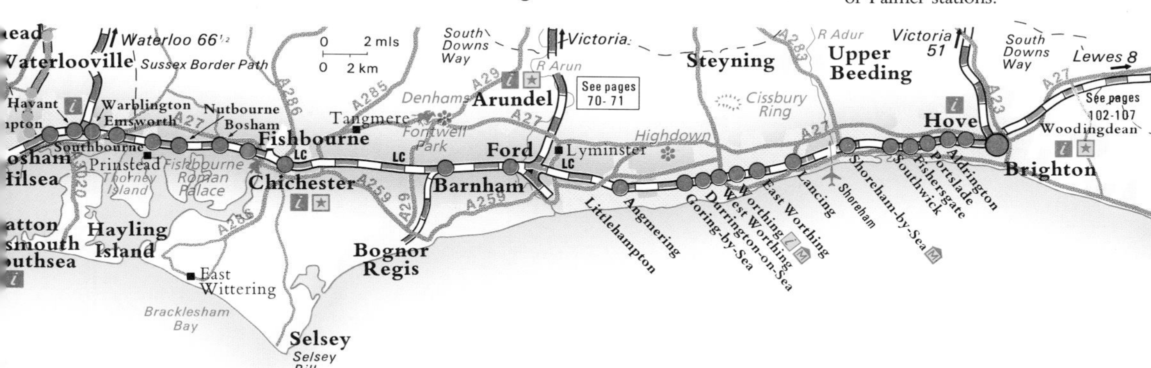

The Sussex Border Path (see page 62). The path can be joined from Rye.
The Wayfarer's Walk (see page 79). The path can be joined from Havant.
The Wealdway (see page 56). The path can be joined from Berwick or Polegate stations.
The Cuckoo Trail. Polegate – Heathfield. Official disused railway footpath, 10 miles.
Rye – Winchelsea, see Walk 3 on page 97.

Places to Visit
WAREHAM – PORTSMOUTH

For information on Wareham, Poole, Bournemouth and Southampton, see pages 82–7; for Netley, Bursledon, Swanwick and Portchester, see pages 98–9.

All the usual seaside attractions await those inclined to stroll along Brighton's Palace Pier

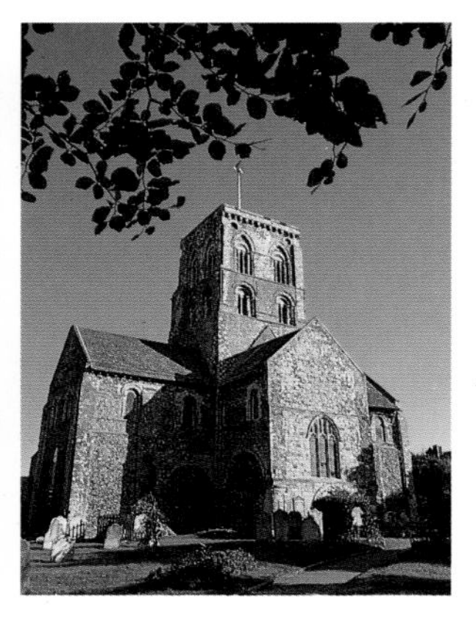

Shoreham's Church of St Mary de Haura

PORTSMOUTH – BRIGHTON

For information on Portsmouth and Havant, see pages 78–81; for Brighton, see pages 67–8.

FISHBOURNE
Fishbourne Roman Palace, Salthill Rd. Largest Roman palace

continued on page 103

the sea is completely hidden by indeterminate suburbia. **West Worthing**, **Worthing** and **East Worthing** all serve a built-up area whose boundaries are inseparable, but Worthing at least has the traditional air of a seaside resort, with the pier and esplanade only a short walk from the big station, which dates largely from 1909. The original 1845 station, modernised in 1911, looking like a two-storey house, can still be seen.

Leaving East Worthing, there is a sudden break in the urban surroundings, allowing a quick view of Sompting Church with its Saxon tower, well placed against the steep side of the South Downs that rise up to Cissbury Ring. Around **Lancing**, the bungalows return but soon after the station there is a magnificent view northwards up the valley of the River Adur, with the extraordinary chapel of Lancing College on a crest in the foreground. Built between 1868 and 1911, this huge and decorative gothic structure is the main feature of an interesting range of Victorian school buildings, dramatically placed against the Downs. By the line is Shoreham airport, with its 1930s terminal, and then the train crosses the Adur with Shoreham beach and the sea to the south and the harbour ahead. Old Shoreham, grouped around its impressive French-style church, can be seen on the river bank to the north, while all around the station, **Shoreham-by-Sea**, is New Shoreham, a town created by the port which has been busy since the Middle Ages and continues to be so. Here again is a splendid and huge church, Flemish in style, full of Norman details and rising high above the houses. From Shoreham station, the line runs beside the Adur estuary and the harbour, a long inlet parallel to the sea, with plenty of maritime views of yachts, ships, docks, cranes and lighthouses, and in the background the powerful presence of the former Portslade power station. A series of stations in quick succession serves the area, **Southwick**, **Fishersgate**, **Portslade** and **Aldrington** and then the train reaches **Hove**, a large station with a covered cab drive outside. Although inseparable from its larger neighbour, Brighton, Hove has a quality of its own, with handsome houses, a pleasant seafront and a good museum. Deep cuttings through the chalk and a tunnel now take the train into **Brighton** (see page 68).

BRIGHTON – HASTINGS
40 miles

Brighton–Eastbourne

Trains for Eastbourne and Hastings soon branch eastwards from the London line, to be carried high above the town and the London Road on

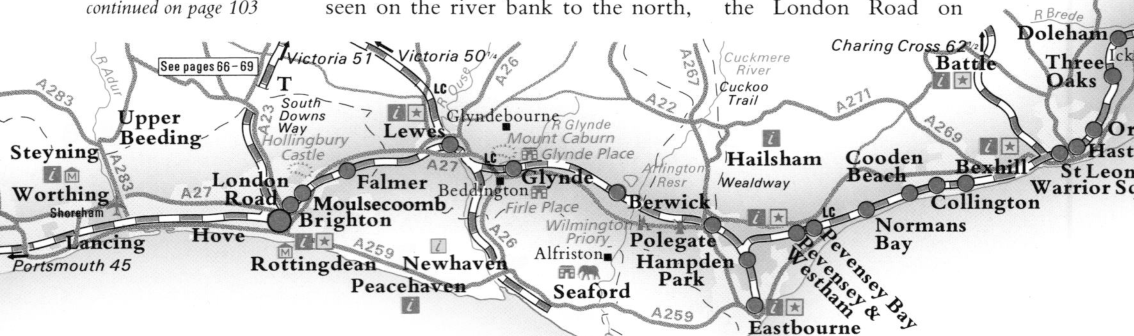

J U Rastrick's great, curving brick viaduct of 1846, whose 27 arches dominate the surrounding landscape. The first station is **London Road**, and then the line runs through cuttings to **Moulsecoomb**, set on the side of the Downs below Hollingbury Castle hillfort. Leaving Brighton behind, the train runs along the side of the Downs to **Falmer**, with good views southwards and, to the north, the buildings of the University of Sussex, initially designed from 1958 by Sir Basil Spence. With the A27 alongside, the line continues along the side of the Downs to enter **Lewes** from the south, passing the remains of the priory. (For Lewes, see page 69.)

Flint-built Glynde Place dates from the 1560s

As it leaves Lewes, the line runs briefly beside the Ouse before branching eastwards away from the Newhaven and Seaford branch (see pages 68–9). The train crosses the River Glynde, with, to the south, Beddingham Church and, to the north, the steep flanks of the Downs leading up to Ranscombe Camp and the hillfort at Mount Caburn. The next station is **Glynde**, serving a little village set in the river valley and surrounded by major country houses. Just to the north is 16th-century Glynde Place, remodelled in the 18th century, with the Palladian church near by. A mile further north is Glyndebourne, famous for its summer season of operas set in the 1934 opera house with its park and lake, while one and a half miles south of Glynde is Firle Place, an 18th-century mansion concealing a Tudor heart.

The train continues along the valley, with the Downs to the south and a more open landscape to the

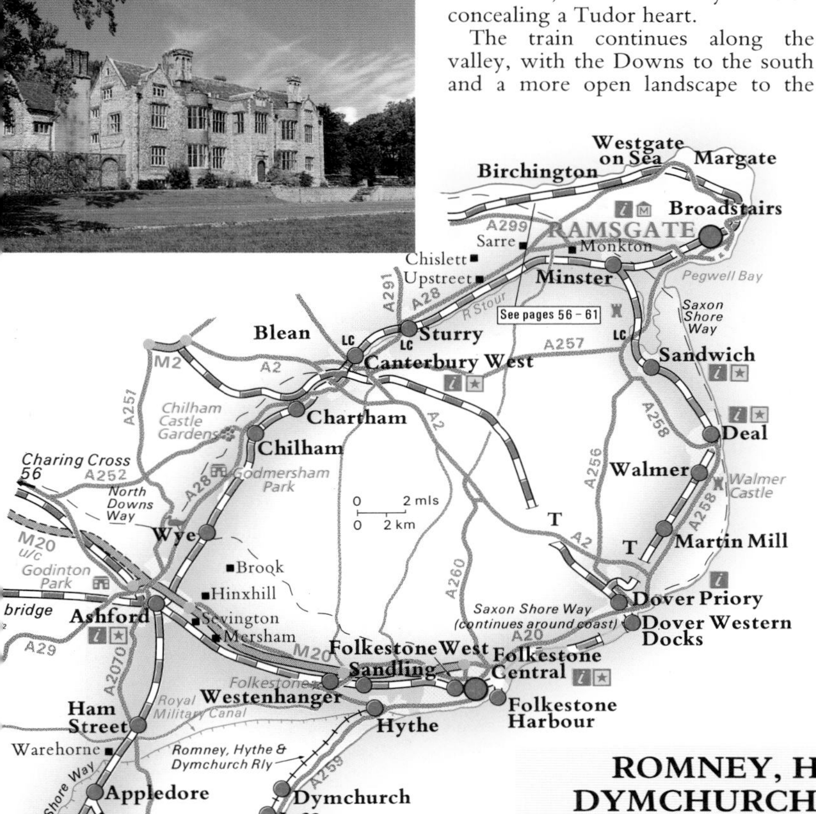

in Britain, with numerous mosaic pavements.
CHICHESTER **District Museum**, 29 Little

Fireback, Anne of Cleves' House Museum, Lewes

London. Local history, archaeology and geology. **Guildhall Museum**, Priory Park. Branch of District Museum in medieval Greyfriars church. Contains local archaeological finds (open Jun–Sep). **Mechanical Music and Doll Collection**, Church Rd, Portfield. Barrel and dance organs, street pianos, musical boxes. Also Victorian china dolls. **Pallant House Gallery**, 9 North Pallant. Queen Anne town house with period rooms, collection of modern British art, and temporary exhibition gallery. **St Mary's Hospital**, St Martin's Sq. Refounded *c.* 1240. Interesting hall with wagon roof.

continued on page 104

ROMNEY, HYTHE & DYMCHURCH RAILWAY

HYTHE – DUNGENESS *13½ miles*

Built in the 1920s as a one-third scale miniature main line, this is the longest and most fully equipped 15-inch gauge railway in the world. It runs across the distinctive landscape of the Romney marshes, linking little holiday resorts with spectacular and isolated beaches. At the end of the line is Dungeness lighthouse and the power station. As well as daytrippers, the trains carry children to and from the local school at New Romney.

The railway has a fleet of steam locomotives, based on the main line express engines of the 1920s and 1930s, which evoke in a particular way the heyday of steam.

Services: Daily from Easter to end September, weekends in March and October
For information: General enquiries (0679) 62353
Access: Nearest BR station Sandling (1½ miles), or bus connection from Folkestone to Hythe

BARNHAM **Fontwell Racecourse** (contact TIC for race meetings). **Denhams**, Fontwell. Unique 20th-century walled garden, planted for overall, all-year interest (open Apr–Nov).
FORD for Arundel, 1¾m N, see page 71.
GORING **Highdown Garden**, 1m N. Gardens laid out in chalk pit. Rock plants, flowering shrubs and daffodils. Good views.
WORTHING **Worthing Museum and Art Gallery**. Archaeology, Downland display, history of Worthing, pictures and large costume collection.
SHOREHAM **Marlipins Museum**. Maritime and local history (open May–Sep).

north, to **Berwick**. The station is one mile north of the village, but the walk is worth it for the murals in the church by Duncan Grant and Vanessa Bell. With their home, Charleston, a few miles to the south, this is true Bloomsbury country. Leaving Berwick with Arlington Reservoir to the north, the line crosses the Cuckmere, with fine views southwards along the valley towards the sea. With Wilmington Priory and the 'Long Man of Wilmington', outlined in the chalk face of the Downs, to the south, the line now curves round to enter **Polegate**, with the Victorian church and the windmill to the south. The former railway line that ran northwards from Polegate is now an official walkway (see Cuckoo Trail, page 102). From Polegate the train turns south towards **Eastbourne**, away from the Downs, passing **Hampden Park** and then running across a flat landscape into Eastbourne.

Eastbourne owes much to the Victorians, including its well-preserved pier

BRIGHTON – HASTINGS

For information on Brighton and Lewes, see pages 67–9; for St Leonards and Hastings, see pages 62–3.

GLYNDE **Charleston Farm House**, Firle. 17th- to 18th-century farmhouse, once home to Vanessa and Clive Bell and Duncan Grant (open Apr–Oct). **Firle Place**. Mainly Georgian house with Tudor core. Contains European and English Old Masters, Sèvres porcelain and fine English and French furniture (open Jun–Sep). **Glynde Place**, Glynde. Elizabethan manor altered in mid-18th century, with pictures, bronzes and historical documents (open Jun–Sep).

continued on page 105

Eastbourne

An extravagant and spacious structure, built in 1866 and later extended, the splendid station is a rich mixture of Italianate and French styles with a powerful clock tower at the centre of its asymmetrical façade. The station is well placed for the town centre, but there is no immediate feeling of the seaside. A walk along Terminus Road will soon lead to familiar 19th-century terraces, the front and the pier. Eastbourne is entirely a 19th-century town, created by the coming of the railway, and it has grown enormously since, spreading along the coast in both directions, and becoming a rather genteel resort. The few older buildings include the church, the 18th-century Manor House, now the Towner Museum, and the Earl of Wilmington's former 18th-century mansion, Compton Place.

Eastbourne – Hastings

The train leaves as it came in, for the

Pevensey Castle was built within Roman Walls soon after the Norman invasion

line to Eastbourne was built as a branch off the original coastal railway constructed in the 1840s by the Brighton, Lewes & Hastings Company. It then swings eastwards across the flat marshland of the Levels with the sea away to the south. The first station is **Pevensey & Westham**, and the ruins of both the Roman fort and the Norman castle are clearly visible to the north, along with two good churches. These all reflect Pevensey's former importance as a strategic harbour and one of the original Cinque ports. William the Conqueror is supposed to have led his Normans ashore here in 1066, but the river is now little more than a stream and the sea has receded to the south.

After Pevensey Bay, the line runs closer to the sea and between **Normans Bay** and **Cooden Beach** it is virtually on the shore, with fine views of the Martello Towers, dunes, groynes, beach huts and boats. The landscape of flat marshland, fragmented by streams and scattered with cows and caravans, has a curious appeal. From Cooden, the town takes over and the train enters **Bexhill**. There is little to be seen of the town from the big station, except its dominant suburbs spreading along the line, but the sea is actually close at hand. Apart from its many 19th-century churches, Bexhill's main claim to fame is the Art Deco De La Warr Pavilion, designed in 1933 by Mendelsohn and Chermayeff and still the heart of the seafront. East of Bexhill, the old-fashioned seaside atmosphere returns, with low cliffs above the stony beach and plenty of old wooden beach huts and then the outskirts of **St Leonards** take over. The train joins the main line from London to enter **Hastings** (see page 63) through a series of cuttings and tunnels.

HASTINGS – ASHFORD

26½ miles

Hastings – Rye

From Hastings station, with its excellent views of the Old Town, the train swings inland to **Ore**, and then, after a tunnel, comes into open country. The next station is **Three Oaks**, remote and hidden in woodland, with a fine timber-framed farmhouse visible to the north-east. Even more remote is **Doleham**, a station with no village at all, and then the line turns eastwards to follow the River Brede, the valley enclosed to the north by a line of wooded hills. To the south is Icklesham, whose church has a fine Norman tower, and then the train crosses the Brede and reaches **Winchelsea**. This medieval town is south of the station, across the marshes. Little can be seen but it is only a short walk and well worth while. Originally planned in the 13th century as a port for the French wine trade, Winchelsea lost its connection with the sea 300 years later when the harbour was closed by silting. What remains is still largely a medieval town, with three impressive town gates, a large but incomplete church and a grid pattern of little streets whose attractive houses make it delightful and easy to explore. The line continues across the marshes to **Rye**, with the ruins of Camber Castle clearly visible to the south.

Rye

Rye is a small town and its attractions are so well known that it tends to suffer from overcrowding. Its charms are far more appealing out of season. The station, set to the north of the town, is an elegant Italianate building, whose formal classicism belies its date of 1851. With the windmill and the River Rother near by, and the town on its hill to the south, it is a natural starting point for visits. Narrow streets lined with pretty houses bring a definite flavour of Italy to the marshlands of Sussex. At its centre is the church, with houses clustered around, and near by is the Ypres Tower, the remains of the 13th-century castle. The steep streets are filled with attractive 17th- and 18th-century buildings, and in between are sudden views out over the marshes and along the Rother to the sea. The river, filled with boats, skirts round the town and then runs straight for two miles to the

View down Mermaid Street, best known of Rye's steep, cobbled streets

Winchelsea's Strand Gate, one of three that survive from the original walled town laid out in medieval times

sea. A Cinque port, Rye still has a busy harbour, with its own little village, to the south, guarded by a Martello Tower. At one time, a branch railway linked the harbour to the main line.

Rye – Ashford

Rye hill dominates the landscape for miles as the train goes north straight across a vast, open marshland to **Appledore**. The Royal Military Canal runs parallel to the west, at the foot of a line of distant hills, and all around is the distinctive flat landscape, cut by innumerable streams and dotted with sheep and wild flowers. Far to the south, the towers of Dungeness lighthouse and power station stand on the horizon, served by a freight-only branch line from Appledore. Appledore village is away to the west, by the canal, but its church can be seen. North of Appledore, the train crosses the canal, with Warehorne's isolated and handsome church close by, and then the marshes are left behind as it enters the woodlands around **Ham Street**. Woods and farmland now accompany the line as it goes north towards **Ashford**, entering the station past the remains of the railway works that gave the town its importance in the 19th century. A busy junction with routes in five directions, Ashford may well come into its own again with the opening of the Channel Tunnel, for it is likely to be the only intermediate terminal for international train services on the English side.

ASHFORD – RAMSGATE

via Canterbury 29½ miles

There are two direct routes from Ashford to Ramsgate, one inland via the Stour valley and Canterbury West, the other round the coast via Folkestone, Dover and Deal (see below). In addition, a third route runs from Canterbury East to Dover, described on pages 59–60, and so travellers can plan an interesting variety of round trips to enjoy to the full the contrasting scenery of east Kent.

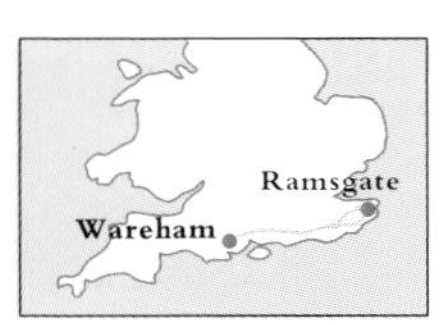

BERWICK **Clergy House**, Alfriston (NT), 2½m S. Mid-14th-century. Exhibition room and garden (open Apr–Oct). **Drusillas Zoo Park**, Alfriston, 1m S. Collection of small mammals, rare breeds, penguins, flamingo lagoon and Japanese garden.
POLEGATE **Polegate Windmill**. Tower mill (1817) with restored machinery (open May–Oct). **Wilmington Priory**, 2½m E. Remains of Benedictine priory with collection of bygone agricultural implements (open Mar–Oct).
EASTBOURNE **Coastal Defence Museum**, Tower 73, King Edward's Pde. Martello Tower displays 19th-century defence equipment (open Etr–Oct). **Eastbourne Redoubt Fortress**, Royal Pde. Extensive fortification built in 1804. Houses Sussex Combined Services Museum (open Etr–Oct). **Lifeboats Museum**, Grand Pde. Displays details of work carried out by Eastbourne lifeboats and RNLI in general. **Towner Art Gallery and Local History Museum**, High St, Old Town. Large collection of 19th- and 20th-century British art.
PEVENSEY & WESTHAM **Old Minthouse**, High St. Built in 1342, interior altered in 1542 by Dr Andrew Borde, then court physician to Henry VIII. Contains 18 rooms, carvings, frescos and small museum. **Pevensey Castle**. 3rd-century Roman fort containing medieval castle.
BEXHILL **Bexhill Museum**, Egerton Rd. Local archaeology, geology, marine biology and social history. **Bexhill Museum of Costume and Social History**, Old Manor Gardens, Old Town. Set in small gardens the museum displays costumes, 1740–1960 accessories, toys and dolls (open late Mar–early Oct).

continued on page 106

Chilham, on the Pilgrims' Way to Canterbury, has retained its medieval heart

Ashford – Canterbury

Leaving the town behind, the train enters the valley of the Stour, crossing the river into a landscape of rolling farmland, with views to the east of distant church towers at Hinxhill and Brook, and ahead to the little town of **Wye**. The line passes near the former racecourse shortly before the station, with the river's meandering route near by. Wye is just to the east, a compact and decorative little Georgian town grouped round the church and the college, whose 15th-century heart has been progressively expanded in more recent times to fulfil the needs of the agricultural students. A crown carved into the chalk Downs can be seen away to the east. From Wye to Chilham the train continues along the valley, cutting through the steadily steepening flanks of the Downs. Set in this attractive landscape is 18th-century Godmersham Park, a handsome classical house with Jane Austen associations. As the train approaches **Chilham**, the castle and church can be seen standing high to the west among the woodlands, a tantalising introduction to a village that still has a strong medieval atmosphere. The station is to the east, down in the valley. Flooded gravel pits and lakes flank the line as it runs through fruit and hop fields to **Chartham**, whose grand 13th-century church stands near the station. Ahead is Canterbury, with the cathedral clearly in view as the train enters the city's outskirts. Near by, curving away to the south, is the old brick viaduct that carried the long-closed line to Folkestone. **Canterbury West** is a classical station of 1846, set well to the north of the city centre, but offering fine views of the cathedral.

Canterbury – Ramsgate

From Canterbury, the line continues by the Stour to **Sturry**, and then

Canterbury Cathedral dominates the surrounding ancient buildings and narrow streets

HASTINGS – ASHFORD

For information on Hastings, see pages 62–3.

WINCHELSEA **Winchelsea Museum**, Court Hall. Restored 14th-century court hall housing collections illustrating history of this Cinque port (open May–Sep).
RYE **Lamb House** (NT), West St. 18th-century house, home of Henry James from 1898 until his death in 1916. Attractive garden (open Apr–Oct). **Rye Museum**, Ypres Tower. 13th-century, 3-storeyed fortification containing collections of Cinque port material, medieval and other pottery from Rye kilns, and local history (open Etr–Oct). **Rye Town Model**, Son et Lumière, Strand Quay. New heritage centre illustrating history of Rye using sound and light show, and town model (open daily Etr–Nov).
ASHFORD **Ashford Local History Museum**, Central Library, Church St. **Godinton Park**, 2½m NW. Gabled house dating from 1628, with fine panelling and carving, portraits, furniture and china. 18th- and 19th-century garden layout with topiary work (open Etr wknd and Jun–Sep). **Intelligence Corps Museum**, Templar Barracks. Items concerning the corps from both world wars and up to the present day (open by appointment only).

ASHFORD – RAMSGATE

For information on Dover and Canterbury, see pages 56–61. For Ashford, see above.

WYE **Wye National Nature Reserve.** Bird sanctuary.
CHILHAM **Chilham Castle Gardens**. Overlooking River Stour. Bird of Prey Centre (open Apr–Oct).
FOLKESTONE **Eurotunnel Information Centre** (2m). Models, videos, etc covering design and construction of Channel Tunnel.

continued on page 107

enters a very different landscape, with the river winding its way across flat marshland and alongside huge lakes. With the Stour close by, the train passes the remote villages of Upstreet and Sarre, with the Norman tower of Chislet's church away to the north, and then the line swings east to follow the river's course across the marshes towards its estuary. Monkton is to the north, and to the south is the huge, open landscape of the Levels. The next station is **Minster**, with the massive Norman and 13th-century church and the adjacent abbey close by. Just east of the station is the junction with the coastal line to Ramsgate. From here the marshland is left behind, with the train running through fruit fields and into a long cutting that leads to Ramsgate. Pegwell Bay is to the south, out of sight, and there is no view of Ramsgate itself. For Ramsgate, see pages 59–60.

ASHFORD – RAMSGATE
via Dover 43 miles

Ashford – Dover

South from Ashford, the line runs through an open landscape, following the course of the East Stour River. Sevington's remote church is to the north, followed by Mersham's, with its massive west window, close by the line. This area has a number of fine 17th- and 18th-century farms and manors, but none is as striking as the remains of the large 14th-century fortified manor beside the track at **Westenhanger**. This is the station for Folkestone racecourse, which is just to the south. The landscape now becomes hillier and more wooded as the line cuts its way through the Downs. At **Sandling** station the track of the former branch to Hythe can still be seen.

A tunnel and cuttings take the line into Folkestone, passing the English terminal of the Channel Tunnel, with freight exchange sidings and the massive road vehicle shuttle terminal. (See also page 113.) **Folkestone West** is the next station and from here eastwards, the track is elevated high above the town with fine views southwards. The train crosses the high, curving Foord viaduct, carried 100 feet in the air on 19 brick arches, and on its way out of the town passes the junction with the branch line that takes boat trains steeply down through the town and over a viaduct across the harbour to Folkestone Harbour station. The train enters a tunnel, and then emerges on to a dramatic stage, with white cliffs forming the backdrop and the sea the foreground. The line runs along the base of the cliffs, in and out of cuttings and tunnels, railway theatre at its best. The two long tunnels, Abbot's Cliff and Shakespeare Cliff, were massive engineering works during the building of the line in the 1840s, and the journey along beside the sea into Dover is a fitting memorial to the ambitions of the Victorian railway builders. The train now passes below Dover's Western Heights, and swings north away from the branch leading to the Western Docks station. Another tunnel leads to **Dover Priory** station. For Dover, see pages 56–61.

Dover – Ramsgate

The line runs northwards up the valley, with Dover hidden from view before curving sharply eastwards away from the London line. From the curve there are splendid views of Dover castle, away to the south. Another tunnel and a cutting take the line away from the hills and into a more open landscape. The next station is **Martin Mill** and then the train runs through farmland to **Walmer**, where the station is quite a way west of the sea and the 16th-century castle, the official residence of the Warden of the Cinque Ports. There is no town as such, for Walmer is really an extension of Deal. Approaching **Deal** station, the line comes nearer to the sea, and the delightful front is only a short walk away. Fishing boats are drawn up on the stony beach beside the small pier, and along the front are pretty houses painted in soft colours, the famous Time Ball tower and, to the south, the castle. Deal represents the traditional English seaside at its best.

Leaving Deal with Sandown Castle and the sea on the distant horizon to the east, the line crosses the flat marshland of the Lydden valley to **Sandwich**. To the west are the rather unexpected remains of the once extensive Kentish mining industry. Far to the north is a distant view of Ramsgate. Developed for the wool trade in the 13th century, Sandwich was once a Cinque port. However, silting closed the harbour in the 17th century, and the town today is far smaller than it was in the Middle Ages. What remains is still a medieval town and its narrow streets and old churches give it a particular, unspoilt quality, rare in Britain.

From Sandwich the train follows the Stour, passing a fine windmill and the site of the Roman fort at Richborough Castle to the west, while to the east is Richborough Harbour, hidden by factories and the dramatic cooling towers of the power station. By the power station is a more modern windmill, designed to generate electricity. The train now crosses the Stour and Minster marshes before joining the Ashford–Ramsgate via Canterbury line just east of **Minster** station. Far to the east is the mouth of the Stour, the traditional landing site of St Augustine in AD 597.

Fishing boats at Deal

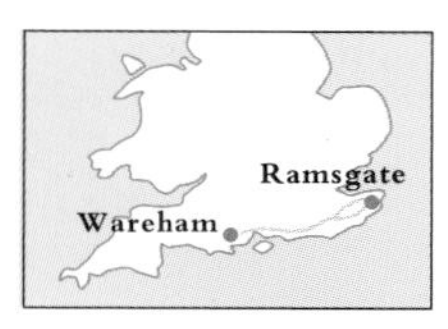

Museum and Art Gallery, Grace Hill. Town's history, also natural history, etc.
Martello Tower.

WALMER **Walmer Castle**. Built by Henry VIII. Official residence of the Lord Warden of the Cinque Ports (open all year, but closed when Lord Warden is in residence).

DEAL **Deal Archaeological Collection**, Deal Library, Broad St. Archaeological finds from the Deal area spanning 5,000 years.
Deal Castle. Built by Henry VIII, with a massive central citadel. Contains exhibits of Iron Age weapons, early pottery and relics of Deal's history.
Maritime and Local History Museum, 22 St George's Rd. Exhibits of local boats, model sailing ships and bygones (open daily spr BH–Sep). **Time-Ball Tower**, Victoria Pde. 4-storey museum of maritime communication, built in 1821 with working time-ball (open spr BH–Sep).

SANDWICH **The Guildhall Museum**. Collection of ancient and interesting items.
The Precinct Toy Collection, 38 Harnet St. Doll's houses, Noah's arks, dolls and clockwork toys (open Etr–Oct).
Richborough Roman Castle, 1½m N. The conquering Roman army landed here in AD 43. Massive stone walls built in 3rd century to combat Saxon sea attacks.

Along the North Downs

READING – TONBRIDGE *66 miles*

This is one of the most interesting and varied cross-country journeys in southern England, with much of its route running along below the North Downs from Guildford to Tonbridge. The wooded slopes and chalk scarps form a dramatic background to the north, while to the south the landscape rolls away towards Sussex and the Weald. There are plenty of small towns and villages to break the journey, and from several there is easy access to the North Downs Way.

Running beneath the escarpment of the North Downs

See pages 78-81

Tourist Information Centres
READING Town Hall, Blagrave St (0734) 566226
FARNBOROUGH The Library, Pinehurst (0252) 513838
GUILDFORD Guildford House Gallery, 155 High St (0483) 444007
TONBRIDGE Tonbridge Castle, Castle St (0732) 770929

Walks
The Kennet and Avon Canal (see page 18). The towpath can be joined from Reading.
The North Downs Way (see page 56). The path can be joined from Wanborough, Guildford, Shalford, Dorking or Betchworth stations (see Walk 5 on page 97).
The Wealdway (see page 56). The path can be joined from Tonbridge station.

Places to Visit

For information on Reading, Winnersh and Wokingham, see pages 14–15, 92–3;

continued on page 109

The windmill on Reigate Heath, used as a church

There are few direct services from Reading to Tonbridge, and so most journeys involve a simple change of trains at Redhill. Some trains do not stop at all stations between Reading and Redhill.

Reading – Guildford
From Reading, trains follow the Waterloo–Reading route as far as **Wokingham** (see pages 92–3). The line then runs straight through a landscape of woods and farmland to **Crowthorne**. From here, the line acquires a definite military flavour, with Wellington College in the woods to the east and Sandhurst to the south. The line is flanked by pine and heathland as it approaches **Sandhurst**, and then it swings into the open valley of the Blackwater with the Royal Military Academy, which was established here early in the 19th century, visible to the east. **Blackwater** is the next station, with York Town, named after the Grand Old Duke of York, to the east. Passing under the M3, the train follows the Blackwater valley south to **Farnborough North** and **North Camp** with the military presence all around. The airfield is well away to the west, out of sight. A series of lakes flanks the line, which then crosses the Basingstoke Canal and swings away to the east, leaving Aldershot to the west. **Ash**'s church is by the line and then, after the station, the distinctive military landscape finally gives way to more open countryside. The track is elevated to **Wanborough**, a station a long way from its attractive brick and flint village on the side of the Hog's Back to the south, and there are fine views northwards towards Fox Hills and Normandy. After Wanborough, Guildford Cathedral comes into view, its bulky shape clear on its mound. A long cutting then takes the line into **Guildford** (see page 79).

Guildford – Redhill
Leaving Guildford, the train tunnels under the Downs and runs beside the Wey Navigation, passing a pretty lock, before branching eastwards to cross the river and its watermeadows, with the spire of Shalford's 1846 church in the background. **Shalford** serves a village whose early 19th-century cottages have managed to maintain an independent quality, despite Guildford's proximity, and then the line runs straight to **Chilworth**, a station isolated from its village. Chilworth Manor with its 17th-century garden is up on the hillside to the north and above it is the church, dramatically placed high above the valley. The train now curves round Albury and Shere, with their churches and Albury Park hidden by woods, but there are excellent open views southwards. A high embankment takes the line above **Gomshall**'s Victorian cottages, and to the south is Abinger Hammer, a main-road village with a fine range of buildings. East of Gomshall, the wooded tops of Hackhurst Downs and White Downs rise high above the line and then long cuttings take the train towards Dorking.

Dorking West is the first of the town's three stations but the next, **Dorking Deepdene**, is the best placed for the town centre. Dorking's best feature is probably its meandering main street, lined by buildings of varied age and interest. Leaving Deepdene, the train crosses the London line, with Dorking's main station just to the north, and then the steep flank of Box Hill dominates the line as it crosses the Mole. The Downs are now close at hand, their steep, wooded sides broken by the great white scars of former quarries. **Betchworth** has a good cottage-style station, well to the north of its village, and then the line moves away from the Downs for its approach to **Reigate**. Colley Hill rises to the north of this typical suburban Surrey town, whose best features are its large church and its 1728 arcaded town hall. Little remains of the castle, but the former priory contains a fine *trompe-l'œil* painted staircase of 1703. Reigate now spreads inseparably into **Redhill**, a town that barely existed before the coming of the railway. The approach is marked by the spiky spires of Redhill's Victorian churches, and then the train curves sharply round to enter the station. Some trains terminate here, but Tonbridge trains generally leave from the same platform.

Betchworth
Reigate
Redhill
Nutfield
Godstone
Salfords
Victoria 21
M25
A25
A22
A23
A217
M23
R Mole
2 mls
2 km
Victoria – Brighton
See pages 60-69
Horsham
Brighton 30
Victoria
Oxted
Charing Cross – Hastings
See pages 62-63
Crowhurst
East Grinstead
Uckfield
Edenbridge
R Eden
Penshurst
Hever
Chiddingstone
Bough Beech Reservoir
Penshurst Place
Hildenborough
Charing Cross 29½
Leigh
A21
A227
A26
Ashford 26½
TONBRIDGE
Wealdway
Hastings 33

Redhill–Tonbridge

The Tonbridge line branches eastwards just south of Redhill station and the train crosses a more open landscape to **Nutfield**. The Downs are now well to the north, but on the lower hills the Tudor-style façade of Nutfield Priory, a heavy mansion built in the 1870s, can clearly be seen. The line passes under the M23 and then runs through cuttings and a tunnel towards **Godstone** station, which is so far south of its village that its own community has grown up around it. The landscape is now more open, with views south towards East Grinstead and north towards the now distant line of the Downs. To the south is Crowhurst's pretty church, with its simple bell turret and then the train crosses over the East Grinstead and Uckfield lines, the latter in a cutting that breaks dramatically into the tunnel below.

The next station is **Edenbridge**, well to the north of the town centre, and from here there is a long straight run to **Penshurst** through a rolling landscape dotted with oast houses, old farms and cottages. The River Eden runs to the south and the castles at Hever and Chiddingstone stand close by it, but hidden from view. To the north are the curving walls of Bough Beech Reservoir. Penshurst station, like so many on this route, is well away from its village and it is a two-mile walk south from Penshurst station to Penshurst Place. A long cutting leads from Penshurst to **Leigh**, where the station is, for once, well placed for the pretty village. The line is then elevated with good views southwards over the Medway and its lakes and watermeadows. The train then crosses the river and runs above and beside it towards its terminus at **Tonbridge**. A short walk north from the station along the High Street leads to the best part of Tonbridge, where the castle ruins stand overlooking the river. The Medway is navigable from Tonbridge eastwards and so the old quays are often crowded with boats. Rowing boats can be hired by the castle gardens.

Tonbridge: a pleasant river walk along the Medway gives good views of the castle ruins

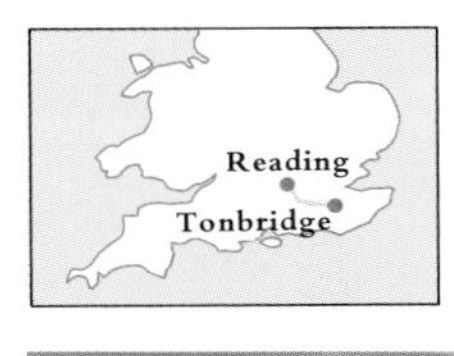

Penshurst Place, famous for its fine chestnut-beamed Great Hall

for Guildford, see pages 78–9; for Dorking, see pages 76–7; for Tonbridge, see page 62.

ASH For **Aldershot** see page 87.
CHILWORTH **Albury Park**, Albury, 2m E. Country mansion by Pugin (open May–Sep).
REIGATE **Priory Museum**, Bell St. House of 1235 converted into Tudor mansion, of which the hall fireplace is the finest surviving relic. Painted staircase by Verrio (1710). House now used as a school, with small museum with changing displays (museum open Weds all year).
Old Windmill, Reigate Heath. 220-year-old mill converted into a church in 1882. Restored 1964.
PENSHURST **Penshurst Place**, 2m S. Birthplace of Sir Philip Sidney in 1554. Chestnut-beamed Great Hall is one of the oldest and finest in England. State rooms splendidly furnished. Extensive Tudor gardens and toy museum (open Apr–Oct).

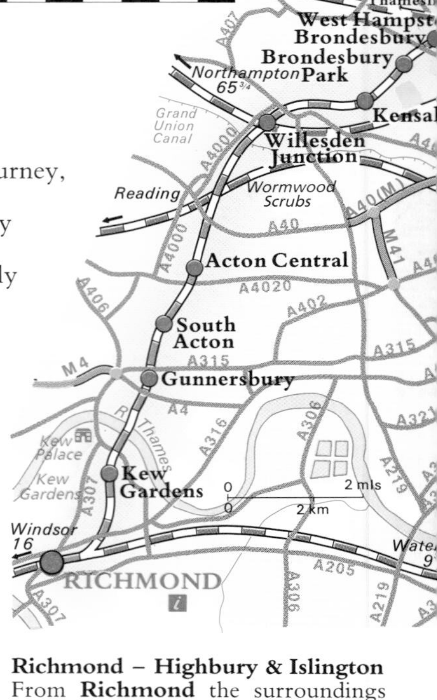

The North London Line

RICHMOND – NORTH WOOLWICH *22½ miles*

The Thames is at the start and finish of this unusual journey, whose semi-circular route through some of the less familiar regions of north London gives ample opportunity for the leisurely study of back gardens and the varied styles of the capital's domestic architecture. From the early 19th-century Georgian terraces of Brondesbury and Canonbury to Dockland's post-Modernism, all periods are well represented.

Tourist Information Centres
London Tourist Board
26 Grosvenor Gdns
(071) 730 3488
Richmond Old Town Hall, Whittaker Ave
(081) 940 9125

Richmond Park is home to red and fallow deer

Places to Visit
RICHMOND **Ham House.** A 17th-century house containing superb Charles II and early Georgian furnishings, and a portrait gallery.
KEW GARDENS **Kew Gardens (Royal Botanic Gardens).** The gardens cover 300 acres and contain over 50,000 different living plants. The Palm House, an early example of glass and wrought iron, was added in 1848, and the Chinese Pagoda, standing ten storeys high (163ft), in 1761.
Kew Palace. Built in 1631. Opened to the public in 1899, it remains much as it was in George III's time (open daily Apr–Sep).
Queen Charlotte's Cottage. Used by the royal family as a summer house and a place to take tea. The interior is designed to give the impression of a tent (open Apr–Sep, wknds & BH only).

continued on page 111

This route is an important slice of history, keeping alive the memory of one of London's more obscure, but remarkably successful, independent Victorian railway companies. Between 1850 and the 1870s the North London Railway, in conjunction with other, and generally larger, companies, opened a line from Richmond in Surrey to Blackwall, with a branch to an impressive terminus at Broad Street in the City of London, adjacent to Liverpool Street. The importance of this line's route, and the secret of its success, was that it crossed, and had connections with, all the major companies' lines out of London north of the Thames. These large and powerful railways were therefore, to some extent, dependent upon the little North London for access to London's expanding docklands, east of the Isle of Dogs.

Successful also on its own terms as a passenger-carrying railway, the North London remained independent until 1922, when it was finally absorbed into the group that was to become the LMS. In the early 1980s the grand but little used Broad Street terminus was finally closed, and from 1985 the route was extended to a new terminus at North Woolwich, incorporating the remains of another of London's historic independent companies, the North Woolwich Railway. Today, Network SouthEast's modern trains provide a vital link to the Docklands and an unusual way to explore North London.

Richmond – Highbury & Islington
From **Richmond** the surroundings are pleasant and suburban to **Kew Gardens**, an elegant station with decorative ironwork and a pub on the platform. The Royal Botanic Gardens are close by. The elevated line then crosses the Thames, with a view westwards to the tall chimney of the Kew Bridge Steam Museum, housed in the former waterworks. From **Gunnersbury** the line runs between typical railway terraces through **South Acton** and **Acton Central** passing Wormwood Scrubs, to the east, and crossing the Grand Union Canal before reaching **Willesden Junction**. Another selection of back gardens leads to **Kensal Rise** and **Brondesbury Park**, with its smart station, and then there are some fine early 19th-century Georgian terraces beside the line. After **Brondesbury** and **West Hampstead**, with the line flanked by trees and Hampstead's handsome houses, the train comes to **Finchley Road & Frognal**, and then a tunnel takes it under Hampstead to **Hampstead Heath** station.

Kew Gardens: the Rose Garden and Palm House, an early example of glass and wrought iron

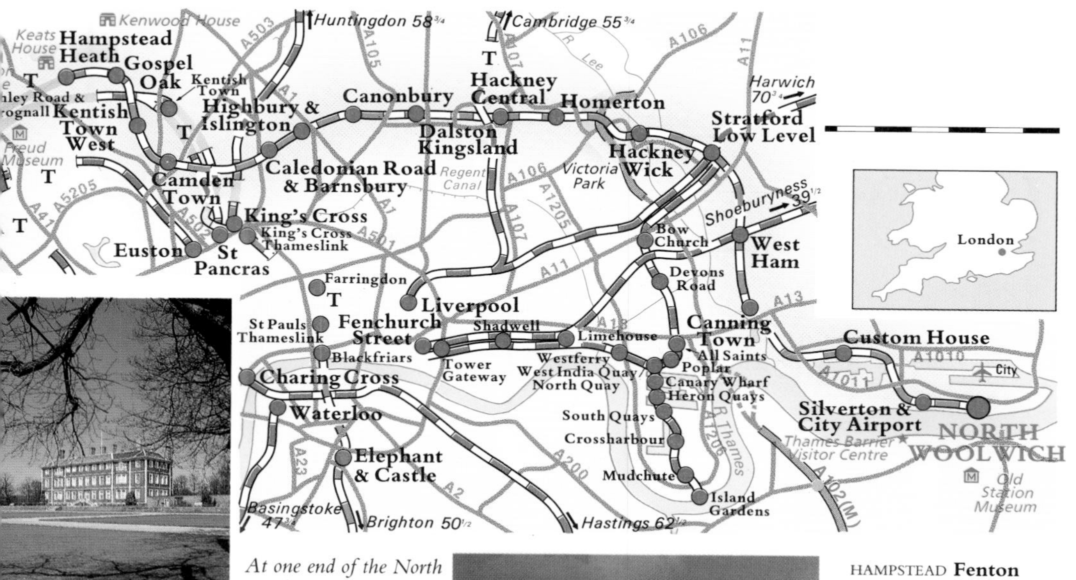

At one end of the North London Line, Ham House in Richmond (left) and, at the other, the Thames Barrier (right)

There are good views northwards across the Heath to Parliament Hill. From **Gospel Oak** the line curves round on a long, brick viaduct to **Kentish Town West**, and then swings east, with the giant egg cups of TVam's studios just to the south and, on the far horizon, the Telecom Tower. **Camden Road** is a large and decorative station, and then there is a good view of the towers and pinnacles of St Pancras, away to the south. After **Caledonian Road & Barnsbury**, a long, brick-lined cutting leads to **Highbury & Islington**.

Canonbury – North Woolwich

Canonbury is overlooked by smarter, early 19th-century terraces, and then the remains of the line to the former Broad Street terminus can be seen to the south just before **Dalston Kingsland** station. **Hackney Central** is elevated, with a good view of the surrounding towers, but **Homerton** is more domestic, with back gardens by the line. To the south is Victoria Park, and to the north the Lea valley, and then from **Hackney Wick** the rising towers of the Canary Wharf development can be seen far to the south. The train crosses the Lea Navigation and the River Lea and then comes to **Stratford Low Level**, where there is a connection with the Docklands Light Railway line to Island Gardens.

The next station is **West Ham**, opened in the late 1970s, and from here the route follows the former North Woolwich Railway south to **Canning Town** and then along beside the Royal Victoria Dock to **Custom House**. Now used for sailing and pleasure boating, the Royal Victoria, opened in 1855, was the first of the three Royal Docks. Regeneration is under way, and the Docklands City Airport is now beside the Royal Albert Dock, served by the new station called **Silvertown & City Airport.** The train now passes Tate & Lyle's sugar refinery, with its stylish Art Deco central clock tower, and then comes into the **North Woolwich**

terminus. Adjacent is the original 1854 Italianate station which now houses the Great Eastern Railway Museum. The Woolwich ferry is a short walk away, and there are fine river views across to Woolwich, west to the Thames Barrier and east to the marshlands that flank Gallions Reach.

Thameslink

Thameslink is a new service that runs through the heart of London via an old, recently re-opened freight line, to connect places north of the Thames such as Bedford, Luton and St Albans to destinations south such as Brighton, Bromley, Croydon, Epsom, Guildford, Sevenoaks and Sutton.

In London, passengers can join Thameslink at Blackfriars, St Paul's Thameslink, Farringdon and Kings Cross Thameslink. Monday–Friday peak services also run from Moorgate, Barbican and St Pancras, and there is an off-peak service from London Bridge. Thameslink also serves Gatwick and Luton airports, whilst at Kings Cross there is a direct connection with London Underground's Piccadilly Line to Heathrow.

Apart from the obvious convenience of Thameslink, the trains offer passengers exciting and unusual views of the City of London and the Thames from Blackfriars Bridge as they cross the heart of London.

HAMPSTEAD **Fenton House** (NT), Windmill Hill. A William and Mary mansion built about 1693, set in a walled garden. Display of furniture, Oriental and European porcelain. Benton Fletcher collection of early keyboard instruments. Summer concerts (open Mar–Oct).
Freud Museum The former wartime home of Sigmund Freud, housing a museum devoted to the history and development of psycho-analysis. It contains many of his personal effects, including his now famous couch.
Keats House. The two Regency houses of John Keats and his lover and nurse Fanny Brawne have now been converted into one building to form a museum devoted to the poet's life (open all year, Wed–Sun).
Kenwood, Iveagh Bequest. Fine collection of paintings.
NORTH WOOLWICH **The Museum of Artillery in the Rotunda**. A rotunda that once stood in St James's Park houses collections of guns, muskets, rifles and artillery.
North Woolwich Old Station Museum, Pier Road. Displays history of Great Eastern Railway, collection of rolling stock, railway ephemera, etc.
Royal Artillery Regimental Museum. The old Military Academy houses the story of the Royal Regiment of Artillery.
Thames Barrier Visitors Centre. Built to prevent the possibility of disastrous flooding, the Thames Barrier is the world's largest movable flood barrier, spanning a third of a mile.

CROSSING THE CHANNEL

The grand age of the Boat Train which linked London with other capitals in Europe is long gone, but it paved the way for the cross-Channel services available today

SOUTHERN ENGLAND IS PARTICUlarly well served by ports offering regular cross-Channel services to the Channel Islands, France, Belgium and Holland. The list includes Weymouth, Poole, Portsmouth, Newhaven, Folkestone, Dover, Ramsgate, Sheerness and Harwich. All can be reached by Network SouthEast and in most places the station is near the ports. The number of ports, and the many routes they offer, are in part a legacy of late 19th-century competition between independent railway companies keen to gain a share of the lucrative cross-Channel freight and passenger traffic. Indeed, the development of regular cross-Channel services in the Victorian era was largely due to the railways, with many companies seeing their ports and their steamers as a natural extension of their routes on the British mainland. During this period, for example, the London & South Western Company was responsible for the great expansion of Southampton and Portsmouth, while Newhaven, and the prestigious service to Paris via Dieppe, was very much the jewel in the London, Brighton & South Coast's crown. The proliferation of services from the Kent ports of Folkestone, Dover and Ramsgate was the result of competition between the London, Chatham & Dover and South Eastern Companies, who were virtually in a state of war until their final merger in 1899. Their intense rivalry led to the creation of some other ports long since abandoned – and whose commercial viability must have been questionable even at the time – for example, Port Victoria at the far eastern tip of the Isle of Grain. The expanding holiday trade during the Edwardian era, marked by the growth of resorts such as Deauville and Le Touquet, encouraged further development, but the major boost in cross-Channel services really came from the experience of World War I, when vast quantities of men and materials had to be moved regularly to and from France. Dover's dominance as the major cross-Channel port dates from that period.

The 1920s and the 1930s were the golden era of train travel, and cross-Channel services boomed accordingly, with a fleet of fast and efficient railway steamers linking London with the capitals of Europe. These were the days of luxury trains such as the *Orient Express*, when crossing the Channel was but one stage in an interconnected railway journey between London and Istanbul. In some cases the trains actually went on the ship. The *Night Ferry*'s specially built Wagons-Lits ran directly between London and Paris and Brussels, with the sleeping cars crossing overnight on the train ferry while their passengers slept. Most famous of all was the *Golden Arrow*, a luxury day service linking Paris and London via Dover.

Today, boat trains are a rarity, and those 'Channel Trains' that run regularly from Victoria to Newhaven, Folkestone and Dover lack the glamour of their famous predecessors. However, Network SouthEast still runs many services to the Channel ports that connect with the ferry, hovercraft, Seacat and jetfoil routes operated by Sealink, P&O, Hoverspeed and others, making possible a wide choice of day, weekend and longer visits to French ports. A variety of day trip packages, involving combined rail and ferry or hovercraft tickets for a discount price, are available and the best of these allow visitors several hours in France for shopping, exploring, eating or just enjoying the atmosphere of the country.

Many trains are also timetabled to form the first part of a through service by rail and sea to the capitals of Europe. Journeys from London to Paris and Brussels are run on a regular daily basis, and from these it is possible to travel on by train to faraway destinations such as Rome, Madrid, Berlin, Copenhagen or Budapest on scheduled services. Many daily international services depart from the ports of Oostende, Calais and Hoek van Holland to destinations as far away as Berlin and Moscow.

THE CHANNEL TUNNEL

WHEN IT OPENS IN JUNE 1993, THE Channel Tunnel will revolutionise cross-Channel travel. The all-rail, twin-bore tunnel from Folkestone to Sangatte, near Calais, will create a fixed link between the road and rail networks of Britain and France, facilitating travel and trade within the single European market. The tunnel will be used both by a continuous service of special shuttle trains carrying cars, coaches and freight vehicles from the British to the French terminals, and by through, express passenger trains from London and other British cities to Paris and other European destinations.

The best way to understand the complex technology and the extraordinary implications of the largest privately funded engineering project this century, and to see how a Victorian dream is being fulfilled, is to visit the Eurotunnel Exhibition Centre near Folkestone. Models, videos, etc cover all aspects of the design, construction and use of the Tunnel. Combined rail and entry tickets are available, and there is a regular bus service from Folkestone Central station to the Centre included in the ticket.

For information on opening times etc, telephone (0303) 270111.

CHANNEL PORTS AND SERVICES

Weymouth
Trains from Waterloo
Condor Weymouth
Hydrofoil services to the Channel Islands and St Malo (March–October)
Tel (0305) 761551
Westward Ferries
Service to Cherbourg
Day trips available
Tel (0305) 761773

Poole
Trains from Waterloo
Brittany Ferries
Service to Cherbourg (summer only)
Tel (0202) 666466
British Channel Island Ferries
Service to Guernsey and Jersey
Tel (0202) 681155

Portsmouth
Trains from Waterloo
P&O European Ferries
Services to Cherbourg and Le Havre
Day trips available
Tel (0705) 827677
Brittany Ferries
Services to St Malo and Caen
Tel (0705) 751833
Hoverspeed Seacat
Service to Cherbourg
Day trips available
Tel (0705) 755111

Newhaven
Trains from Victoria
Sealink Dieppe Ferries
Service to Dieppe
Day trips available
Tel (0233) 647047

Folkestone
Trains from Victoria
Sealink British Ferries
Service to Boulogne
Day trips available
Tel (0233) 647047

Dover
Trains from Victoria and Charing Cross
Sealink British Ferries
Service to Calais
Day trips available
Tel (02337) 647047
P&O European Ferries
Services to Boulogne, Calais, Oostende and Zeebrugge
Day trips available
Tel (0304) 203388
Hoverspeed
Services to Boulogne and Calais. Day trips available
Tel (0304) 240241

Ramsgate
Trains from Victoria and Charing Cross
Sally Line
Service to Dunkerque
Day trips available
Tel (0843) 595522

Sheerness
Trains from Victoria
Olau Ferries
Service to Vlissingen
Tel (0795) 666666

Harwich
Trains from Liverpool Street
Sealink British Ferries
Service to Hoek van Holland
Day trips available
Tel (0233) 647047
Also, services to Hamburg, Esjberg and Gothenburg *(Scandinavian Seaways)*
Tel (0255) 241234

I SPY ON THE JOURNEY

LOOKING OUT OF THE WINDOW IS ONE OF THE GREAT PLEASURES OF train travel, something that puts it apart from any other form of transport. With a viewpoint high enough to see over walls and hedges and a continually changing panorama as the train makes its way through town or country, there is time to notice an infinite variety of small details. Listed below is a selection of things that can be seen from the windows of Network SouthEast's trains. They are grouped in categories, first those related to the railway, second buildings, and third, features of the landscape. Some are common, some rare, and so each has been given a value to give window-gazing a competitive edge.

HOW FAST IS THE TRAIN GOING?

Look out for mileposts on the offside track, at quarter mile intervals. Count the seconds between two quarter mile posts and divide that number into 900. The answer is the speed in miles per hour.

ON THE RAILWAY

gradient post ⋆
speed restriction sign ⋆⋆
bridge number plate in cast iron ⋆
whistle and SW signs ⋆⋆
old style semaphore signal ⋆⋆⋆
turntable (originally for turning steam engines) ⋆⋆⋆⋆⋆
old water tower (from steam days) ⋆⋆⋆⋆
hydraulic buffers (usually at termini) ⋆⋆
fixed buffers ⋆
level crossing with gates ⋆⋆⋆
train-washing unit ⋆⋆
old-style luggage trolley ⋆⋆
BRUTE (British Rail Universal Trolley) for transporting mail bags etc. on the platform, with high, wire-mesh sides ⋆
platform tractor (for towing BRUTEs, water tanks, etc.) ⋆⋆
platform sweeper, mechanical ⋆⋆
old-style station clock, with hands, showing correct time ⋆⋆⋆
disused station ⋆⋆⋆
steam locomotive ⋆⋆⋆⋆⋆
diesel locomotive ⋆
diesel locomotive with name ⋆⋆
diesel locomotive in freight livery ⋆⋆
diesel shunter ⋆
snow plough ⋆⋆⋆⋆
breakdown train ⋆⋆⋆⋆
de-icing train ⋆⋆⋆⋆
weed-killing train ⋆⋆⋆⋆
track tamper (track repair and maintenance vehicles, usually bright yellow) ⋆⋆
Royal Mail train or carriages (painted bright red) ⋆⋆
train comprising sleeper carriages ⋆⋆⋆
named train with headboard or identification ⋆⋆⋆⋆
pullman train ⋆⋆⋆
carriage with old-style FIRST and NO SMOKING signs (blue double sausage, red triangle) ⋆⋆
initials or monogram of former private railway company, e.g., GWR, LSWR, LT & SR, LB & SCR (often to be found in decorative cast iron, terracotta or brickwork on stations) ⋆⋆⋆
enamel sign in old regional colours (brown Western region, green Southern region, blue Eastern region, maroon Midland region) ⋆⋆⋆⋆

freight wagons:
coal ⋆
oil ⋆
cement ⋆
stone ⋆
railway ballast ⋆
rails ⋆
container ⋆⋆
international ferrywagon ⋆
timber ⋆⋆
fertiliser ⋆⋆
car transporter ⋆⋆
flat trucks with military vehicles ⋆⋆⋆
milk ⋆⋆⋆
old-style guard's van ⋆⋆⋆
nuclear flask ⋆⋆⋆⋆

freight wagons with fish names (to denote class or type of wagon, and often stencilled or painted on the side, e.g., tench, bass, bream, grampus, sealion, seacow, dace, crab, rudd, dogfish⋆ for each fish recorded

BUILDINGS

castle ⋆⋆
cathedral ⋆⋆
church with spire ⋆
windmill ⋆⋆⋆
watermill with wheel ⋆⋆⋆⋆
oast house ⋆⋆
lighthouse ⋆⋆⋆⋆⋆
pier ⋆⋆⋆⋆
power station with cooling towers ⋆⋆
airfield or airport, in use ⋆⋆
gasometer ⋆⋆
thatched house ⋆⋆
cemetery or graveyard ⋆⋆⋆
old-style red telephone box ⋆⋆⋆
lock on a river or canal ⋆⋆⋆
harbour or dock, in use, with cranes and ships ⋆⋆⋆
quarry, in use ⋆⋆⋆
brickfield, with chimneys ⋆⋆⋆

FEATURES OF THE LANDSCAPE

racecourse ⋆⋆⋆
golf course ⋆⋆
tennis court ⋆⋆
swimming pool ⋆⋆
game of bowls, cricket or football being played ⋆⋆
helicopter ⋆⋆
fire engine or ambulance ⋆⋆⋆
bus or coach ⋆
bicycle, being ridden ⋆
houseboat ⋆⋆
sailing boat or windsurfer, in use ⋆⋆
hillfort ⋆⋆⋆
strip lynchets, or terracing on hillside ⋆⋆⋆
campsite ⋆⋆
figure or device carved in hillside ⋆⋆⋆
garden gnome ⋆⋆⋆
fishpond, in garden ⋆⋆
combine harvester ⋆⋆
cattle trough ⋆⋆
scarecrow ⋆⋆⋆

crops:
potatoes
linseed
rape
maize
watercress
apples or pears
hops
other fruit
⋆⋆ for each crop recorded

donkey ⋆⋆
goat ⋆⋆
pigs in field ⋆⋆
black sheep ⋆⋆
bull ⋆⋆⋆
shire or heavy horse ⋆⋆⋆
foal ⋆⋆
llama ⋆⋆⋆⋆⋆
two or more farm animal species in one field (e.g., horses and sheep) ⋆⋆ for each species
rabbit ⋆
fox ⋆⋆⋆⋆
deer ⋆⋆⋆⋆
geese ⋆⋆
swan ⋆⋆
heron ⋆⋆⋆⋆
hawk ⋆⋆
rosebay willowherb ⋆
foxgloves ⋆
Oxford ragwort ⋆⋆
bluebells ⋆
lupins ⋆⋆

Below: *Where the track is not level, gradient posts at the side of the line indicate how steeply it rises or falls. In this case, it drops 1 foot in 236 feet to the left and rises 1 foot in 331 feet to the right*

Above: Mileposts are at quarter mile intervals. This one means it is 53 ¼ miles from London

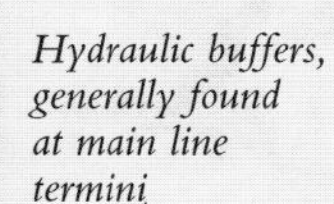

Hydraulic buffers, generally found at main line termini

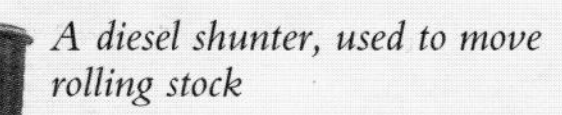

A diesel shunter, used to move rolling stock

Above: Semaphore stop (red) and distant (yellow) signals

Railways and industry are historically and irrevocably linked, and a train journey is an excellent way to appreciate our industrial heritage. Above: Chimneys from the local brickworks are a characteristic feature of the line between Bedford and Bletchley

Left: A weed-killing train, which sprays the line and the embankment, is one of the more unusual maintenance machines to look out for

INDEX OF STATIONS

This index includes all Network SouthEast stations on all routes in this book.

- ☕ Refreshments available at station
- 🚖 Taxi rank at station
- Ᵽ No car park at station
- ♿ Special facilities for the disabled at station
- ⊖ Stations having interchange with London Regional Transport Underground Services

INDEX OF PLACES TO VISIT

Page references not in italics refer to captions

ACKNOWLEDGEMENTS

The Automobile Association wishes to thank the following photographers, libraries and associations for their assistance in the preparation of this book.

ABERDEEN CITY ARTS DEPT, ART GALLERY & MUSEUMS 75 Train Landscape (E Ravilious)
P H BRANNLUND 72 West of Tisbury, 94 Train
BRITISH RAIL Cover St Paul's & Train, 8/9 Alton Station, 11 Approaching Gt Bedwyn, 12 Slough, Littlehampton, 26 Linslade, Train by Canal, 52 Arundel, 73 Houses of Parliament, Clock at Waterloo, 114 Shunter, weed killing train
CHRISTOPHER WOOD GALLERIES 74/5 King's Cross going north (G Earl)
COLIN GARRATT'S STEAM LOCOMOTIVES OF THE WORLD PHOTO LIBRARY 1 Wessex Electric, 2/3 Train going through trees, 26 Signals, 95 Thameslink, 108 Train Reigate – Reading, 114 Gradient sign, mile post, buffer, signal
B DENTON 10 Train near Twyford, 29 Newbury to Bedwyn, 114 train and brickfield
MUSEUM OF LONDON 40/1 Charing Cross Station
NATIONAL GALLERY 75 Rail, Steam and Speed (Turner)
NATIONAL RAILWAY MUSEUM 68 Brighton Station, 74 Letchworth Station, 75 Poster 'South for Winter', 112 Golden Arrow
D SMYTH 38 Digswell Viaduct
M S TRIGG 73 Train near Brockenhurst
D WARWICK 28 Bursledon Bridge, 29 Cholsey, 52 Hastings line near Wadhurst, 85 near Beaulieu Road
ANDY WILLIAMS PHOTO LIBRARY Cover Windsor Castle

All remaining pictures are held in the AA Photo Library, with contributions from:

M Adleman, D Austin, P Baker, M Birkitt, J Cady, R Czaja, P Enticknapp, R Fletcher, D Forss, B Johnson, A Lawson, S & O Mathews, R Newton, D Noble, B Smith, R Surman, M Trelawney, R Victor, W Voysey, H Williams, T Woodcock

LONDON UNDERGROUND

The Underground – known as the tube – is the quickest and most efficient means of public transport in London. With over 270 stations, the network reaches out from central London to the suburbs and trains run frequently between 5.30 am and 0.15 am. There are no all night services and certain stations are closed at weekends. Network SouthEast stations on the routes included in this book that have an Underground connection are marked in the Station Index.

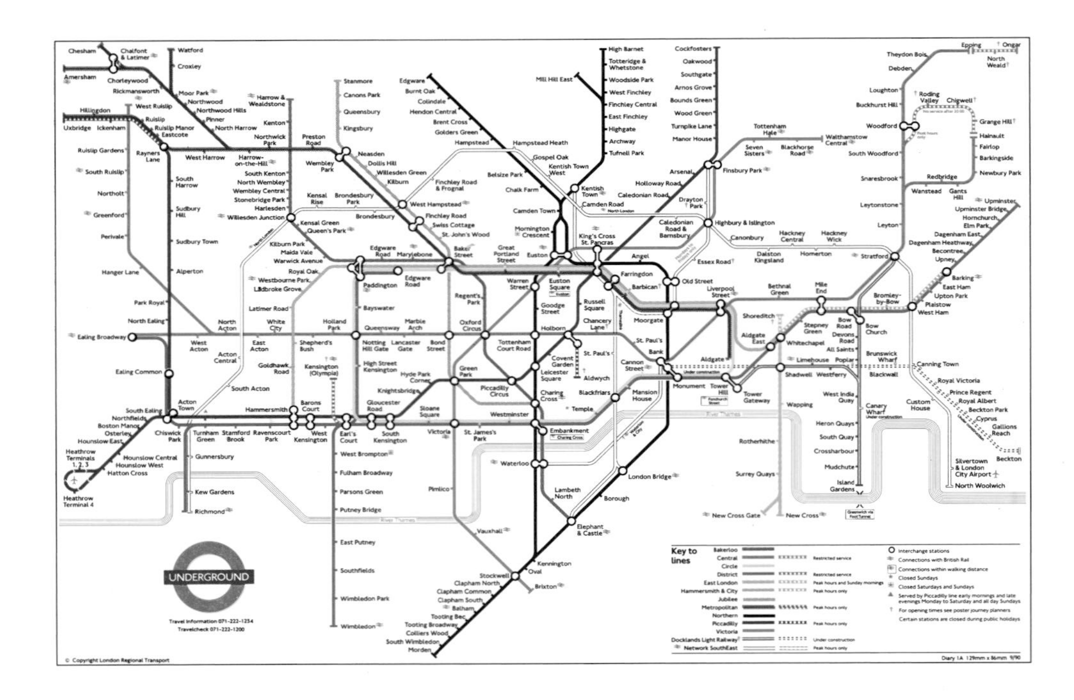